Finding Your Chicago Ancestors

*A Beginner's Guide
to Family History in the City
and Cook County*

Grace DuMelle

First Edition

LAKE CLAREMONT PRESS

www.lakeclaremont.com
Chicago

Finding Your Chicago Ancestors:
A Beginner's Guide to Family History
in the City and Cook County
by Grace DuMelle

Published February, 2005, by:

4650 N. Rockwell St.
Chicago, IL   60625
773/583-7800
lcp@lakeclaremont.com
www.lakeclaremont.com

Publisher's Cataloging-in-Publication
(Provided by Quality Books, Inc.)

DuMelle, Grace, 1958-
      Finding your Chicago ancestors : a beginner's guide
to family history in the city and Cook County / by Grace
DuMelle. -- 1st ed.
      p. cm.
      Includes bibliographical references and index.
      LCCN 2004103412
      ISBN 1-893121-25-9

      1. Chicago (Ill.)--Genealogy--Handbooks, manuals,
etc.   2. Cook County (Ill.)--Genealogy--Handbooks,
manuals, etc.   I. Title.

F548.25.D86 2004   929'.1'07207731
                                      QBI04-200430

10   09   08   07   06   05   10 9 8 7 6 5 4 3 2 1

Printed in the United States of America by
United Graphics, Inc., of Mattoon, Illinois.

Table of Contents

Publisher's Credits

Cover design by Timothy Kocher. Editing by Laura R. Gabler. Interior design and layout by Michelle Haug. Proofreading by Sharon Woodhouse and Karen Formanski. Indexing by Matt Rutherford and Grace DuMelle.

Notice

Acknowledgments

"Nothing is impossible with God" — Luke 1:37

Many are those who must be thanked for this book's appearance in print:

My grandparents, Joseph and Antonina (Pajak) Konieczny and Frank and Regina (Rebman) Dumelle. Thank you for crossing the ocean. Thank you for the stories that live on with your children, grandchildren, and great-grandchildren.

My parents, Jacob and Dorothy (Konieczny) Dumelle. Thanks, Dad, for sharing your enthusiasm and knowledge of genealogy. Thanks, Mom, for your Scott Foresman proofreading skills and gathering of family information. Margo, Lili, Chris, Colleen, and Cassie: I appreciate your working around my writing and publishing deadlines these past two years.

The librarians, archivists, and staff from whom I've learned so much. Your dedication is inspiring, particularly in dealing with the budget cuts of the past few years. My gratitude goes to Jeanie Child and Phil Costello of the Clerk of the Circuit Court of Cook County Archives; Craig Davis and Kathryn Tutkus of the Harold Washington Library Center; Ellen Engseth of North Park University's F. M. Johnson Archives and Special Collections; Donald Jackanicz and Peter Bunce of the National Archives and Records Administration—Great Lakes Region; Glen Kistner of the Illinois Regional Archives Depository at Northeastern Illinois University; Kathleen Kloss-Safer of the Cook County Bureau of Vital Statistics; Lesley Martin of the Chicago Historical Society; Barbara Moore of the Family History Center in Wilmette, Illinois; Linda Naru of the Richard J. Daley Library of the University of Illinois at Chicago; and Ellen O'Brien, formerly of the Municipal Reference Library at Harold Washington Library Center.

Those in the genealogical community whose expertise and willingness to share has enriched countless families. Your words of encouragement meant a lot. Many of you allowed me to make presentations to your members that helped me formulate the ideas in this book. I'm talking about Thelma Eldridge of the Patricia Liddell Researchers; Peggy Gleich of the British Interest Group of Wisconsin and Illinois; Rita Hodgetts of the Northwest Suburban Council of Genealogists; Rosalie Lindberg of the Polish Genealogical Society of America; Rollie Littlewood of the Wisconsin State Genealogical Society; Carolyn O'Brien of "A Look At Cook" Web site; Craig Pfannkuche of the Chicago Genealogical Society and the Chicago and North Western Historical Society; Kathy Bergan Schmidt of the McHenry County Illinois Genealogical Society; Norman Schwartz of the Chicago Jewish Historical Society; Ted Wachholz of the Eastland Disaster Historical Society; and Michael Wolski of the Historic Pullman Foundation.

My Newberry Library colleagues, present and former. You read or wrote drafts of chapters, scanned or selected photos, made suggestions, and kept cheering me on. I am lucky to have co-workers of such high caliber: Martha Briggs, Susan Fagan, Rhonda Frevert, Scott Holl, Katie McMahon, Ginger Frere, Matt Rutherford, Jack Simpson, and Peggy Tuck Sinko.

The patrons of the Newberry, who come from all over the globe seeking their Chicago ancestors. Your questions and frustrations shaped the presentation of my book. Please let me know how it helped you.

Sharon Woodhouse of Lake Claremont Press, for green-lighting my proposal and showing incredible patience. Her capable staff, especially Karen Formanski and Ken Woodhouse, deserve a round of applause. My admiration for Laura Gabler's editing grew with each chapter I reviewed. Tim Kocher came up with the attention-getting cover design. Michelle Haug, who's made my house histories look so good, did the interior design. Liz Sloan and Bob Nick, photographers extraordinaire, took the author's portraits. Nancy Beskin coordinated the immense research facilities chapter and shot most of its photographs.

Finally, my husband, Walter Podrazik, gave me the invaluable perspective of a ten-time author at every step. Merci beaucoup!

Introduction

Family History:
The Ultimate Reality Show

Get ready to produce, direct, and star in a guaranteed ratings grabber. It's all about you—how you got here, how your ancestors got here, and the influence those folks still have on you in the form of traits and traditions.

Family history is more than filling in names and dates. It's finding the stories *behind* the dry facts, the stories that enable you to better understand your people and yourself.

I never knew my mother-in-law, Julia. She died years before I met my husband. Like so many children, Walter never asked his mom about her childhood and her parents.

Through genealogical research, I've been able to put some pieces together that tell me about the woman who shaped the man I love. Julia lost her father a month and a half after her birth. She was two when she and her brother Gus were orphaned. Their parents were Lithuanian immigrants who married in Chicago. Constantine got blood poisoning from a botched dental visit, giving Julia a lifelong fear of doctors. Her mother, Marijona, so the family story goes, was so depressed at her strapping husband's sudden death that she ate nothing but coffee and sweet rolls for the next two years. The Cook County Hospital physician gave the cause of her death as tuberculosis. She was 25.

I guarantee you that once you find proof of a couple of things, you won't want to stop. Everything literally relates to you! The addictive nature of genealogy has much to do with it being the second most popular hobby in America (after gardening). Another reason is that you can "play" it on so many levels. You can follow one side of the family as far back as possible. You can stay in the recent past and look for living descendants of another branch. You can exchange tips and leads with new friends who share your interest. You can detour down any number of side paths into the history of Chicago and the United States.

What's great about the techniques you'll learn in this book is that you can use them on anybody you're interested in—even beyond your family—from the past owners of your home to the personage the local park is named for. A novelist in Texas asked me to research Mary Todd Lincoln's Chicago neighborhood. I didn't know that her son Robert had brought her to live with him after his father's assassination. Using some of the strategies discussed in Chapter 6 ("Where Did My Ancestor Live?"), I was able to tell my client about the street surface, sewers, streetlights, sidewalks, and city water connections, even though the home had been demolished.

What You'll Find in This Book

When you're just starting out, it's important to know *how* to research as well as *what* to research. Most general genealogy books emphasize the *what*, the types of records: government, religious, military, and so on. *Chicago and Cook County: A Guide to Research* by Loretto Dennis Szucs is excellent at describing area sources and their locations but does not tell readers how to start their research or what steps to follow. There is no discussion of Web sites, so important to genealogy, and the 1930 U.S. census had not been released when the book was published in 1996.

From my experiences on both sides of the reference desk, as a staffer and a professional researcher, I know people think in terms of questions they want answered. They don't think in terms of record groups. So that's the way I organized the book.

The chapters in Part I give you strategies for answering the questions most beginners want to know:

- Where do I start?

- When was my ancestor born?

- When did my ancestor come to America?

- What did my ancestor do for a living?

- Where did my ancestor live?

- Where is my ancestor buried?

You can start with any chapter you're interested in. You don't have to wade through a lot of preliminaries. Most everything you need to know about a particular question is in that chapter, with a minimum of cross-references.

The chapters in Part II help you do research with specifics, such as how to use a microfilm reader or what you can expect at the Cook County Bureau of Vital Statistics. Other chapters in Part II go into depth on topics that show up frequently in the book (for example, how to find ancestors in the U.S. census). Again, pick and choose based on your interests.

Four chapters, two in Part I and two in Part II, have been written by Jack Simpson. Jack heads the Local and Family History section of the Newberry Library, one of the top genealogical facilities in the country. I learned new things from his chapters and I know you will as well.

What You Won't Find in This Book

Finding Your Chicago Ancestors is not an exhaustive listing of every strategy and record source. Each of the chapters could easily be twice or three times as long. A 400-page book would scare you away by its size and price. I didn't want to overwhelm you; as a famous prophet once said, "I have much more to tell you but you cannot bear it now." There's only so much you can absorb at one time.

I didn't mention the exact fee charged for copies and searches and so forth, because I didn't want to outdate the text. Likewise, locations of books in research facilities can change, so I left those out.

You won't find call numbers for library holdings here.

Places use different systems, and it's good for you to get familiar with them. I was also motivated by mental health considerations; I would have been lying awake nights wondering if I got a number wrong.

Lastly, you won't find the *why*, as in, "Why isn't there one central archive for all Chicago records?" or "Why can't people see their deceased parents' public school records?" Discussing why Cook County and Chicago records are in such a piecemeal state and why access is so haphazard would take another book. Just know that this is the state of affairs at the time of publication, and it probably won't change anytime soon.

Your Connection to Chicago

For almost 175 years, this great metropolis on the shores of a freshwater sea has sent a siren call to immigrants internal and external. I'd venture to say that most Americans have some kind of link to the City of Big Shoulders. Whether your people came west from New England in the early days of settlement or north from Mississippi in the Great Migration . . . whether they sailed from Sicily or flew from Budapest. . . you'll find the means to document them.

When you do, you'll be a Chicagoan, if not by birth, then by blood. I've lived in a lot of places and traveled to many more. Chicago is the Capital of Real: real people doing things that really matter. Welcome!

Finding
Your Chicago
Ancestors

A Beginner's Guide
to Family History in the City
and Cook County

Part I

Getting Your Questions Answered

1   Where Do I Start?

by Jack Simpson
Curator of Local and Family History,
the Newberry Library

Beginning family history research is a daunting task, but you can make the process easier by following a simple strategy and avoiding some typical novice errors. First, gather the information that your family currently possesses and interview older relatives. Second, organize the information you have gathered. Third, research historical documents beginning with census records, vital records, and city direc-tories, working backward from the present to the past. Also, avoid these common mistakes: starting on the Internet, working forward from a famous ancestor, and being too rigid or credulous.

❑ Step 1:
Gather Your Family's Information

This book is mainly about how to research using historical documents. For many researchers, though, the most valuable information isn't in a library but rather is stored in your own attic or in the memory of your older relatives. When you begin your research, gather together all of the documents you have on your parents and grandparents, such as death certificates, birth certificates, marriage licenses, naturalization certificates, institutional membership cards, and photographs—anything that might offer information about their lives. These records will provide valuable clues for further research.

Interviewing your relatives is perhaps the most urgent research task. As people age, their short-term memories often weaken, but long-term memory remains strong. People tend to retain vivid memories of their childhood and youth.

When your grandparents or your parents pass away, their memories are lost as well, and a vast storehouse of information is gone. So it is important to interview your parents, grandparents, or other older relatives. If possible, you should record what they tell you on an audio recorder, or at least by taking copious notes. You might ask them to identify people in old photographs or other documents—this sometimes helps evoke memories.

These interviews are important for two reasons. First, your relatives will provide you with details about their lives, which will help guide your research: the names of towns where they were born, the date they arrived at Ellis Island, or the names of their grandparents. Second, they will give you a rich picture of what their lives were like: how they felt about moving to Chicago from Italy, what life was like in Bridgeport in the 1930s, or what kind of relationships they had with their siblings. These emotional and personal details are impossible to recover from historical documents such as censuses and vital records, so recording them is vitally important. There is an art to conducting such interviews. Before you interview, you may want to consult a how-to book, such as *The Oral History Manual* by Barbara W. Sommer and Mary Kay Quinlan. Cyndi's List of Genealogy Sites on the Internet (www.cyndislist.com) features many links to interviewing guides on the Web, under the category "Oral History & Interviews."

❑ Step 2: Organize Your Information

Once you have gathered your family's information, you should organize what you have found using a family tree chart or software. The traditional family tree chart (see Illustration 1.1) shows family relationships and records the dates of births, deaths, and marriages. Related charts called family group sheets or records (see Illustration 1.2) display more detailed information about each family. Large paper charts can be purchased from publishers such as Family

History Network (www.ancestor-circles.com). Smaller charts are available for free on the Internet from a variety of sources—see the Cyndi's List category "Supplies, Charts, Forms, Etc." for links to download forms.

Family tree software is an increasingly popular option for organizing family information. Programs such as Family Tree Maker and Personal Ancestral File allow you to enter your family information into a database. Once your family information is in the database, these programs allow you to display it in a family tree or in a number of other useful ways. Current versions of most family tree software also allow you to enter photographs and other scanned documents into the database.

Most family tree software operates on the GEDCOM (Genealogical Data Communications) standard. GEDCOM is not a personal brand but rather is an industry standard, like VHS is a standard for videotape. When you save a family tree file you have created using one of these programs, you save it as a GEDCOM file. Because most programs use GEDCOM as a standard, GEDCOM files can be shared between users of different programs. If you are somewhat technophobic, don't worry—using GEDCOM files is easy, and the major software programs are very user-friendly. Family Tree Maker is available for purchase from Genealogy.com, and Personal Ancestral File is available to download for free at the Family History Library Web site (www.familysearch.org). For Macintosh users, there is a program called Reunion, available for purchase from Leister Productions (www.leisterpro.com). Family history information gets more complex and confusing as you gather more information and more names, so organizing your information from the start will make your research more efficient.

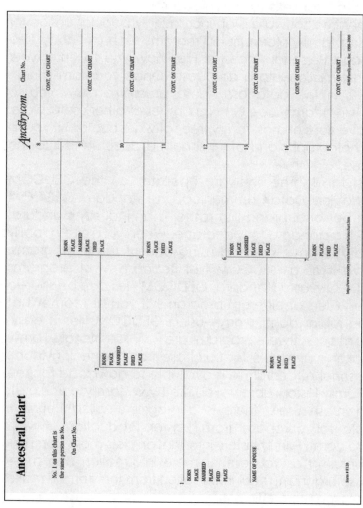

Illustrations 1.1 and 1.2: Forms like these help you keep track of all the people you're tracing. They're a handy reference when you're at a research facility. Courtesy of Ancestry.com.

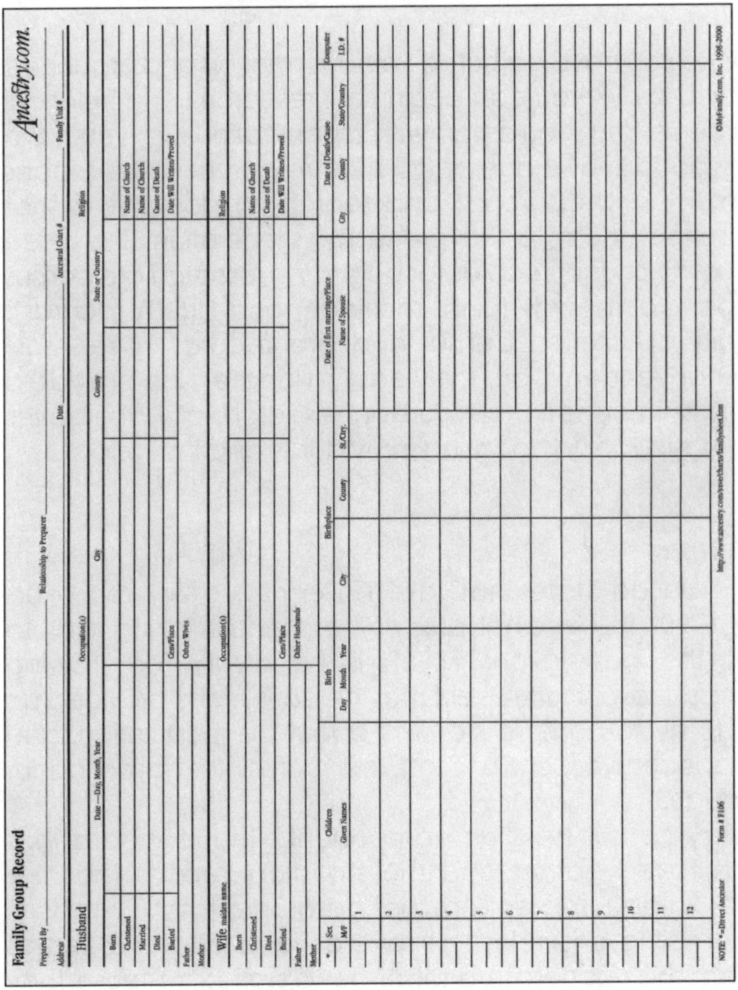

Family Group Record

Ancestry.com.

Prepared By _____ Relationship to Preparer _____

Address _____ Date _____ Ancestral Chart # _____ Family Unit # _____

Husband

Occupation(s) _____ Religion _____

	Date —Day, Month, Year	City	County	State or Country	
Born					
Christened					Name of Church
Married					Name of Church
Died					Cause of Death
Buried		Cem/Place			Date Will Written/Proved
Father		Other Wives			
Mother					

Wife maiden name

Occupation(s) _____ Religion _____

Born					
Christened					Name of Church
Died					Cause of Death
Buried		Cem/Place			Date Will Written/Proved
Father		Other Husbands			
Mother					

*	Sex M/F	Children Given Names	Birth Day	Month	Year	Birthplace City	County	St./Ctry.	Date of first marriage/Place Name of Spouse	Date of Death/Cause City	County	State/Country	Computer I.D. #
		1											
		2											
		3											
		4											
		5											
		6											
		7											
		8											
		9											
		10											
		11											
		12											

NOTE: *=Direct Ancestor   Form # F106   http://www.ancestry.com/save/charts/familysheet.htm   ©MyFamily.com, Inc. 1998-2000

Illustration 1.2

❑ Step 3:
Begin Research Using the Census, Vital Records, and City Directories

Once you have gathered your information and organized what you know, you can begin your research using historical documents. You should start with a generation that you have a fairly good knowledge of (for most researchers, this means parents or grandparents) and search for documents that will connect them to the preceding generation. The three most useful kinds of records for beginning research are census records, vital records (birth, marriage, and death records), and city directories. Census and vital records cover most American residents, are fairly easy to locate, and provide a wealth of information. For urban research, city directories are a basic tool for locating individuals and institutions.

Census

The United States has taken a census every ten years since 1790. The original purpose of census taking was to count the population, which is necessary for drawing congressional districts. Over time, the census also provided an opportunity to compile statistics about the population, and each successive census compiled more information about individuals.

Every census has two components: the raw data that census takers gather and the statistical reports that the Census Bureau derives from that data. The statistical reports are compiled and released several years after the census is taken; they generate a lot of news stories because they show changing demographics. When television reporters talk about the 2000 census, they are talking about the statistical report of the census. But it is the first part of the census, the raw data, that genealogists are interested in. In particular, genealogists are interested in the *population schedules* of the census. These are the sheets where the

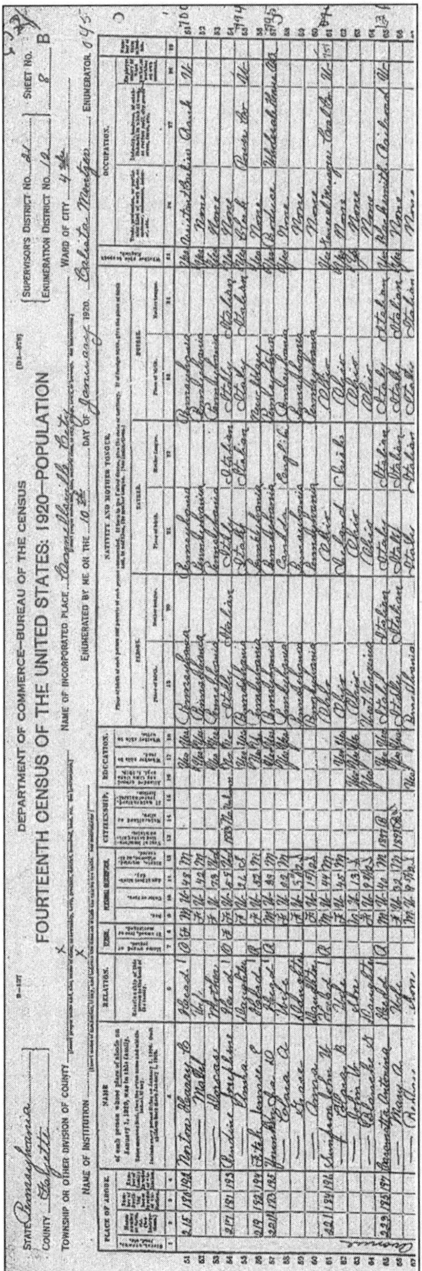

Illustration 1.3: Analyzing the information in the U.S. census can help you trace your family backward. Courtesy of Ancestry.com.

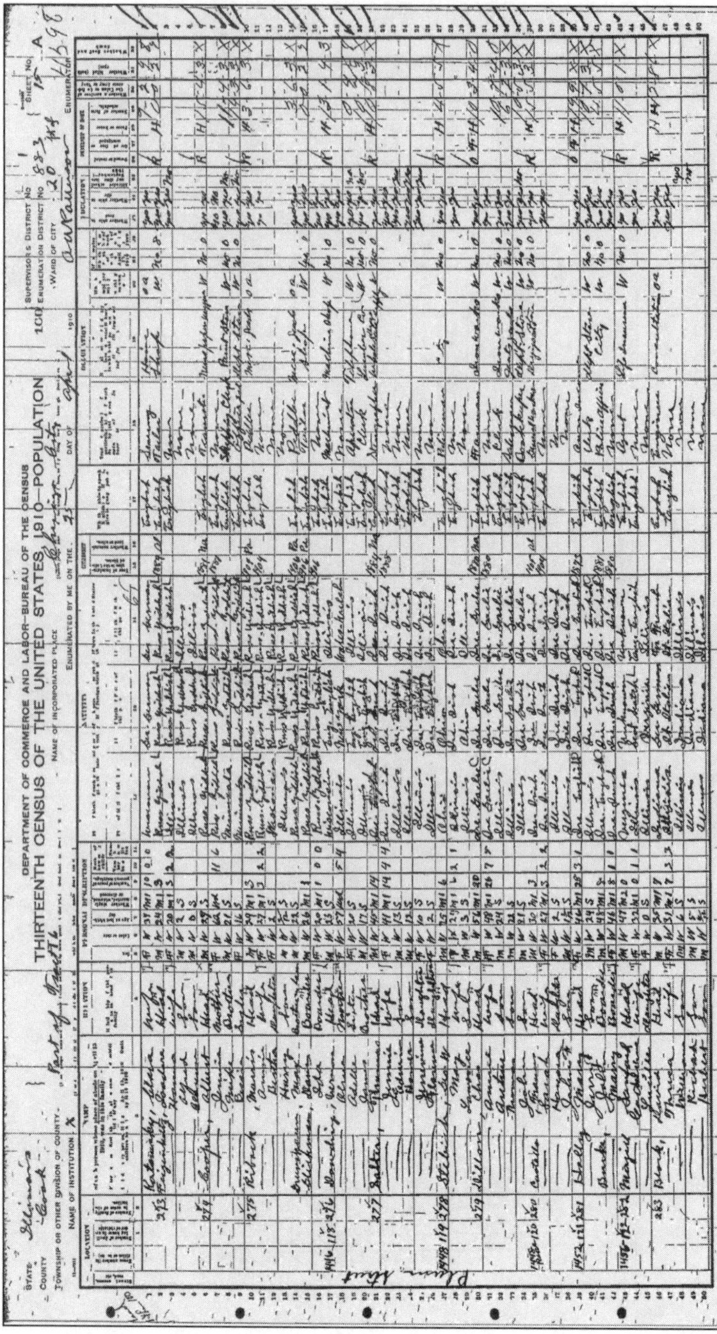

Illustration 1.4: 1910 census entry for the Washington Post cartoonist Herblock (family #283). Courtesy of Ancestry.com.

census taker recorded information on individual households. For privacy purposes, the population schedules are closed to the public for 72 years. The most recent population schedule that is open to the public is from the 1930 census.

Censuses are a great tool for beginners to trace their families backward. My research on my grandfather is a typical example. I knew that my grandfather, John Simpson, grew up in Uniontown, Pennsylvania, and I knew that he shared his father's name, which was also John Simpson. I knew the elder John Simpson was a mine manager. But I didn't know where his parents were from. I found my grandfather John and my great-grandparents John and Clara in the Pennsylvania census of 1920 (see Illustration 1.3). Note that the census shows a great deal about the family: the names and ages of each family member, their occupations, and the address of the family home. Studying this census, I learned that the elder John Simpson was born in Ohio around 1876. Using that information, I was able to search for him as a child in the 1880 census. When I located him, the 1880 census gave me clues as to when and where *his* parents (my great-great-grandparents) were born. In this way, the census can help you trace your family backward and fill in names and dates in your family tree.

Let's try a Chicago example. In 2001 the *Washington Post* cartoonist Herbert Block (who used the pen name Herblock) died at age 91. His obituary in the *Post* noted that he was born in 1909 in Chicago to David and Tessie Block. Searching the census, we find the family living at 1456 Plum Street (see Illustration 1.4). The census indicates that David Block was born in Indiana around 1875 to a German father and a French mother. Theresa Block was born around 1879 in Illinois to Italian parents. These clues can help us move backward another generation. For more information about using the census, turn to Chapter 10 ("Nuts and Bolts of the U.S. Census").

Vital Records

Vital records, meaning birth, death, and marriage records, are another great source of information for beginning genealogists. Like census records, vital records document a large portion of the population. And although vital records are not as accessible as census records, researchers can usually locate them with some effort and a small amount of cash. Vital records, especially birth and death records, are useful because they can connect one generation to another. If you know when and where your grandmother passed away, you can usually locate her death certificate; that certificate usually records her place and date of birth and the names of her parents. See Chapters 5 and 12 ("When (and Who) Did My Ancestor Marry?" and "Nuts and Bolts of Birth and Death Records").

City Directories

City directories are similar to present-day telephone books. They were used by city dwellers to locate individuals and institutions. Most directories consist of three parts: the front matter, an alphabetical directory of individuals, and a classified business directory. Chicago city directories were published for 1839 to 1870 (irregular), 1871 to 1917 (every year), 1923, and 1928–29. City directories for some suburban towns also exist for certain years.

The directory of individuals is the most useful part of the directory for genealogists. Typically, the directory records an individual's home address, work address, and occupation. Generally, people who were not employed outside of the home are not listed in directories—therefore, housewives, retirees, and minors are rarely included. While working-age men account for the bulk of the listings, employed women and female business owners are also listed. Additionally, for several years following a man's death, a widow is often listed. These listings are a good starting point for urban genealogy research, as they are easy to use and fairly inclusive.

Many novice researchers overlook the front matter, but

it is actually one of the most useful sources for urban genealogy research. The front of most city directories contains basic information about the city: lists of organizations, churches, institutions, and government offices, as well as a detailed street guide. This information is useful because it describes the city *in a particular year*. So, if you have an address from a letter in 1906, you can use the 1906 directory to figure out where the address was *that year*. If you have a marriage record from 1895 that mentions a minister's name, you can use the 1895 directory to see which church the minister led *that year*. The city is constantly changing—streets are renamed, churches move, organizations disband—so having an annual snapshot of the state of the city is immensely important for researchers.

The business directory is similar to the Yellow Pages today. This is a good point for beginning research on small businesses. Typically, the business directory is at the back of the city directory. For certain years, separate business directories were also published for Chicago. For more information about city directories, see the list available on the Newberry Library Web site, www.newberry.org.

❏ Three Beginner's Mistakes to Avoid

Working with genealogy researchers at the reference desk, I have seen what methods work well—and also the typical errors that cause frustration. Even if you don't perfectly follow the three steps just outlined, you should certainly avoid the three errors described here.

1. Starting on the Internet

The Internet is a great source for genealogists—an entire chapter of this book is devoted to it (see Chapter 15). However, it is generally a bad starting point for genealogy researchers. The Internet grew organically as more and more users connected their computers to the World Wide Web; it did not follow any organizational plan.

Because of the Internet's inherent disorder, researchers typically rely on search engines to locate information in the digital morass. Most Internet users begin researching a subject by typing some terms into a search engine, such as Google.

For some specific kinds of research, this might be effective. For example, if I want information about Wrigley Field, Google searching is fairly effective. If I type "Wrigley Field" into Google, the top results are informative: a Major League Baseball profile of the park and the Chicago Cubs home page are both in the top five results that are returned. Now, let's try a genealogy Google search. If I type "Simpson genealogy" into Google, I get a long list of results, but after wading through the first 15 results, I still don't find anything about my ancestors. Even if I narrow the search and enter "Simpson genealogy" and "Ohio" as search terms, I don't find any useful information. I do come across a lot of advertisements for commercial genealogy sites.

This kind of searching is inefficient and is discouraging for novices. It can also lead inexperienced researchers down false paths and away from their own family history. Once you have a firm grounding in basic research, the Internet can be very useful, but it isn't a good training ground. When you've done some of your basic research, turn to Chapter 15 to get some strategies for research on the Internet.

2. *Working Forward from a Famous Ancestor*

Families often have a story about how they are related to a famous individual, somewhere back in the foggy past. For instance, I remember hearing, when I was growing up, that my family might be related to Ulysses Simpson Grant. Novice researchers sometimes try to work forward from a supposed famous ancestor of theirs. This is a bad tactic for several reasons. First, it is very difficult to trace a family forward in time. Genealogical documents tell us where people came from, but they don't tell us where people are going. For example, a person's death certificate might say where he was born, but his birth certificate does not indicate where he will die. Second, it is difficult to know which family lines might be connected to you. I would have to research all of Ulysses S. Grant's children and grandchildren to determine if any of them are connected to me. Without having done my own research, it would be difficult to evaluate whether they are connected. When you work backward, you know that each generation you research is connected to you. Finally, "famous ancestors" often turn out to be just famous and not ancestors. This was the case with my family and Ulysses S. Grant.

3. *Being Too Rigid or Too Credulous*

All of the sources for genealogical research mentioned so far are fallible. People lie to census takers, submit mistaken information on death certificates, and misremember dates. Census takers mishear names, indexers misread original records, and amateur genealogists publish error-filled family histories. These errors shouldn't discourage you, but they should make you look at your evidence with a skeptical eye and an open mind. If your ancestor was named Ross Jonson, remember that the census taker might have recorded him as Ross Jansen, R.J. Johnson, or Roy Jensen. If your distant cousin said that your great-grandfather was a world-famous architect, be open to the idea that he was actually a moderately successful construction contractor. If evidence you find in documents doesn't match your family stories, consider both that the stories might be wrong and the documents might be inaccurate.

Where Do I Start?

Points to Remember

❑ *Gather family information:*

• Look for documents of your parents and grandparents (for example, death certificates, marriage licenses, newspaper clippings, membership cards)—anything that might provide information about their lives.

• Assemble photographs and collect information about names, places, and dates.

• Interview older relatives and take notes, either written or recorded. Ask for help in identifying photographs and documents. Ask about their lives and past generations. Ask about relationships.

❑ *Organize your information:*

• Get into good habits from the beginning. This way, you won't get confused later on with all the information you'll be finding.

• Compile your information on paper forms or using software programs. Paper forms are easy to start with and are often available for free. Software programs let you do more things, but you have to choose, buy, and learn one.

Where Do I Start?

❑ *Begin your research using historical documents:*

• Check U.S. census records. Start with the most recent (1930) and work backward to 1920, 1910, 1900, and so on. Use indexes and always get a copy of the census entry, not just the index entry.

• Look for vital records (birth, marriage, death). Search indexes if you don't know the dates the events occurred. Be open to spelling variations, especially for ethnic surnames.

• Explore all parts of city directories. Find your ancestor's occupation and home and work address in the alphabetical section. Use the front matter to determine locations of churches and other institutions connected to your ancestor. Turn to the classified section for listings of businesses your ancestor operated or worked for.

❑ *Avoid these beginner's mistakes:*

• Jumping on the Internet and name-searching. Work from the known to the unknown, one generation at a time, starting with yourself.

(Continued next page)

Where Do I Start?

• Working forward from a famous ancestor to yourself. Work backward so the connections you make are solid, and then see if anyone turns up related to the famous person.

• Being too rigid. Even if your family has spelled your surname one way, it could have been different in the past, or it could have been written wrong or indexed wrong. Don't pass up variations.

• Believing everything your relatives tell you. Always cross-check your information with other sources.

2 When (and Where) Was My Ancestor Born?

Answering questions of birth date and birthplace are one of the basics of genealogy. In the beginning, you may only know an approximate year and a state or country of birth. Follow the strategies in this chapter to get more specifics about your ancestor. Many of the methods in Chapter 4, "Who Were the Siblings of My Ancestor?", are also effective.

❏ Strategy No. 1:
Birth and Baptismal Records

There are a few things you should know before plunging into the search for official birth records.

First, it was not an Illinois state requirement until 1916 to file birth certificates, so it's hit or miss finding them before that date. Many home births were not recorded with the county or state. You may need to check filings of delayed birth certificates, when your ancestor needed proof of age years later.

Second, pre-1871 Cook County birth records were destroyed in the Chicago Fire that October. But given the spotty registration before 1916, there were probably not that many of them anyway. Family records and religious records are alternative sources.

Third, Illinois law makes birth records confidential for 75 years. That means if you are requesting a birth certificate for someone who was born in 1930 or later (as of this book's 2005 publication date), you must prove you are an immediate family member (spouse, child, sibling) or have a financial interest (for example, legal guardian). If you don't fit one of those categories, you are considered a third party and your request will be denied. The exception is that if you can prove the person is deceased, you can obtain the birth record from the Illinois Department of Public Health. Otherwise, workarounds include getting an immediate family member to make the request (with you paying for it) or looking for other types of records as detailed in this chapter.

Because there are many nuances to Chicago and Cook County birth records, they are detailed separately, in Chapter 12 ("Nuts and Bolts of Birth and Death Records").

Baptismal records typically supply the child's name, the date of birth, the date of baptism, the names of the parents, and the names of the godparents or sponsors, who are often relatives of the parents. Denominations that use baptismal records include Roman Catholic, Eastern-rite Catholic, Orthodox, Episcopalian, Lutheran, and Methodist.

You may find a baptismal certificate among family papers. If not, many baptismal registers have been microfilmed by the Church of Jesus Christ of Latter-day Saints and are available on loan through Family History Centers and the Newberry Library for a fee. Others remain in the custody of the churches or have been removed to denominational archives. The Newberry Library's *Guide to Chicago Church and Synagogue Records* is a good starting point. It is posted on the genealogy section of the library's Web site, www.newberry.org, and can be consulted in person at the Local and Family History reference desk.

For churches in Cook County towns, your work is a bit easier because there are fewer churches of each denomination. It becomes a matter of looking for the one matching your ancestor's religion closest to where the family was living. Local histories can be helpful in discussing churches in existence at the time of the birth; some of these churches may have merged or closed in the interim. Usually the town's public library has a local history collection, or there will be a historical society. Either is a good source for getting answers to your questions.

When records are held by churches, call or write the office administrator to learn the research policy. If possible, go on-site rather than rely on a staffer, who is usually doing the work of three people. If mail research is necessary,

38				
Nro.	Name	Geburts- und Tauftag	Eltern	Pathen
505. 76.	Johann Jakob Martin Theodor	d. 18. Januar 1869. d. 11. Maerz 1869.	Johann Thumel; Karoline geb. Klank	Ferdinand Klank; Jakob Thumer; Maria Thumel; Dorothea Thumel.
506. 77.	Wilhelm Friedrich August	d. 13. December 1868 d. 14. Maerz 1869	Friedrich Stahnke; Hermine geb. Saß	Friedrich Stahnke; Louis Stahnke; August Saß; Johanne Saß.
507. 78.	Max Friedrich Wilhelm	d. 4. Januar 1869 d. 14. Maerz 1869.	Karl Dabbert; Charlotte geb. Bretz	Wilhelmine Wilk; Friedrich Nienmeyer; Max Wartmann;
508. 79.	Karoline Ida Anna	d. 29. Februar 1868. d. 17. Maerz 1869.	Heinrich Breyer; Friedericke geb. Mühlhahn	Karoline Heling; Karoline Miehlke; Anna Breyer;
509. 80.	Friedericke Johanne Karoline	d. 18. Maerz 1869 d. 18. Maerz 1869.	Johann Temmer; Maria geb. Lemlow	Johann Schwerin; Friedericke Stewand; Karoline Schmidt;
510.	Karl Rudolph	d. 8. Maerz 1869	Karl Behnke;	Karl Behnke; Gustav Behnke;

Illustration 2.1: Pre-Chicago Fire baptismal register from a German Lutheran church in Chicago. Notice that you can't scan the name column for the surname, because that's given in the fourth column, "Eltern" (parents). The father's name is listed first and then the mother's name, with her maiden name following the abbreviation "geb." (short for the word born). The third column means "Birth and Christening Day." There is often a span of several months between the two days. The fifth column gives the names of the godparents. Judging by the last names, many are related to the parents. You may discover the relationships in obituaries and probate records. Source: First St. John Lutheran Church, Chicago, Baptisms 1867–1878, Microfilm 1262, Reel 1, Newberry Library. Microfilm image courtesy Concordia Historical Institute, St. Louis, Missouri.

always include a donation and an appreciation of the staffer's time.

❏ Strategy No. 2: Birth Announcements

I have seen only a few birth announcements in the Chicago newspapers in my years of research, and they give the barest of information—parents' names and child's name. I would not spend too much time looking for Chicago birth announcements.

You may have more luck if your ancestor was born in a suburb where births were considered newsworthy in the local paper. For instance, the Northwest Suburban Council of Genealogists has compiled a book, *Births as Published in Paddock Publications, Arlington Heights, Illinois*, that includes the Cook County towns of Arlington Heights, Mount Prospect, Palatine, and South Barrington. The years covered are 1900 to 1920. The book is available at the Mount Prospect Public Library and the Newberry Library, among others.

❏ Strategy No. 3: Census

The United States takes a census every ten years. One of the standard questions is the age of each individual. Starting in 1850, the census also asked for the birthplace (the state or country of birth).

Based on your ancestor's age in the census, you can calculate the approximate year of birth. Say the age is seven in 1930. The birth year then would be 1923 or 1922, depending on when the birthday fell in relation to the date the census was taken. (The day and month the data was collected appears at the top of each census page.)

In the 1870 and 1880 censuses, the month of birth is given if the child was born within the year. The 1900 census collected the month and year of birth in addition to age (see Illustration 7.4 in Chapter 7). You may also see a notation like this, "5/12," for your ancestor. It means your ancestor was five months old at the time.

Try to get as many census entries as you can for your ancestor, so you have a basis of comparison. You may discover he or she doesn't age at all in ten years! People did not have to show proof of age to the census taker, and whoever answered the door—perhaps a child, a servant, or a landlady—might be used as the informant. Especially with birthplace, don't fall into the trap of jumping into research for other states or countries based solely on the census report of where your ancestor was born. You need to assemble and compare as much documentation as possible before deciding how to move forward.

The 1930 census is the most recent one available. See Chapter 10 ("Nuts and Bolts of the U.S. Census") for instructions on how to find your ancestor's entry in the censuses up to 1930. The 1940–2000 censuses will not be released (for privacy reasons) until 72 years have passed. You can obtain the information for a fee if you prove you are an heir of the person and that the person is deceased. Request Form B6–600 from the following:

Personal Census Search Unit
U.S. Census Bureau
P.O. Box 1545
Jeffersonville, IN 47131
812/218-3046
fax: 812/288-3371

This is what the most recent censuses asked regarding age and birthplace:

- 1940 census: age, birthplace
- 1950 census: age, birthplace if foreign born
- 1960–90 censuses: age
- 2000 census: age, birth date

❏ Strategy No. 4: School Records

Elementary school. High school. College. Think beyond these familiar boundaries to the types of schools your ancestor may have attended, such as:

- art school
- beauty or barber school
- Bible or Sunday school
- business school
- dental school
- flight school
- library school
- medical school
- nursing school
- seminary (Protestant, Catholic, Jewish)
- teachers' college
- trade or technical school

You may be able to find clues from diplomas, licenses, union cards, yearbooks, and the like. If your ancestor attended any type of school, that school should have records of enrollment information that would include birth date and possibly birthplace. Getting that information will depend on the policies of the individual school. Your chances are best if you can show your ancestor is deceased, that you are a descendant, and that you are not interested in grades or disciplinary records but rather you are looking for what's called *directory information*: name, address, years attended, participation in sports, and items of a similar biographical nature.

From the beginning, there have been two major school systems, public and private. Public elementary and high schools were and continue to be operated by boards of education in Chicago and other towns. Chicago continues to operate trade schools (now called vocational schools). Junior colleges run by the Chicago Board of Education became independent in 1966, and a teachers' college was turned over to the state of Illinois in 1965.

On the private side, many religious bodies (such as Lutheran, Episcopalian, and Greek Orthodox) operated schools (and still do). The Roman Catholic Archdiocese of Chicago developed an extensive network of elementary and high schools, as well as minor and major seminaries for educating priests. The boundaries of the Archdiocese at its beginning in 1843 encompassed all of Illinois. Later, the dioceses of Quincy (1853), Alton (1857), Peoria (1877), Rockford (1908), and Joliet (1948) were formed, so the present boundaries are confined to Cook and Lake Counties. Contact the respective dioceses for records of schools formerly in the Archdiocese of Chicago.

A whole book could be devoted to all the schools of Chicago and Cook County. I'm going to concentrate here on the two largest systems.

Chicago Public Schools

Sitting on the shelves of the Chicago Public Library and the University of Illinois at Chicago are enormous books called *Board of Education Proceedings*. These unwieldy volumes are a hidden source of birth dates for thousands of Chicagoans.

Starting in the 1933–34 school year and continuing through the 1971–72 school year, each *Proceedings* volume lists the birth dates of elementary school graduates. The dates begin about where the *Cook County Birth Index 1871–1916* leaves off and continue to about 1958.

The lists of elementary school graduates come after the graduation lists for Chicago Normal College (a teachers' college), junior colleges, high schools, evening high schools, and prevocational schools. Names are listed alphabetically within each school, so be prepared for a bit of looking. In each *Proceedings* book, there are two sections of graduates: one in June, toward the back of the book, and one in January or February, toward the front.

The Harold Washington Library Center holds the 1933–34 to 1971–72 volumes. The Richard J. Daley Library at the University of Illinois at Chicago has 1960–61 to 1971–72. I stumbled across these while researching a case for a client in Sweden.

Finding his half sister's birth date enabled me to obtain (with authorization from my client) her birth certificate and her parents' marriage certificate. I learned from the *Proceedings* that she was a graduate of Lake View High School. The school has an alumni association, which forwarded my letter to her and allowed me to put her in touch with her relative.

Roman Catholic Schools

If the school you're looking for is still open, send a written request directly to the school. Be patient—the priority of a school's office administrators and registrars is current students, not those who attended years ago. Always express appreciation and send a donation.

The Archives of the Archdiocese of Chicago holds records for approximately 250 closed schools (elementary and high schools). The Archdiocese policy states that researchers are only allowed "directory information." Per the Archdiocese:

> This includes: name and address, telephone number, birthday, birthplace, major field of study, participation in school activities, weigh[t] and height of members of athletic teams, dates of attendance, awards received, previous schools attended, the student's photograph, and the parish in which the student resides. This information is taken from the student's record at the time the student attended the school. Current information is not available from the Archives under any circumstances.

There is a fee per name for this service, and all requests are conducted by mail. A request form may be printed from their Web site; you need to include a copy of a photo ID as well as a cashier's check or money order (no personal checks). Contact:

Archdiocese of Chicago's Joseph Cardinal Bernardin Archives & Records Center
711 W. Monroe Street
Chicago, IL 60661

ADMISSIONS TO THE
HIGH SCHOOL DEPARTMENT

The following named pupils are entitled to admission to the High School Department, June, 1935:

AGASSIZ SCHOOL	Date of Birth	ALCOTT SCHOOL	Date of Birth		Date of Birth
Allen,	6-29-1921	Angelica,	7- 6-1921	Rheinberger,	12-20-1921
Allen,	8- 9-1922	Bachrach,	10-25-1922	Roberts,	5- 6-1922
Allseitz,	3-19-1922	Baker,	7- 5-1921	Roberts,	9-25-1920
Becker,	12- 6-1920	Bartkus,	6-12-1921	Ruf,	6- 4-1921
Beystehner,	10- 2-1922	Bates,	6- 5-1921	Runge,	9-30-1921
Biss,	8- 7-1922	Benjamin,	6-15-1921	Saidla,	6- 3-1921
Blixt,	11-11-1920	Boring,	11- 1-1920	Schmidt,	1-20-1921
Brown,	6- 8-1921	Brandt,	5-12-1921	Schmidt,	12- 7-1919
Budill,	2-12-1922	Bressler,	2-25-1922	Schrot,	2-27-1922
Callaghan,	8-13-1921	Carr,	3-28-1921	Searle,	8-25-1920
Carter,	8-28-1920	Casmano,	7-11-1920	Selander,	6- 9-1918
Cnudde,	11-22-1921	Christacatos,	1- 2-1922	Seuffer,	4-28-1921
Crowell,	1-16-1920	Ciaccio,	10- 7-1920	Shoub,	8-23-1921
Crowell,	1-16-1920	Clifford,	2-21-1920	Sim,	9-18-1921
Daniel,	11-14-1921	Corrigan,	3- 8-1922	Slagel,	5- 7-1921
Dankan,	2- 5-1921	Dallman,	11-22-1921	Stark,	10- 4-1921
Delwo,	9- 2-1921	Dalporto,	8- 3-1921	Steger,	11-16-1919
Demopoulos,	10-18-1919	Eckert,	8- 2-1922	Stevens,	9- 6-1922
Dennos,	11-28-1921	Elias,	12- 1-1919	Stueckl,	11-23-1921
Dichiaro,	7-26-1920	Elias,	5- 5-1921	Sutherland,	11- 5-1919
				Vittorson,	12- 2-1919
				Vine,	3-27-1921

Illustration 2.2: Sample of elementary school graduates from the 1934–35 Chicago Board of Education Proceedings. First names are omitted to respect the privacy of individuals who may still be alive. Source: Proceedings, July 9, 1934, to June 26, 1935, Harold Washington Library Center.

312/831-0711
fax: 312/831-0610
http://archives.archchicago.org
info@chgocatholicarchives.org (general inquiries)

❑ Strategy No. 5:
Social Security Application

When an individual applies for a Social Security number, the information he or she gives is very valuable (from a genealogist's perspective) precisely because it comes from the horse's mouth. One principle of genealogy is to put more weight on documents created by the person than documents created about the person. Still, you must compare such documents with what you find elsewhere and be ready to reinterpret them in light of new evidence you might uncover.

The Social Security application (known as Form SS–5) provides the exact date and place of your ancestor's birth, the names of your ancestor's parents, and your ancestor's mother's maiden name. It also gives the place where your ances-

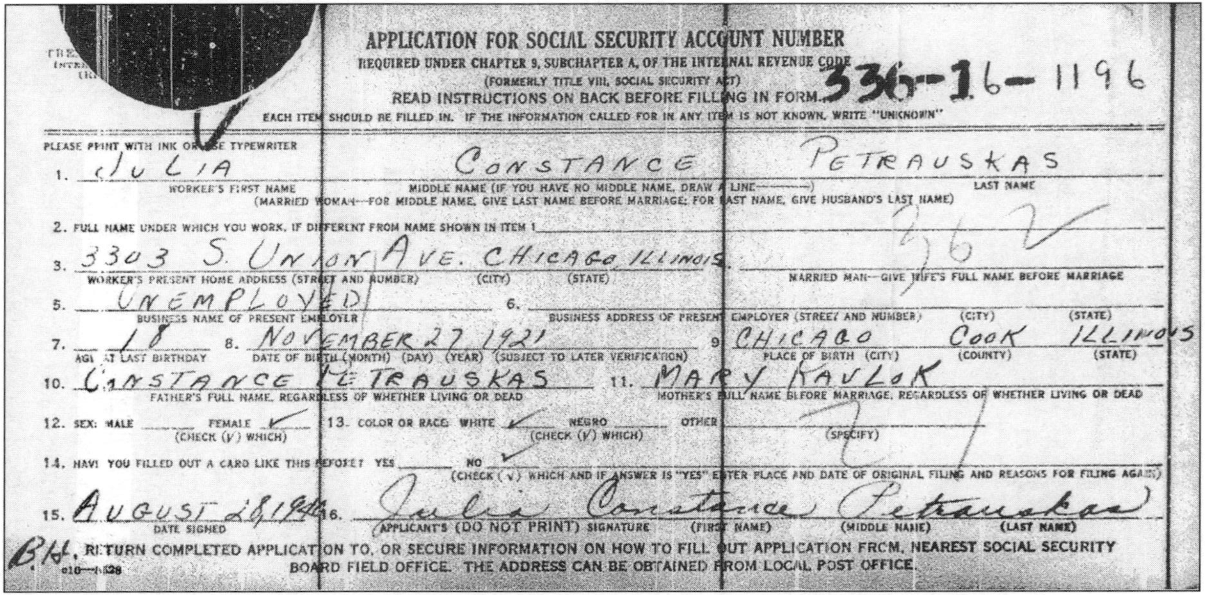

APPLICATION FOR SOCIAL SECURITY ACCOUNT NUMBER
REQUIRED UNDER CHAPTER 9, SUBCHAPTER A, OF THE INTERNAL REVENUE CODE
(FORMERLY TITLE VIII, SOCIAL SECURITY ACT)
READ INSTRUCTIONS ON BACK BEFORE FILLING IN FORM. 336-16-1196
EACH ITEM SHOULD BE FILLED IN. IF THE INFORMATION CALLED FOR IN ANY ITEM IS NOT KNOWN, WRITE "UNKNOWN"

PLEASE PRINT WITH INK OR USE TYPEWRITER

1. JULIA — WORKER'S FIRST NAME; CONSTANCE — MIDDLE NAME (IF YOU HAVE NO MIDDLE NAME, DRAW A LINE———) (MARRIED WOMAN—FOR MIDDLE NAME, GIVE LAST NAME BEFORE MARRIAGE; FOR LAST NAME, GIVE HUSBAND'S LAST NAME); PETRAUSKAS — LAST NAME

2. FULL NAME UNDER WHICH YOU WORK, IF DIFFERENT FROM NAME SHOWN IN ITEM 1

3. 3303 S. UNION AVE. CHICAGO ILLINOIS — WORKER'S PRESENT HOME ADDRESS (STREET AND NUMBER) (CITY) (STATE)

4. MARRIED MAN—GIVE WIFE'S FULL NAME BEFORE MARRIAGE

5. UNEMPLOYED — BUSINESS NAME OF PRESENT EMPLOYER

6. BUSINESS ADDRESS OF PRESENT EMPLOYER (STREET AND NUMBER) (CITY) (STATE)

7. 18 — AGE AT LAST BIRTHDAY

8. NOVEMBER 27 1921 — DATE OF BIRTH (MONTH) (DAY) (YEAR) (SUBJECT TO LATER VERIFICATION)

9. CHICAGO COOK ILLINOIS — PLACE OF BIRTH (CITY) (COUNTY) (STATE)

10. CONSTANCE PETRAUSKAS — FATHER'S FULL NAME, REGARDLESS OF WHETHER LIVING OR DEAD

11. MARY KAVLOK — MOTHER'S FULL NAME BEFORE MARRIAGE, REGARDLESS OF WHETHER LIVING OR DEAD

12. SEX: MALE ___ FEMALE ✓ (CHECK (✓) WHICH)

13. COLOR OR RACE: WHITE ✓ NEGRO ___ OTHER ___ (SPECIFY) (CHECK (✓) WHICH)

14. HAVE YOU FILLED OUT A CARD LIKE THIS BEFORE? YES ___ NO ✓ (CHECK (✓) WHICH AND IF ANSWER IS "YES" ENTER PLACE AND DATE OF ORIGINAL FILING AND REASONS FOR FILING AGAIN)

15. AUGUST 28 1940 — DATE SIGNED

16. Julia Constance Petrauskas — APPLICANT'S (DO NOT PRINT) SIGNATURE (FIRST NAME) (MIDDLE NAME) (LAST NAME)

B.H. RETURN COMPLETED APPLICATION TO, OR SECURE INFORMATION ON HOW TO FILL OUT APPLICATION FROM, NEAREST SOCIAL SECURITY BOARD FIELD OFFICE. THE ADDRESS CAN BE OBTAINED FROM LOCAL POST OFFICE.

Illustration 2.3: Julia Petrauskas filed this application for a Social Security number in 1940. She was unemployed at the time, so there is no information on where she was working. She gave her birth date and birthplace and the names of her parents. I believe she was in error when she provided Constance as her father's first name. It is stated as Constantine or Konstantin on other documents, such as her delayed birth certificate and her parents' civil marriage record. Julia was a month and a half old when her father died. She must have been told later that her middle name came from her father's name. So even though Julia supplied the information on this application, the weight of other evidence makes me discount Constance as her father's name. Courtesy of Walter J. Podrazik.

tor was living and the name and address where he or she was working at the time the application was made.

Applications for deceased individuals can be obtained from the Social Security Administration. There is a rather high fee (slightly lower if you supply the Social Security number), but it is well worth it. Both Ancestry.com (subscription Web site) and RootsWeb.com (free Web site) generate form letters with every hit on the Social Security Death Index. When writing your own letter, give your ancestor's name and birth and death dates, and request a photocopy of Form SS–5. Address it to:

> Social Security Administration
> Office of Central Records Operation
> Attention: FOIA Workgroup
> P.O. Box 17772
> 300 N. Greene Street
> Baltimore, MD 21290

❑ Strategy No. 6:
Post-1906 Naturalization Records

If your ancestor was an immigrant or the child of an immigrant, naturalization records can be a good source, but only if the immigrant filed court papers in 1904–06 or after. Beginning in those years, much more information was required to be on record, as procedures were reformed by the creation of the Immigration and Naturalization Service (now known as U.S. Citizenship and Immigration Services). For dates prior to 1904, all you will find in Cook County is the name and signature of the immigrant, the country of birth, and the names of witnesses.

Beginning in 1904, the Declaration of Intention to become a U.S. citizen asked for the month, day, and year of birth and the locality and country of birth. The Petition for Naturalization, filed a few years after the declaration, asked again for specific birth date and birthplace and also provided space to list the immigrant's children and their dates and places of birth. By listing the children, the petition can overcome the lack of birth registration that was prevalent for home births in Cook

County up until 1916.

Just so you know, you generally won't find naturalization records for female ancestors prior to 1922. That year, the Married Women's Act was passed, stating that all alien married women had to apply for citizenship on their own, instead of obtaining derivative citizenship through their spouses.

For examples of naturalization records and instructions on finding them, see Chapter 9 ("When Did My Ancestor Come to America?").

❑ Strategy No. 7: Death Records

Public health officials are sticklers for knowing a person's age at death, to calculate mortality rates. Consequently, death certificates in Cook County have always asked for the deceased's age, but not always for the date of birth. Even if it is asked, grieving relatives may fail to supply it (see Illustration 9.2). Similarly, the death certificate collects the place of birth, but you may get vague answers, such as "Illinois" or "Sicily," depending on who was the informant.

Church death registers may record the date of birth as well as the date of death. They may or may not give the place of birth. See Illustration 8.6.

Tombstones may give the age in terms of years, months, and days, allowing you to calculate the date of birth. Places of birth and death often appear on the tombstone.

An age is usually given in a death notice or an obituary; the date of birth is less commonly provided. Obituaries have better chances of stating the place of birth, though I have seen the county of origin in Ireland mentioned in a death notice. (For tips on finding death notices and obituaries, see Chapter 11, "Nuts and Bolts of Newspaper Searching.") These are just a few of the sources that may contain your ancestor's birth date and birthplace.

When (and Where) Was My Ancestor Born?

Points to Remember

❑ *Many births prior to 1916, and many home births, were not recorded:*

• Check for filings of delayed or corrected birth certificates.

❑ *Pursue religious records and family records as alternatives to pre-Chicago Fire birth records.*

❑ *Be aware of the 75-year confidentiality rule for Illinois birth records.*

❑ *Finding baptismal records is a three-step process:*

1. Determine your ancestor's religion at the time of baptism.

2. Identify likely churches in the area at that time.

3. Research the current location of records.

(Continued next page)

When (and Where) Was
My Ancestor Born?

❏ *Check birth announcements only if your ancestor was born in a suburb.*

❏ *Be prepared to pay for unreleased 1940–2000 census information (deceased individuals only— you must prove you're an heir).*

❏ *Determine where your ancestor attended school:*

• If your ancestor attended a specialty school, check to see if the school still exists and what its policy is on releasing student information.

• If your ancestor attended a Chicago public school, check the *Board of Education Proceedings* for birth dates from about 1917 to 1958.

• If your ancestor attended a Roman Catholic school, check with either the school, if it's open, or the Archdiocesan Archives, if the school's closed.

When (and Where) Was My Ancestor Born?

❑ *Look at Social Security applications:*

• Because these are created by the person rather than about the person, they hold valuable information. But you should cross-check these documents with other information.

❑ *Look at naturalization records post-1906:*

• These are good for finding an immigrant's exact birth date and birthplace and also birth dates and birthplaces for an immigrant's children.

❑ *Look at death records:*

• Check all types: death certificates, church death registers, tombstones, and death notices or obituaries.

3   Who Were the Parents of My Ancestor?

I hear this question over and over at the reference desk of the Newberry Library. Genealogists always want to go back another generation, always want to fill another space on the family tree.

To be successful in locating the parents, you have to do your homework first. In his 2001 book Black Roots, Tony Burroughs talks about falling into the trap of trying to go back too quickly. (This is an excellent beginner's guide for everyone, by the way.) Go broad before you go deep. That means researching all the siblings of your ancestor, not just your direct line. The siblings had the same parents as your ancestor, and the clues to the parents will be found among their children. It is often easier, for example, to find records about your grandmother's brother, because his last name did not change. Among his records will be information about his parents, which is just as valid for your grandmother. The bonus of sibling research will be seeing family dynamics from different perspectives: your Uncle Frank getting married when his youngest sister, your Aunt Dorothy, was eight months old. That brings home the span of ages in that family. So look for the types of records discussed in this chapter for each sibling in your ancestor's family, as well as for your ancestor.

❑ Strategy No. 1:
Birth and Baptismal Records

The logical place to start is with a birth certificate or baptismal record because they name the parents. Birth certificates will usually provide additional data on the parents, such as their address, ages, place of birth, and mother's maiden name. Baptismal certificates aren't as rich

Illustrations 3.1 and 3.2: Compare the information collected on the Cook County birth certificate (Illustration 3.1) with that on the St. George Church baptismal certificate (Illustration 3.2). The parents' birthplace on the birth certificate is given only as "L.R." (Lithuanian Republic). There are two spellings of the mother's maiden name: one interpreted by a Polish midwife on the birth certificate and one by a Lithuanian priest on the baptismal certificate. Deciphering handwriting will be one of the biggest challenges in your research. Images courtesy of Walter J. Podrazik.

in detail, typically including just the parents' names and the mother's maiden name.

A common misconception is that genealogical libraries have copies of birth certificates. There are only two places in the Chicago area that have them: the Family History Center in Wilmette and the Illinois Regional Archives Depository (IRAD) at Northeastern Illinois University. See Chapter 12 ("Nuts and Bolts of Birth and Death Records") for a complete rundown on these and other places to obtain birth certificates.

Not all religious denominations create baptismal records. Those that do include Roman Catholic, Eastern-rite Catholic, Orthodox, Episcopalian, Lutheran, and Methodist.

If you don't know your ancestor's religion, ethnic identity is one starting point—Scandinavians are generally Lutheran, Italians generally Catholic, Germans either Lutheran, Catholic, or Jewish. See where the family lived at the time of the birth, and determine which places of worship were located nearby (see Chapter 6, "Where Did My Ancestor Live?"). Then you'll have to find out what happened to the records. Are they at the same church? at a church it merged with? in an archive? Have they been microfilmed by the Latter-day Saints? Finding your ancestor's baptismal records among family papers makes the whole process a lot easier! That's another reason for doing your homework, as discussed in Chapter 1 ("Where Do I Start?"). For more on finding religious records, see strategy number 5 in this chapter.

❏ Strategy No. 2:
Delayed and Corrected Birth Certificates

If you are stymied finding your ancestor's birth certificate, check for delayed or corrected filings.

Delayed Birth Certificates
With home births common, many people did not have birth certificates. It was not a state requirement until 1916, and even after that time, the midwives and physicians who

were supposed to file the certificates often did not. Later, when people needed proof of birth for school or a job, they had to apply for a delayed birth certificate. There was a big surge in the 1940s because of the requirements for war work and the armed services.

When you go through the *Cook County Birth Index 1871–1916*, you may see a reference like this:

Stern, Solly   Oct. 31, 1896   D.S. #120381

"D.S." = Delayed Series and "O.D.S." = Old Delayed Series. Both of these mean your ancestor's birth record was filed years after the fact. That should alert you to proceed with caution regarding information about your ancestor's parents. Include the abbreviation when you request the certificate at Cook County Bureau of Vital Statistics—this should help in locating it. You'll find contact information for the Bureau in Chapter 12, "Nuts and Bolts of Birth and Death Records."

Only a few of the delayed certificates are indexed in the *Cook County Birth Index 1871–1916*. The majority are on seven reels of microfilm that make up *Chicago Delayed Birth Indexes, 1871–1948*, which is available on loan through Family History Centers and the Newberry Library for a fee. Entries are not in strict alphabetical order. In the Chicago area, the Family History Center in Wilmette holds this set. If you would like to order the films at another Family History Center, find the film numbers through the Family History Library catalog (www.familysearch.org/Eng/Library/FHLC/frameset_fhlc.asp). Do a place search for Cook County. Go to "View Related Places" and choose Chicago, then select "Vital Records Indexes."

Corrected Birth Certificates

Sometimes the parents had not chosen a name for the baby when it was born, and the birth certificate was filed with a combination of the father's first initial and the mother's first name. That obviously had to be corrected when the person needed proof of identity. Mistakes in spelling and omitted information are other reasons for corrections.

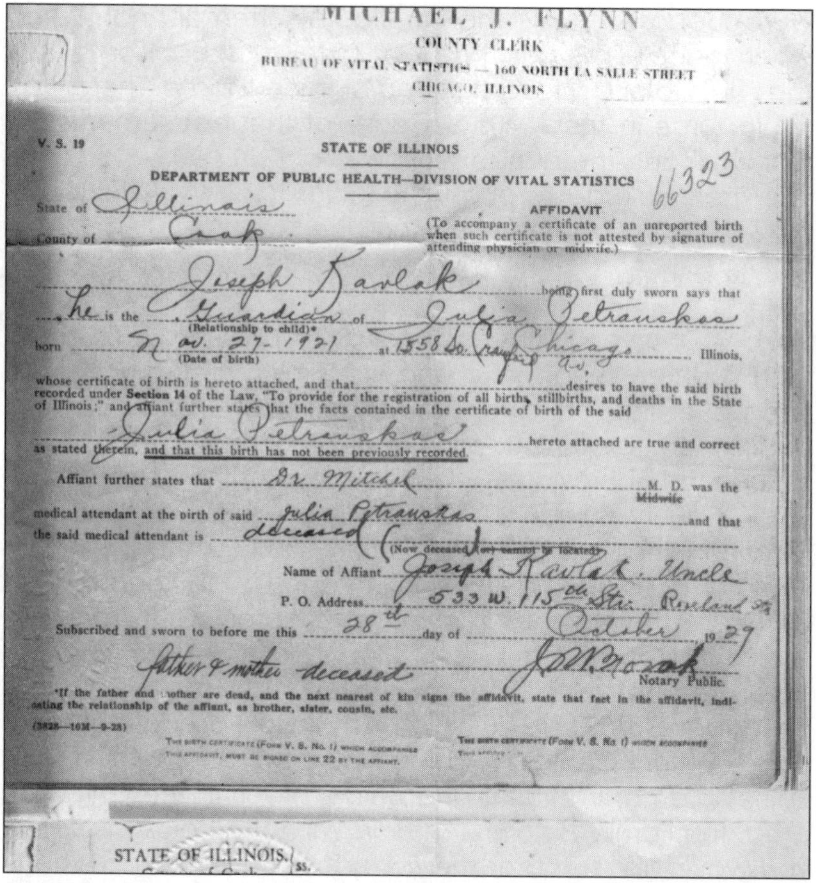

MICHAEL J. FLYNN
COUNTY CLERK
BUREAU OF VITAL STATISTICS — 160 NORTH LA SALLE STREET
CHICAGO, ILLINOIS

V. S. 19

STATE OF ILLINOIS

DEPARTMENT OF PUBLIC HEALTH—DIVISION OF VITAL STATISTICS 66323

State of Illinois

County of Cook

AFFIDAVIT

(To accompany a certificate of an unreported birth when such certificate is not attested by signature of attending physician or midwife.)

Joseph Kavlak being first duly sworn says that he is the Guardian (Relationship to child)* of Julia Petrauskas born Nov. 27-1921 (Date of birth) at 1358 So. Crawford av. Chicago Illinois, whose certificate of birth is hereto attached, and that desires to have the said birth recorded under Section 14 of the Law, "To provide for the registration of all births, stillbirths, and deaths in the State of Illinois;" and affiant further states that the facts contained in the certificate of birth of the said Julia Petrauskas hereto attached are true and correct as stated therein, and that this birth has not been previously recorded.

Affiant further states that Dr. Mitchel M. D. was the ~~Midwife~~ medical attendant at the birth of said Julia Petrauskas and that the said medical attendant is deceased (Now deceased or cannot be located).

Name of Affiant Joseph Kavlak. Uncle

P. O. Address 533 W. 115th Str. Roseland

Subscribed and sworn to before me this 28th day of October, 1929

father & mother deceased

Notary Public.

*If the father and mother are dead, and the next nearest of kin signs the affidavit, state that fact in the affidavit, indicating the relationship of the affiant, as brother, sister, cousin, etc.

(3828—10M—9-28)

The birth certificate (Form V. S. No. 1) which accompanies this affidavit, must be signed on line 22 by the affiant.

STATE OF ILLINOIS, } SS.

Illustration 3.3a: Joseph Kavlak, guardian of Julia Petrauskas, filed an affidavit (a written, notarized statement) in 1929 about Julia's birth in 1921. He stated that the physician involved was deceased, her parents were deceased, and the birth had not been previously recorded.

Facing page: As Julia's uncle, Joseph would have good knowledge of her parents. He provided her mother's maiden name, Kaulakis; evidently he had Americanized his to Kavlak. He also gave the parents' ages at the time of birth, their occupations, and their address. For their birthplaces he merely wrote "Lithuania." He was certainly in a position to provide more details about his sister's birthplace but did not do so. Whether his brother-in-law Constantine was in fact a clerk in 1921 needs to be verified; Constantine's 1922 death certificate stated that he was a laborer. Always check and compare information from different sources. Give the most weight to information recorded at the time of the event by the people involved. Courtesy of Walter J. Podrazik.

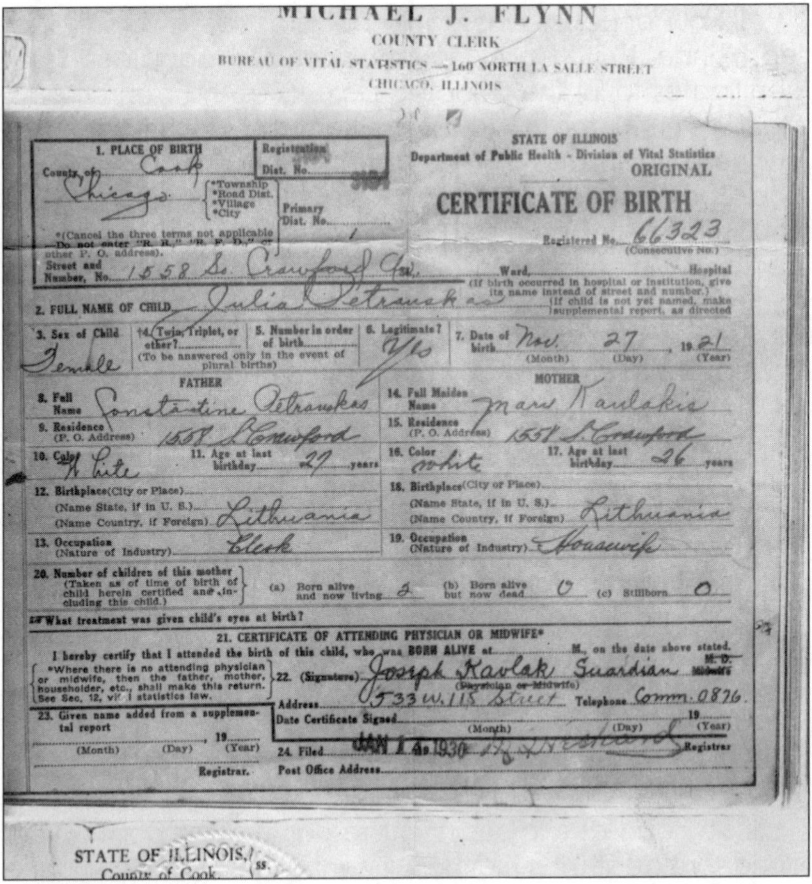

MICHAEL J. FLYNN
COUNTY CLERK
BUREAU OF VITAL STATISTICS — 160 NORTH LA SALLE STREET
CHICAGO, ILLINOIS

STATE OF ILLINOIS
Department of Public Health - Division of Vital Statistics
ORIGINAL

CERTIFICATE OF BIRTH

Registered No. 66323 (Consecutive No.)

1. PLACE OF BIRTH
County of Cook
Chicago *Township *Road Dist. *Village *City
Registration Dist. No.
Primary Dist. No.
*(Cancel the three terms not applicable—Do not enter "R. R.," "R. F. D.," or other P. O. address).
Street and Number, No. 1558 S. Crawford Av. Ward. Hospital
(If birth occurred in hospital or institution, give its name instead of street and number.)

2. FULL NAME OF CHILD Julia Petrauskas (If child is not yet named, make supplemental report, as directed)

3. Sex of Child Female
†4. Twin, Triplet, or other? (To be answered only in the event of plural births)
5. Number in order of birth
6. Legitimate? Yes
7. Date of birth Nov. 27, 1921 (Month) (Day) (Year)

FATHER
8. Full Name Constantine Petrauskas
9. Residence (P. O. Address) 1558 S. Crawford
10. Color White
11. Age at last birthday 27 years
12. Birthplace (City or Place) (Name State, if in U. S.) (Name Country, if Foreign) Lithuania
13. Occupation (Nature of Industry) Clerk

MOTHER
14. Full Maiden Name Mary Kaulakis
15. Residence (P. O. Address) 1558 S. Crawford
16. Color white
17. Age at last birthday 26 years
18. Birthplace (City or Place) (Name State, if in U. S.) (Name Country, if Foreign) Lithuania
19. Occupation (Nature of Industry) Housewife

20. Number of children of this mother (Taken as of time of birth of child herein certified and including this child.) (a) Born alive and now living 2 (b) Born alive but now dead 0 (c) Stillborn 0

What treatment was given child's eyes at birth?

21. CERTIFICATE OF ATTENDING PHYSICIAN OR MIDWIFE*
I hereby certify that I attended the birth of this child, who was BORN ALIVE at ....M., on the date above stated.
*Where there is no attending physician or midwife, then the father, mother, householder, etc., shall make this return. See Sec. 12, vital statistics law.
22. (Signature) Joseph Kavlak Guardian ~~M.D. Midwife~~ (~~Physician or Midwife~~)
Address 533 W. 115 Street Telephone Comm. 0876
Date Certificate Signed (Month) (Day) 19 (Year)
23. Given name added from a supplemental report (Month) (Day) 19 (Year) Registrar.
24. Filed JAN 1 1930 Registrar
Post Office Address

STATE OF ILLINOIS, } ss.
County of Cook.

Illustration 3.3b

If your ancestor was legally adopted, be aware that at least since 1935, Cook County changed adoptees' birth certificates to list the adoptive parents as the birth parents. Starting in 1971, the law also permitted using a false birthplace on these certificates (source: Loretto Dennis Szucs, *Chicago and Cook County: A Guide to Research*, 1996, page 37). So you will not get accurate information from an amended certificate in connection with an adoption.

Corrected names are usually but not always indexed in *Cook County Birth Index 1871–1916*. Other types of corrections rarely show up in that index. The Latter-day Saints (LDS) microfilmed *Chicago, Illinois Birth Corrections and Indexes, 1871–1915*. As with the index to the delayed births, entries are not in strict alphabetical order. These microfilm reels are available on loan at LDS Family History Centers and the Newberry Library for a fee; for film numbers, consult the Family History Library catalog (www.familysearch.org/Eng/Library/FHLC/frameset_fhlc.asp). Do a place search for Cook County. Go to "View Related Places" and choose Chicago, then select "Vital Records Indexes."

❏ Strategy No. 3: Death Records

It's a good idea to begin your research at the point of your ancestor's death. It is the most recent event in time, using the genealogical principle of working backward from the present to the past. And once you have a death date, you can look for a death certificate, an obituary or a death notice, funeral home information, and tombstones, all of which can lead you to your ancestor's parents.

Death Certificates

There are several important things to keep in mind concerning death certificates:

• Pre-1871 death certificates were destroyed in the Chicago Fire that October.

```
VS 400.1                                              Use ONLY on Original Records
  (2/64)              STATE OF ILLINOIS              ✶ Filed with County Clerk.
              AFFIDAVIT AND CERTIFICATE OF CORRECTION

Concerning the record of:  Birth                    No. 8711
FULL NAME Stella Klames                                              birth
                                                       whose stillbirth occurred
                                                             death

at  Chicago        in the County of  Cook    , Illinois on the 12 day of February 19 10
In keeping with the provisions of Paragraph 73-22 of the Vital Statistics Act, Paragraphs 73-1 through 73-29, Chapter 111½, Illinois
Revised Statutes, 1961, I hereby certify under oath that the following items appearing on the original certificate identified above are in-
correct or missing and should be corrected as follows:

     ITEM NO.  1        omitted          Stella Klames
and SHOULD READ   was incorrectly given as   Stefanie Klimek
     ITEM NO. 8        omitted          Blanche Klames
and SHOULD READ   was incorrectly given as   Blanche Klimek
     ITEM NO. 10       omitted          John Klames
and SHOULD READ   was incorrectly given as   John Klimek
     ITEM NO.          omitted
and SHOULD READ   was incorrectly given as
     ITEM NO.          omitted
and SHOULD READ   was incorrectly given as
     ITEM NO.          omitted
and SHOULD READ   was incorrectly given as

                              Signed Stefanie Klimek Federowski
  Add 10 E. Braiton, Chicago, Ill.  Relationship  Self
Subscribed and sworn to before me this  27      day of   July          19 66
  Add 130 N. Wells, Chicago, Ill.   Signed
                                    Title      -Notary Public
                        Documents Accepted as Supporting Evidence   February 13, 1910
 1. Baptismal Record                               Date made
 2. Saint Salomea Church                           Date made
 3. 118th St. & Indiana Ave                        Date made
 4. Chicago, Illinois                              Date made
 5.                                                Date made

Accepted for filing on the      day of        19     By   J. A.
                                                   Title

    FORMS FURNISHED BY BUREAU OF STATISTICS – ILLINOIS DEPARTMENT OF PUBLIC HEALTH
                         SPRINGFIELD, ILLINOIS 62706
```

*Illustration 3.4: In 1966 Stefanie Federowski (nee Klimek) filed a correct-
ed birth certificate. Using her baptismal record as evidence, she
showed that her maiden name had been spelled incorrectly for herself
and her parents and that she had been given a different first name on
the certificate than what she grew up using.*

    *Knowing the proper spelling of the parents' names will make a
huge difference in your research. The corrected certificate also gives
you notice of a religious record to pursue for more information about
the parents.* Source: Birth Corrections, Klafta–Pittel, FHL Film #0378365,
part of *Chicago, Illinois Birth Corrections and Indexes, 1871–1915.*

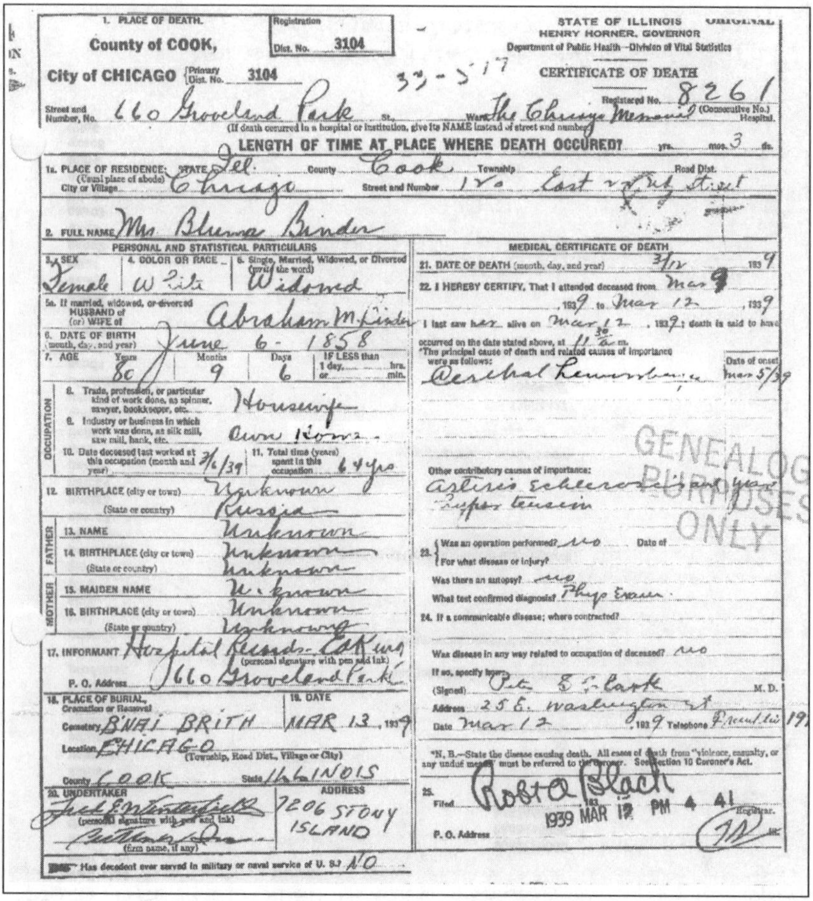

1. PLACE OF DEATH. County of COOK, Registration Dist. No. 3104

City of CHICAGO Primary Dist. No. 3104 33-517

STATE OF ILLINOIS ORIGINAL
HENRY HORNER, GOVERNOR
Department of Public Health—Division of Vital Statistics
CERTIFICATE OF DEATH

Registered No. 8261 (Consecutive No.)

Street and Number, No. 660 Groveland Park St., Ward The Chicago Memorial Hospital.
(If death occurred in a hospital or institution, give its NAME instead of street and number)

LENGTH OF TIME AT PLACE WHERE DEATH OCCURED? yrs. mos. 3 ds.

1a. PLACE OF RESIDENCE: STATE Ill. County Cook Township Road Dist.
(Usual place of abode) City or Village Chicago Street and Number 170 East 72nd Street

2. FULL NAME Mrs Bluma Binder

PERSONAL AND STATISTICAL PARTICULARS		MEDICAL CERTIFICATE OF DEATH
3. SEX Female	4. COLOR OR RACE White	5. Single, Married, Widowed, or Divorced (write the word) Widowed

5a. If married, widowed, or divorced HUSBAND of (or) WIFE of Abraham M. Binder

6. DATE OF BIRTH (month, day, and year) June 6 - 1858

7. AGE Years 80 Months 9 Days 6 IF LESS than 1 day, hrs. or min.

OCCUPATION
8. Trade, profession, or particular kind of work done, as spinner, sawyer, bookkeeper, etc. Housewife
9. Industry or business in which work was done, as silk mill, saw mill, bank, etc. Own Home
10. Date deceased last worked at this occupation (month and year) 3/6/39 11. Total time (years) spent in this occupation 64 yrs

12. BIRTHPLACE (city or town) Unknown
(State or country) Russia

FATHER
13. NAME Unknown
14. BIRTHPLACE (city or town) Unknown
(State or country) Unknown

MOTHER
15. MAIDEN NAME Unknown
16. BIRTHPLACE (city or town) Unknown
(State or country) Unknown

17. INFORMANT Hospital Records - Eaking
(personal signature with pen and ink)
P. O. Address 660 Groveland Park

18. PLACE OF BURIAL, Cremation or Removal
Cemetery B'NAI BRITH 19. DATE MAR 13, 1939
Location CHICAGO (Township, Road Dist., Village or City)
County COOK State ILLINOIS

20. UNDERTAKER Fred F. Winterfield (personal signature with pen and ink) ADDRESS 7206 STONY ISLAND
(firm name, if any)

Has decedent ever served in military or naval service of U. S.? NO

21. DATE OF DEATH (month, day, and year) 3/12 1939

22. I HEREBY CERTIFY, That I attended deceased from Mar 9, 1939 to Mar 12, 1939
I last saw her alive on Mar 12, 1939; death is said to have occurred on the date stated above, at 11:30 a.m.
The principal cause of death and related causes of importance were as follows: Cerebral Hemorrhage Date of onset Mar 5/39

Other contributory causes of importance: arterio sclerosis 3 yrs; hypertension

GENEALOGY PURPOSES ONLY

23. Was an operation performed? no Date of
For what disease or injury?
Was there an autopsy? no
What test confirmed diagnosis? Phys Exam.

24. If a communicable disease; where contracted?
Was disease in any way related to occupation of deceased? no
If so, specify how.
(Signed) Pete E. Clark M.D.
Address 25 E. Washington st
Date Mar 12, 1939 Telephone

*N. B.—State the disease causing death. All cases of death from "violence, casualty, or any undue means" must be referred to the Coroner. See Section 10 Coroner's Act.

25. Filed Robt A. Black 1939 MAR 13 PM 4 41 Registrar.
P. O. Address

Illustration 3.5: A clerk named Eaking in the Hospital Records Department was the informant for Bluma Binder's death certificate in 1939. Consequently, particulars of Bluma's birthplace and her parents could not be provided. You would have to search other sources, such as obituaries, tombstones, and the records of Bluma's siblings. Source: Cook County Bureau of Vital Statistics.

• It was not a state requirement until 1916 to file a death certificate.

• Recent certificates are confidential for 20 years. (You have to be a blood relative or the executor of the estate to obtain a death certificate within that time.)

• Parents' names and birthplaces were not listed on certificates until 1910, according to Loretto Szucs in her 1996 book. But checking the city directory for names at the deceased's address may lead you to the head of household. This technique is especially useful if you're tracing a common surname.

Even if your ancestor died after 1910, you may not get information on your ancestor's parents—it depends on who the informant was. A hospital clerk had no personal knowledge and relied on what was taken down at the time of admitting. You may get lucky when a blood relative supplies the information, or that person may have been so stressed and grief stricken that the details are incomplete or incorrect. Always cross-check the details on the death certificate with as many sources as you can before accepting them. See Chapter 12 for locating death certificates.

Obituaries or Death Notices

You may or may not find the parents listed in your ancestor's death notice or obituary. Certainly if one or both parents survived your ancestor, they would be mentioned. If your ancestor was a person of note, it is more likely that his or her parents would be remarked upon, to compare and contrast their circumstances with what your ancestor became.

A death notice, because it is a paid listing that concentrates on the funeral arrangements, is less apt to include the names of deceased parents. But often there are exceptions. That's why it's important to search places such as:

• Chicago newspapers (for most of Chicago's history, there have been at least four dailies)

> HOFFMANN—Anton R. Hoffmann, beloved
> husband of Eulalia, fond mother of Mrs.
> Louriee Haase and Anton Jr., son of the
> late George and Sophia Hoffmann, brother
> of Mrs. Louise Tenwick and the late Olaf
> Hoffmann. Funeral Tuesday, Oct. 3, 2
> p. m., from his late residence, 3903 N. Kil-
> dare-av.; interment Mount Olive. Mem-
> ber of B. P. O. E. Lodge No. 1295.

Illustration 3.6: This death notice does include the names of deceased parents and mentions a medical miracle: Anton was the mother of two children! A humorous example of the mistakes to watch for in your research. Note the acronym B.P.O.E. (Benevolent and Protective Order of the Elks). Mention of Anton's passing, and possibly more biographical information, may appear in The Elks magazine or lodge records. Source: Chicago Daily News, October 2, 1933.

- neighborhood newspapers

- ethnic newspapers

- suburban newspapers (for ancestors who lived outside the city)

- trade journals covering particular fields or professions

- religiously affiliated newspapers (for example, the publication of the Roman Catholic Archdiocese of Chicago, currently called *The Catholic New World*). See Chapter 11 ("Nuts and Bolts of Newspaper Searching") for more information.

Funeral Home Information

Part of a funeral home's service is to compile biographical information about the deceased. Uses include a written obituary, a funeral program, or a eulogy by a member of the clergy. The information also helps the funeral director advise the family about government programs defraying burial costs, such as Social Security and Veterans Affairs benefits.

The amount of biographical information collected varies

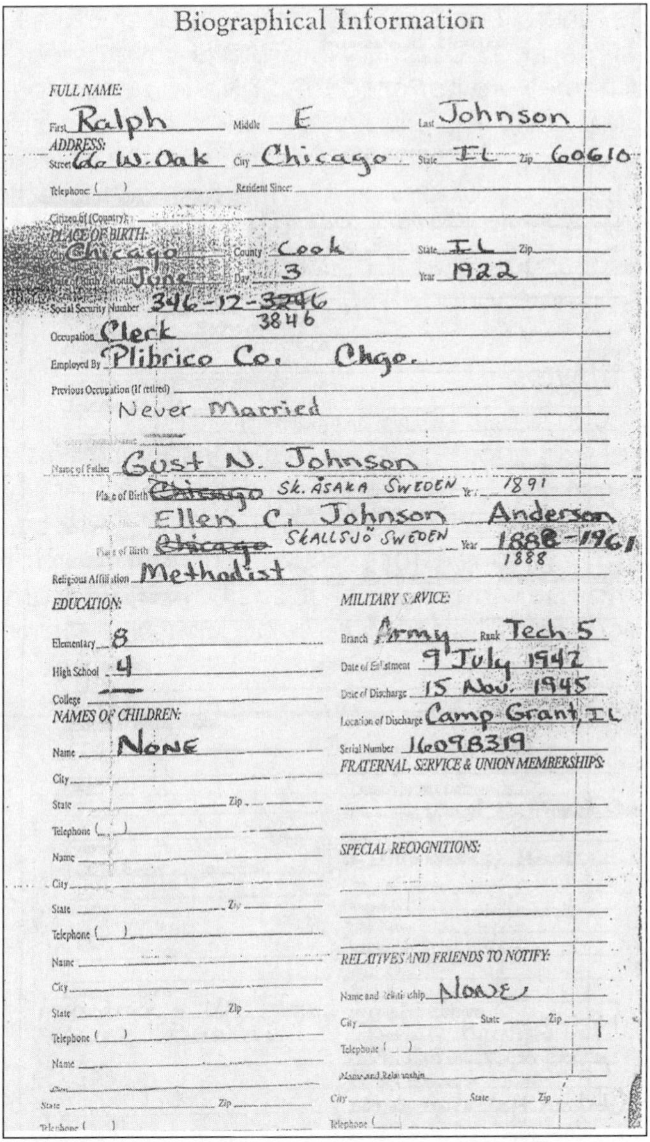

Biographical Information

FULL NAME:

First Ralph Middle E Last Johnson

ADDRESS:

Street 66 W. Oak City Chicago State IL Zip 60610

Telephone ( ) Resident Since:

Citizen of (Country):

PLACE OF BIRTH:

City Chicago County Cook State IL Zip

Date of Birth/Month June Day 3 Year 1922

Social Security Number 346-12-3246 3846

Occupation Clerk

Employed By Plibrico Co. Chgo.

Previous Occupation (If retired)

Never Married

Name of Father Gust N. Johnson

Place of Birth ~~Chicago~~ Sk. ÅSAKA SWEDEN Year 1891

Ellen C. Johnson Anderson

Place of Birth ~~Chicago~~ SKALLSJÖ SWEDEN Year 1888-1961 1888

Religious Affiliation Methodist

EDUCATION:

Elementary 8

High School 4

College —

NAMES OF CHILDREN:

Name NONE

City

State Zip

Telephone ( )

Name

City

State Zip

Telephone ( )

Name

City

State Zip

Telephone ( )

Name

City

State Zip

Telephone ( )

MILITARY SERVICE:

Branch Army Rank Tech 5

Date of Enlistment 9 July 1942

Date of Discharge 15 Nov. 1945

Location of Discharge Camp Grant, IL

Serial Number 16098319

FRATERNAL, SERVICE & UNION MEMBERSHIPS:

SPECIAL RECOGNITIONS:

RELATIVES AND FRIENDS TO NOTIFY:

Name and Relationship NONE

City State Zip

Telephone ( )

Name and Relationship

City State Zip

Telephone ( )

Illustration 3.7: Page of biographical information gathered by the funeral home handling the arrangements of Ralph E. Johnson. It gives his parents' exact birthplace in Sweden, their years of birth, and his mother's maiden name. Only their names are listed on his 1992 death certificate. No death notice or obituary ran in the newspapers, making the funeral home's information extremely valuable. Courtesy of Ralph Johansson.

with the funeral home. It may or may not include the names of the deceased's parents. *Note: Unlike government offices, funeral homes are not obliged to give you any information.* Some feel that the privacy of their clients is paramount. Others are open to genealogists' requests. Be polite and be brief when you call or stop by. The funeral home staff are taking time from their work to look up information for you. Always offer to pay for photocopies and send a written thank-you note for anything you receive.

Tombstones

You can find much valuable information on the tombstones of your ancestors, often including their parents' names. Grave markers of Jews, for instance, list the father's name in Hebrew. You should make a point of visiting the cemetery, locating your ancestor's grave, and photographing it. There may be other clues on it, such as fraternal emblems, references to military service, or occupational symbols. You

Illustration 3.8: The Hebrew inscription on this tombstone reads, "Here is buried Reuben A., son of Mr. Abraham Stern. Died the third day of Kislev in the year 5685." The JewishGen Web site (www.jewishgen.org) has a converter that translates Hebrew dates; in this case, the date is November 30, 1924. Courtesy of Gerald Stern.

may be lucky enough to find one with a photograph of your ancestor.

Note: Cemetery records will not give you the names of your ancestor's parents. The records that cemeteries keep are concerned with location of the grave, maintenance, and payment. What a person did in life and who that person's parents were have no bearing on cemetery operations, so that information is not collected. If your ancestor is buried in a family plot, the records will tell you the names of the others in the plot but will not provide relationships. From the cemetery's point of view, there is no reason to document that. If you know this going in, you will save yourself frustration at the cemetery office.

❑ Strategy No. 4: Census

In the past, generations lived together more than they do now; parents often lived with an adult child. That's why it's important to pull the census for all the siblings of your ancestor; the parent might have lived with an unmarried daughter or with a son who had a large house for his own family.

Starting in 1880 and continuing through 2000, the U.S. census asked for each person's relationship to head of household. You will be able to spot "mother-in-law" or "father" on the page. Other relatives may also give clues. If a sister-in-law is listed, her last name could be the maiden name of the wife.

In the 1880 and 1930 censuses, you can search indexes by your ancestor's name and see who's in the household. In other census years, you have to know the name of the head of household. The head is the husband for a married couple; if your ancestor was single, he or she may be head of household, or he or she may be listed as a boarder or lodger in a rooming house or hotel, with the proprietor considered head of household. In cases of a widow, often an elder, unmarried son is listed as head. In head of household indexes, only the heads and anyone in the same house with a last name different from the head are listed. For more on finding your

Illustration 3.9: The Adams family consists of Albert H. Adams, head of household, age 53; Clare E. Adams, his wife, age 54; Jean Adams, their daughter, age 19; and Minnie A. Crofoot, his mother-in-law, age 76. Because Minnie's relationship to Albert is given, it's pretty likely she is Clare's mother (Minnie could also be the mother of a first wife, now deceased or divorced). You could then make a good guess that Clare's maiden name was Crofoot, which you need to verify through research on Minnie. You can't, however, discount the possibility that Minnie, a widow, is using her second husband's name. For late twentieth century research, remember that increasing numbers of women kept their maiden names and will be found in records that way. Source: 1930 U.S. Census, Reel 504, ED 16–2250, Sheet 15B, Lines 76–79.

---

ancestor's entry, see Chapter 10 ("Nuts and Bolts of the U.S. Census").

A word of caution: If you find a parent in the census, avoid the trap of jumping into research in other states based solely on the census report of where the parent was born. Census takers wrote down what they were told— they did not ask for proof. They could have gotten their information from a child who answered the door or an adult who wasn't really clear on the ancestry of everybody in the household. Take the census information and weigh it with other evidence before making a hypothesis to test in your next search.

❑ Strategy No. 5: Marriage Records

In most other parts of the country, genealogists can easily locate the parents of an ancestor by accessing civil marriage applications or marriage bonds. The problem with Cook County is that it was not until 1968 that names of parents were recorded. But even if you wanted to obtain

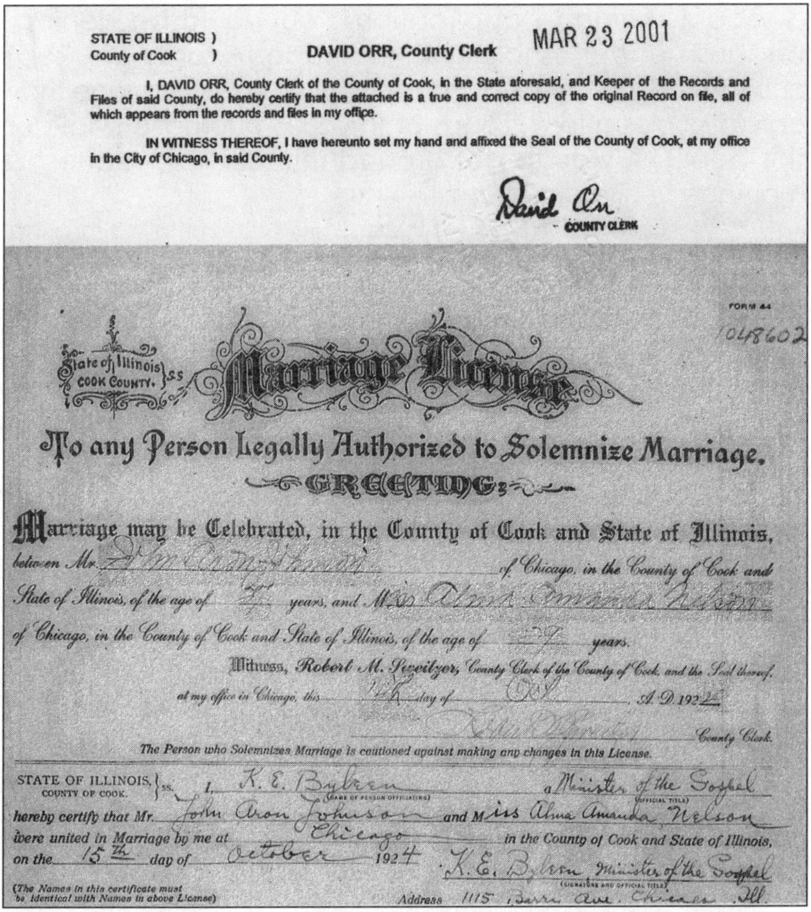
STATE OF ILLINOIS)
County of Cook)

DAVID ORR, County Clerk

MAR 23 2001

I, DAVID ORR, County Clerk of the County of Cook, in the State aforesaid, and Keeper of the Records and Files of said County, do hereby certify that the attached is a true and correct copy of the original Record on file, all of which appears from the records and files in my office.

IN WITNESS THEREOF, I have hereunto set my hand and affixed the Seal of the County of Cook, at my office in the City of Chicago, in said County.

David Orr
COUNTY CLERK

FORM 44

1048602

State of Illinois, COOK COUNTY. } SS

Marriage License

To any Person Legally Authorized to Solemnize Marriage.

GREETING:

Marriage may be Celebrated, in the County of Cook and State of Illinois, between Mr. [illegible] of Chicago, in the County of Cook and State of Illinois, of the age of [illegible] years, and Miss Alma Amanda Nelson of Chicago, in the County of Cook and State of Illinois, of the age of [illegible] years.

Witness, Robert M. Sweitzer, County Clerk of the County of Cook, and the Seal thereof, at my office in Chicago, this [illegible] day of Oct A. D. 192[illegible]

[illegible] County Clerk.

The Person who Solemnizes Marriage is cautioned against making any changes in this License.

STATE OF ILLINOIS, } ss. COUNTY OF COOK. I, K. E. Byleen (NAME OF PERSON OFFICIATING) a Minister of the Gospel (OFFICIAL TITLE) hereby certify that Mr. John Aron Johnson and Miss Alma Amanda Nelson were united in Marriage by me at Chicago in the County of Cook and State of Illinois, on the 15th day of October 1924 K. E. Byleen Minister of the Gospel (SIGNATURE AND OFFICIAL TITLE)

(The Names in this certificate must be identical with Names in above License)

Address 1115 Barry Ave. Chicago Ill.

Illustration 3.10: Shown here is the 1924 civil marriage certificate for Swedish immigrants John Aron Johnson and Alma Amanda Nelson. The names of the couple's parents are not given. I pursued the church records by looking for the minister K. E. Byleen in the 1923 Chicago city directory. He turned out to be Reverend Karl E. Byleen, pastor of Lake View Swedish Baptist Church, located at the southeast corner of Barry Avenue and Clifton Avenue. The church was not listed in today's telephone books, so I went to the address and found that the building had been converted into condominiums. To track down the records, I need to find out if the church merged with another congregation or if its records were sent to an archive. See the section on Swedish research in Chapter 16, "Ethnic Resources." Source: Cook County Bureau of Vital Statistics.

a recent marriage application, you would be denied, because under Illinois law, marriage records are kept confidential for 50 years. Only the parties to the marriage may obtain copies after 1955 (as of the 2005 publication date of this book). A way to get around this rule is to request a marriage verification from:

Illinois Department of Public Health
Division of Vital Records
605 W. Jefferson Street
Springfield, IL 62702
217/782-6553

For a fee, the IDPH will search its files from 1962 to the present and verify the date of, place of, and parties to a marriage. Once you have the date and the name of the spouse, you can look for a wedding announcement or a religious record that will give you the names of the parents of the bride and groom.

Religious records are really the most helpful marriage records to get. Most denominations kept marriage registers with the bride and groom's names, their place of origin, their parents' names, and the names of witnesses. Early religious marriage records may be the only ones available, due to the loss of all county vital records in the Chicago Fire of 1871.

There are two ways to find religious records for your ancestor. One is to find out where your ancestor was living and look for nearby places of worship, assuming you know your ancestor's religion (see Chapter 6). Then you'll need to find out if the church still exists and where the records are. Scott Holl's *Guide to Chicago Church and Synagogue Records* is a tremendous help. It gives locations of archives and film numbers of records that the Latter-day Saints have microfilmed. It is available at the Local and Family History reference desk at the Newberry Library and is posted on the genealogy section of the Newberry Web site, www.newberry.org.

To find religious records in Cook County towns, first determine if the church or synagogue is still in existence. A history of the town can be helpful; check with the local library or historical society. Many histories are held by the Newberry Library and the Chicago Historical Society. If the place of worship exists, call or write the office administrator to learn its research policy. If possible, do your research in person rather than rely on a staffer who has a million other things to do besides answer genealogical requests. Mail requests should always be accompanied by a donation and an appreciation of the staffer's time.

If the place of worship no longer exists, the town history may tell you if it merged with another, and that place should have the records. If it has closed, the records are generally sent to denominational archives; Holl's guide can help with that. Records of closed synagogues may be with the former rabbi's family, or the Chicago Jewish Historical Society may know their whereabouts. Contact:

Chicago Jewish Historical Society
618 S. Michigan Avenue
Chicago, IL 60605
312/663-5634

The second method of finding religious records is to obtain the civil marriage certificate, decipher the name of the officiant, and research what congregation he or she was affiliated with. This only works if your ancestor was married by a priest, minister, or rabbi. Justice of the peace records from 1871 to 1963 were jettisoned in the early 1970s under Illinois law. It's possible a judge may have kept a log of the marriages he or she performed and that such a log would be in a collection of his or her papers, but it would be quite a task to locate that and there would be no guarantee that the judge recorded the names of the couple's parents.

There are several ways to obtain the civil marriage certificate. You'll generally need to look in an index first to get the date. You can get a rough idea from the date of birth of the first child or the date your ancestor first shows up married in the census. IRAD has an index to Cook County marriages from 1871 to 1904. The Illinois State Archives has a searchable database on its Web site (www.sos.state.il.us/departments/archives/marriage.html) for pre-1900 marriages. Volunteers have entered Cook County records from 1833 to December 1895 as of January 2005. Listings prior to 1871, when the records went up in flames, are taken from *Sam Fink's Index*. Fink was a genealogist who went through Chicago newspaper notices to compile a listing covering 1833 to 1871. His index has been microfilmed; the Newberry Library has it, and you can also get it on loan for a fee through Family History Centers. The Latter-day Saints have an index for 1871 to 1916 (with a few before and after those dates), obtainable on loan for a fee at the Newberry Library or at local Family History Centers.

Outside of the preceding parameters, you'll have to rely on the Cook County Bureau of Vital Statistics. The bureau works on a two-tier pricing system: one fee if you supply the certificate number and a higher fee if you don't know it. A bureau staffer will search a year before and a year after the year you specify for a fee and will also search additional years for an extra fee per year.

You can save yourself money by doing the searching yourself. The Latter-day Saints have microfilmed Cook County marriage licenses from 1871 to 1920; these reels are available on loan at the Newberry Library or at local Family History Centers for a fee. IRAD has some of these Latter-day Saints reels (1871–1900), and so does the Family History Center in Wilmette.

Tip: If you can't find your ancestor's marriage record in Cook County, check records for Lake County, Indiana. Crown Point, the county seat of Lake County, was the Midwest equivalent of Las Vegas wedding chapels from 1915 to 1940—no blood tests, no waiting, heavily advertised. The *Index to Marriage Records, Lake County, Indiana, 1805–1920 Inclusive* is available at the Newberry Library; the Lake County Public Library, Merrillville, Indiana; and the Allen County Public

Library in Fort Wayne, Indiana. For 1920 to 1940, contact the Recorder's Office in the Lake County courthouse in Crown Point. This office also has the marriage applications. Keep in mind, though, that people who got married in Crown Point were often eloping or throwing others off their tracks, so the information they provided should be viewed critically and verified with other documentation.

Who Were the Parents of My Ancestor?

Points to Remember

❏ *Go broad before you go deep:*

• Research all the siblings of your ancestor before focusing on your ancestor's parents.

❏ *Siblings of your ancestor had the same parents:*

• The clues to the parents will be found among their children.

❏ *Look for the following records for each sibling of your ancestor, as well as your direct line, to find the names of the parents:*

• birth certificates (possibly delayed or corrected)

• baptismal certificates or registers

• death information

• U.S. census

• marriage records

4   Who Were the Siblings of My Ancestor?

With large families common up to the 1950s, it can be frustrating tracking down all the siblings of your ancestor. Children often died before adulthood, and finding their names and death dates can be quite a project. Remarriage of parents may lead you to your ancestor's half brothers and sisters. There may be adoption or illegitimacy in the family. Following are some strategies to use in finding your ancestor's siblings.

___

❑ Strategy No. 1: Census

Starting in 1880 and continuing through 2000, the U.S. census asked for each person's relationship to the head of household. Select one of those census years when your ancestor would have been a child living with his or her family. So you can make a positive ID, you need to know your ancestor's approximate age and at least one other fact about him or her, such as the country or state of birth. In the 1880 and 1930 censuses, you can search indexes by your ancestor's name. In the other census years, you have to know the name of the head of household. If your ancestor's parents were alive at that point in time, the father would be head of household. If the mother was widowed, she would be head of household. You may find your ancestor living with a relative or in an orphanage.

❑ Strategy No. 2: Death Notices and Obituaries

Usually when the announcement of a person's death is made in the newspapers, the survivors are listed. A brother or sister is closely related enough to be included, whereas a niece or nephew or lesser relation may not be, for reasons of space.

The difference between a death notice and an obituary is that a death notice generally concentrates on the funeral arrangements, while an obituary usually focuses on the details of a person's life. Keep in mind when searching for death notices or obituaries that for most of its history, Chicago has had *at least* four daily newspapers. There were also (and continue to be) neighborhood newspapers and ethnic newspapers. If you don't find the notice in one paper, keep checking other newspapers that existed during that year (see the selected list in Chapter 11, "Nuts and Bolts of Newspaper Searching"). The Illinois Newspaper Project (www.library.uiuc. edu/inp) is very helpful for finding newspapers by date. Harold Washington Library Center has the most complete, convenient collection of Chicago newspapers.

Because the Chicago area has had so many newspapers through the years, not much headway has been made in indexing them. The very early years have been done because the issues were only two or four pages long, and the more recent years have been completed, thanks to advances in imaging technology. However, there's a huge gap between the 1850s and 1970s that is inaccessible without knowing your ancestor's death date. Do not attempt to search without it— your eyeballs will fall out. Chicago is after all the third largest city in the United States.

Once you have an exact death date (see Chapter 12, "Nuts and Bolts of Birth and Death Records"), start with that date and keep searching for a week. If the newspaper had morning and evening editions, check both, as there can be slight variations. For example, one edition might say at the end of the notice, "St. Louis papers please copy." That's a clue that the deceased or one of the survivors had ties to St. Louis, and you should check there for more information. (See Chapter 12 for tips on Cook County town searches.)

When you find the death notice or obituary, if it's a good one, it will give the married names of women and their

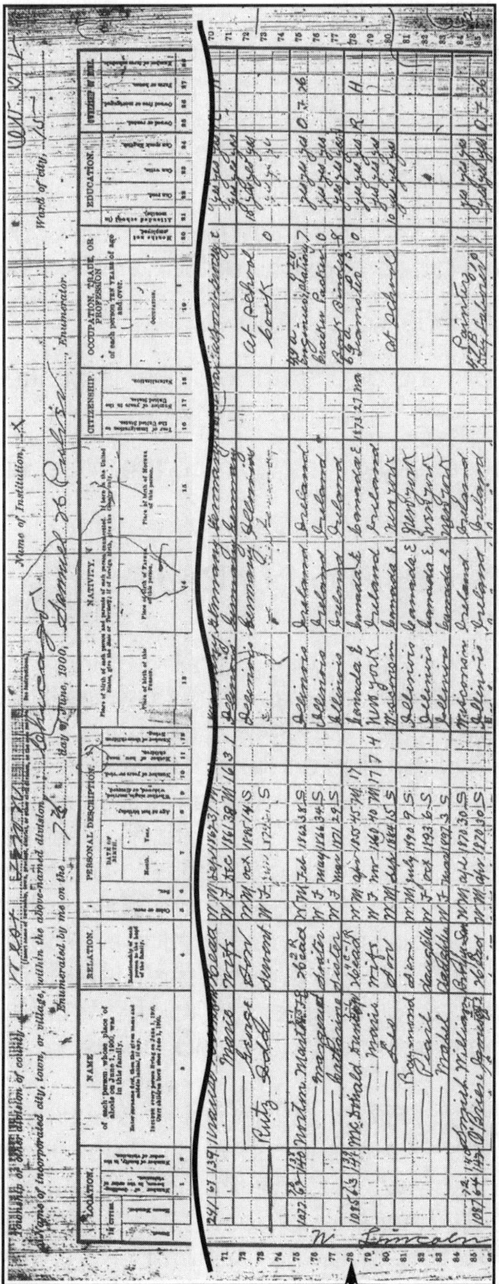

Illustration 4.1: Say you were looking for the siblings of Raymond McDonald. You know his father's name, Duncan, so you are able to locate the family in the 1900 census. It shows that Raymond is 9 years old and has three other siblings at home: an older brother, Leo, age 15, and two younger sisters, Pearl, 6, and Mabel, 3. The 1900 census gives the month and year of birth. But wait—there's more. The 1900 and 1910 censuses asked women how many children had been born to them and how many were alive. Raymond's mother, Maria, said she had seven children and four were still living. Looking at the ages of the surviving children, you can hypothesize when the other births occurred and research accordingly. Source: 1900 U.S. Census, Reel 264, ED 481, Sheet 8, Lines 78–84.

spouse's first name. It will also state where the survivors reside, so you can concentrate on records from that location to find more about them. If you don't find siblings listed in a death notice or an obituary, it can mean any of the following:

• The sibling died before the deceased.

• The sibling is "dead" to the family (for example, the sibling was in prison, had a baby out of wedlock, and so on).

• The sibling's whereabouts are unknown.

• The newspaper or funeral director mistakenly omitted mention of the sibling.

Because of these various explanations, it's important to search for all possible notices.

❏ Strategy No. 3: Proof of Heirship

If your ancestor's estate went through probate, there will be a document called *proof of heirship* in the case file. It is a record of testimony taken from a surviving spouse or child concerning who would be considered heirs of the deceased.

Questions are asked about the number of marriages and children the deceased had. If the children are married, the court will ask about their spouses and children. You often find surprising information, such as there being more siblings than you thought, because some of them died in infancy. You will not get exact dates of birth, but the children are listed in birth order, and their ages at death are given, so you have a nice narrow range to get the death certificate and then learn the date of death.

The criteria for your ancestor's estate being probated is dependent not on whether he or she made a will but on the size of the estate. I don't know what the size has to be under Illinois law. I automatically check for probates, because they have such good information: inventories of property (sometimes everything in the house), funeral bills, wills, addresses of

JENNIE RAYNER, CHICAGO FIRE SURVIVOR, DIES

Miss Jennie Rayner, 72 years old, 1348 Cleveland avenue, who came to Chicago from Michigan sixty-nine years ago and saw her parents' home on the north side destroyed in the great fire three years later, yesterday died in St. Luke's hospital. Miss Rayner, who lived alone, entered the hospital a month ago.

Until a year ago, when her health began failing, Miss Rayner was a seamstress. Surviving her are two sisters, Mrs. Albert Reinert, 5549 North McVicker avenue, and Mrs. Clara Henry of Sterling, Kas.

Obituary: *Chicago Daily News,*
August 26, 1937, p. 9.

RAYNER—Jennie Rayner, late of 1348 Cleveland avenue, Aug. 24, 1937, sister of Mrs. Clara Henery, Mrs. Minnie Reiner and the late William J. Rayner. Services at chapel, 5501 N. Ashland avenue, Saturday, Aug. 28, at 2 p. m., under auspices of Golden Rod chapter, No. 205, O. E. S, Interment Arlington. Also member of St. James' branch, Girls Friendly Society.

Death Notice: *Chicago Daily News,*
August 26, 1937, p. 28.

Illustration 4.2: Jennie Rayner's obituary provides the names of two surviving sisters, Mrs. Albert Reinert and Mrs. Clar_ Henry. Jennie's death notice in the same edition clears up the first name for Mrs. Henry—it's Clara, not Clark—but spells the last name as "Henery." The other sister's first name, Minnie, is given in the death notice, but again a spelling variation is introduced for the surname, which is given as "Reiner." You will have to gather other examples of the surnames to determine which are the correct spellings. The best way is to locate records with signatures and see how Minnie and Clara spelled their surnames. Possibilities include letters, wills, deeds, court records, and marriage records.

Notice how Jennie's brother William is only mentioned in the death notice. He predeceased her. Both the obituary and death notice provide unique information that is not repeated. That's why you need to search for both types, for all the days they were published, in all possible newspapers. Courtesy of Eleanor Baird.

the heirs, and so on.

Probate case files from 1871 to 1963 for Chicago and suburbs are available here:

Cook County Circuit Court Archives
Richard J. Daley Center
50 W. Washington Street, Room 1113
Chicago, IL 60602
312/603-6601
www.cookcountyclerkofcourt.org

Staff can search the indexes and provide certified or uncertified copies for a fee. Search forms are available online, through the mail, or at the office. If you go in person, search the 1871–1967 name indexes to obtain the case number. Request the file; it usually takes a week to come from the warehouse, so be sure to call to ensure it's in before you return for it. You'll need to show ID and fill out a form to look at the file, and you'll have a month to review it.

For probates dating from 1964 to the present, go the Probate Division in the Daley Center, Room 1202 (312/603-6441). There are book indexes by year and computer indexes for more recent cases. Search by name in both instances. You need to show ID to review the file. Photocopy fees apply. To my knowledge, the Probate Division does not offer search services. Tip: The files are not supposed to leave Room 1202, but it's been my experience that many of them do and cannot be located by staff.

❏ Strategy No. 4: Divorce Records

Many times researchers get the divorce decree but overlook the case file. This is a mistake. A divorce case always has a bill of complaint, which sets out the facts of the marriage and the reasons the complainant or plaintiff gives for wanting a divorce. In the complaint will be the marriage date and place of the parents and the birth dates or ages of the children. The question of custody and support of the

Proof of Heirship Testimony, Jan. 11, 1897

Q. *What is your name?*   A. Helene Chorengel.

Q. *Where do you live?*   A. 884 Milwaukee Avenue.

Q. *In the City of Chicago, Cook County, Illinois?*   A. Yes, sir.

Q. *How old are you?*   A. Fifty-seven years old.

Q. *You are the widow of Gerd Friedrich Chorengel, deceased, are you?*
    A. Yes, sir.

Q. *How old was he when he died?*   A. Seventy-one years old.

Q. *How old was he when you first became acquainted with him?*
    A. About thirty-three years old.

Q. *You are thoroughly familiar with his family history, are you?*
    A. Yes, sure.

Q. *How many times was Gerd Friedrich Chorengel ever married?*
    A. Twice.

Q. *Only twice?*   A. Yes, sir.

Q. *What was the name of his first wife?*   A. Anna.

Q. *Is she living?*   A. No, sir.

Q. *Did she die before the death of Gerd Friedrich Chorengel?*   A. Yes, sir.

Q. *And before his marriage to you?*   A. Yes, sure.

Q. *Did they live together as husband and wife up to the time of her death?*
    A. Yes, sir.

Q. *How many children were born to Gerd Friedrich Chorengel and his
first wife?*   A. Four.

Q. *Give me their names beginning with the eldest or first born?*
    A. Johann Friedrich Chorengel.

Q. *Is he living?*   A. Yes, sir.

Q. *About how old is he?*   A. About fifty-four years old.

Q. *What is the name of the second child?*   A. August Wilhelm.

Q. *Is he living?*   A. Yes, sir.

Q. *How old is he?*   A. About forty-three years old.

Q. *Give me the name of the third child?*   A. Carl Heinrich.

Q. *Is he living?*   A. Yes, sir.

Q. *Give me the name of the fourth child?*   A. Diedrich Anton.

Illustration 4.3: My client was researching Carl Heinrich Chorengel. She knew that his father, Gerd Friedrich Chorengel, had been married twice. The proof of heirship gave her the name of the first wife and the fact that that wife's fourth child died shortly after birth. It also told her that three children by the second wife had died in infancy and (Cont.)

Proof of Heirship Testimony, Jan. 11, 1897, cont.

Q. Is he living?   A. No, sir.

Q. How old was he when he died?   A. Three days old.

Q. And died before the death of his father, Gerd Friedrich Chorengel?
A. Yes, sir.

Q. Are these four children that you have named all the children that were ever born to Gerd Friedrich Chorengel and his first wife?   A. Yes, sir.

Q. You are his second wife?   A. Yes, sir.

Q. And you lived together as husband and wife up to the time of his death?
A. Yes, sir.

Q. How many children were born to Gerd Friedrich Chorengel and your-self?   A. Four.

Q. Give me their names beginning with the eldest or first born?
A. Hannah.

Q. Is Hannah living?   A. Yes, sir.

Q. How old is she?   A. Thirty-eight years old.

Q. Is Hannah married?   A. Yes, sir.

Q. What is her husband's name?   A. George Toborg.

Q. Is he living?   A. Yes, sir.

Q. What is the name of the second child born to Gerd Friedrich Chorengel and yourself?   A. Johann Diedrich.

Q. Is he living?   A. No, sir, he is dead.

Q. How old did he live to be?   A. Seven months.

Q. Did he died before the death of his father, Gerd Friedrich Chorengel?
A. Yes, sir.

Q. What was the name of the third child?   A. It was a dead born child.

Q. What was the name of the fourth child?   A. Theresa Wilhelmina.

Q. Is she living?   A. She is dead.

Q. How old did she live to be.   A. Nine weeks.

Q. Did she die before the death of her father, Gerd Friedrich Chorengel?
A. Yes, sir.

Q. Were these four children that you have named all the children that were ever born to Gerd Friedrich Chorengel and yourself?   A. Yes, sir.

---

provided the names of two of them; furthermore, Hannah (the eldest) was still alive at the time of Gerd's death. Carl Heinrich, therefore, came from a family of eight children, half of whom died as infants.
Source: Estate of Gerd Friedrich Chorengel, Docket 38/225, No. 13, Box 6167, Proof of Heirship, Cook County Circuit Court Archives.

children will be discussed in other parts of the file.

Divorce records for Chicago and suburbs from 1871 to 1986 are held at the Cook County Circuit Court Archives. To find them, you'll need to consult alphabetical indexes by the name of the plaintiff or defendant and by the type of court (Circuit Court or Superior Court). There is no master index, so you'll need to have a rough idea of when the divorce occurred. Staff at the archives will search for divorce cases for a fee and get you a complete uncertified copy of the file for another fee. Forms are available online, by mail, or at the archives office. (See contact information in the preceding section.)

Tip: If you don't find either party in the indexes for Circuit Court or Superior Court, try the indexes that cover divorce files from about 1900 to 1963 in Calumet City, Chicago Heights, and Blue Island. Many couples filed in these towns because of lower court costs. The Illinois Department of Public Health in Springfield has a statewide index from 1962 to the present. Staff there can search it by the husband's name for a fee. Forms are available online (www.idph.state.il.us) or by mail.

If you still don't find your ancestor, consider the possibility that he or she filed in Nevada or another state or never filed at all, choosing abandonment over legal niceties.

STATE OF ILLINOIS   }
COUNTY OF COOK   } SS   157145

                    IN THE SUPERIOR COURT OF COOK COUNTY

JULIA PATERABAS   )
       VS   )   BILL FOR DIVORCE
JOHN PATERABAS   )

TO THE HONORABLE JUDGES OF THE SUPERIOR COURT OF COOK COUNTY
                    IN THE STATE OF ILLINOIS
                    IN CHANCERY SITTING:

        Your oratrix, JULIA PATERABAS, of Chicago,
Cook County, Illinois, respectfully represents unto the
Court that she is an actual resident of the said county
of Cook, and is now and has been a resident of the State
of Illinois for over one year last past; that on to-wit,
May 9th, 1916 at Chicago, Illinois she was lawfully
married to one JOHN PATERABAS, the defendant herein named
and from that time until April 17th, 1927, lived and
cohabited with him as his wife, and during all that time
faithfully performed all her duties and obligations as
a wife , bearing with her husband's faults and errors,
and striving to make their home and family comfortable
and happy.

        Your oratrix further represents, that the
said JOHN PATERABAS, wholly regardless of his obligations
as a husband, a few years after the said marriage, com-
menced the excessive use of intoxicating liquors, and
fore more than two years last past has been guilty of
habitudal drunkenness; that he has for several days at a

Illustration 4.4: The bill of complaint (here called bill for divorce) in the Paterabas divorce case states that Julia and John Paterabas were married May 9, 1916, in Chicago and had one child, Stella, ten years old at the time of the filing, May 14, 1927 (the filing date is not shown here but appears

-2-

time been on sprees and remained in an intoxicated condition and has been frequently unfit to attend to his
usual occupation and business during that period; that
while he is thus intoxicated, he is very quarrelsome and
ill-treats your oratrix, using abusive language and
opprobrious epithets, rendering your oratrix' condition
intolerable, and her life burdensome;

    Your oratrix further represents that the said
JOHN PATERABAS, wholly disregarding his marriage vows and
obligations toward your oratrix, has ever since said marriage
been guilty of extreme and repeated cruelty toward your
oratrix, that is to say, that the said JOHN PATERABAS
on divers days and times since said marriage, has beaten
struck, kicked and choked her, and has neglected to furnish
her and their child with proper and necessary food and
clothing, and particularly, that on to-wit, June 24, 1926
the said JOHN PATERABAS, struck your oratrix a violent blow
in her face with his fist, pulled her hair and otherwise
greatly injuring your oratrix; and that afterward, on to-wit,
April 17, 1927 the said JOHN PATERABAS, struck your oratrix
violent blows in her face and over her head and body, as
a result of which your oratrix face became discolored and
on each of said occasions and on numerous other occasions has
used toward your oratrix the most obscene, profane and
opprobrious language, rendering her life miserable.

    Your oratrix further represents that as the issue
of such marriage she has had by the said JOHN PATERABAS,
one child, viz., Stella Paterabas, now aged 10 years; and that
in consequence of his drunken habits and abusive language
the said JOHN PATERABAS is a person wholly unfit to have the
care, custody and education of said children.

on the cover sheet). From these two pieces of information, you can hypothesize that Stella was born in early 1917. Source: Paterabas vs. Paterabas, Case 27 S 457145, Cook County Circuit Court Archives.

Who Were the Siblings of My Ancestor?

Points to Remember

❏ *You may have difficulties tracking down all of your ancestor's siblings for various reasons, such as:*

• Some siblings may have died as children.

• Some siblings may be half brothers or sisters (legitimate or not).

• Some siblings may be the result of adoption (informal or formal).

❏ *Check the U.S. census:*

• Look for your ancestor as a child to get names and ages of siblings.

❏ *Check death notices and obituaries:*

• Search for both types in all possible newspapers (daily, neighborhood, ethnic) for all pertinent days.

❏ *Check for a probate and proof of heirship:*

• Proof of heirship provides information on all potential heirs, including spouses and children, of the deceased.

Who Were the Siblings of My Ancestor?

❑ *Get the divorce case file,*
not just the divorce decree:

• The bill of complaint in the file gives the date and place of the parents' marriage and the birth dates or ages of the children.

5   When (and Who) Did My Ancestor Marry?

by Jack Simpson
Curator of Local and Family History,
the Newberry Library

Marriage records are a cornerstone of genealogy research. In this chapter, you'll learn how to locate civil marriage records in Cook County. Because locating these records can be extremely difficult, you'll also learn about alternative sources for marriage information.

❏ Strategy No. 1: Civil Marriage Records

In Illinois, marrying couples submit an application to marry, and the county government records marriages on a certificate. The certificate is issued to the married couple, and the county clerk keeps a copy. It is also possible to request a copy of the application to marry, but prior to the twentieth century, these applications essentially duplicate the information on the certificate. (In the 1920s, the birth dates of the couple were added, in 1962, their street addresses, and in 1968, their birthplaces and parents' names. Source: Loretto Dennis Szucs, *Chicago and Cook County: A Guide to Research*, 1996, page 480.)

Illustration 5.1 is a typical marriage certificate. It includes the full name of the groom (given as Konstantine Petrauskis), the maiden name of the bride (given as Mary Kavlak), and their ages (26 and 19, respectively). In Lithuanian, the suffixes –as and –is both are used for male surnames, hence the variant spellings of "Petrauskis" here and "Petrauskas" in Illustrations 2.3 and 3.3. The certificate also gives the date of the marriage (January 3, 1914) and the minister or official who performed the marriage (C. Ambrozaitis, described as a

Catholic priest). The name of the minister is a useful piece of information because it will often lead you to the name of the church, which can provide additional records. By looking up the minister in the city directory for the year of marriage, you can determine which church the minister belonged to. For example, checking the 1914 Chicago city directory, we find Charles Ambrozaitis listed as a pastor at Our Lady of Vilna Church (see Illustration 5.2).

Cook County Marriage Certificates

The Chicago Fire of 1871 destroyed all of the county records prior to that year, so the oldest existing civil marriage records date from 1871. If you know the name of the bride or groom, the date of the marriage, and the certificate number,

Illustration 5.1: Cook County civil marriage record gives the date the license was taken out (December 29, 1913) and the date of the marriage. (January 3, 1914). Courtesy of Walter J. Podrazik.

AMBROSIA CHOCOLATE CREAM CO I E Block pres;
   Saml R Block sec 73 E South Water
Ambrosine Jos express 765 Dekoven
Ambrosio Antonio lab h 1002 S State
—Arthur tailor 2001 S Western av
—Frank lab h 1138 Taylor
—Fred barber h 1132 Taylor
—Marchioli lab h 908 Orleans
—Patrick lab h 829 S Bishop
—Vincent lab h 1002 S State
—Vitto lab h 1002 S State
Ambrosius Andrew clk 333 W Lake h 7232
   Champlain av
—Jos A treas; Bridgeport clothing co 3246
   S Halsted h 7010 Eberhart av
Ambrosne Michael stonectr h 1503 N Wash-
   tenaw av
Ambrowicz Geo lab h 4531 Justine
—Michael lab h 4531 Justine
Ambrowitz Michael lab h 415 N Desplaines
Ambroz John painter h 8264 Anthony av
—Jos A machinist h 5337 S Wood
Ambroza Antonia Mrs h 4858 S May
Ambrozaitis Chas Rev pastor Our Lady of
   Vilma R C ch h 2327 W 23d pl
Ambrozas Statnonis lab h 124 W 103d
Ambrozewicz Boleslav electrician h 4447 S
   Honore
—Marcella lab h 2318 Ems
—Marcelin lab h 4447 S Honore
—Peter h 4447 S Honore
—Victor electrician h 4447 S Honore
—Walter tailor h 3117 Lowe av
—Wm lab h 4523 S Honore
Ambrozewski Alex v pres Avondale
   clothing co 2875 Milwaukee av h 2934
   N Lawndale av
—Edmund A salesman 2811 Milwaukee av
   h 2852 Dawson av
—Stanley h 2852 Dawson av
—Thaddeus clk h 2934 N Lawndale av
Ambrozitch Micheal lab h 555 Maxwell
Ambrozy Adelbert iceman h 4302 S Hon-
   ore
—John butcher h 1137 Noble
Ambruchez August lab h rear 382 Kens-
   ington av
Ambruse John lab h 9223 Dobson av
Ambruso Egidio jewelry 768 Taylor
Ambrust Belle Miss clk h 4334 Claren-
   don av
Ambruster Jos H chf clk 1123, 122 S
   Michigan av h 4546 Greenview av
Ambruszkiewicz Paul lab h 3311 Mosspratt
Amba Elsie A Miss stenog 1615, 111 W
   Monroe h 368 N Hamlin av
Ambulatory Pneumatic Splint Mnfg Co F
   I Saemann pres; surgical appliances

Illustration 5.2:
You can find the minister's name and affiliation in the city directory or telephone book. Source: Chicago city directory, 1914, Newberry Library.

you can request a copy of the certificate from the Cook County Bureau of Vital Statistics (see Chapter 14, "What to Expect at Chicago-Area Research Facilities"). Both certificates and applications are closed to the general public for 50 years, but parties to the marriage and close family members may request copies.

There is a request form available on the Cook County Clerk's Web site (www.cookctyclerk.com). A paper version of the form is available at the Newberry Library genealogy reference desk. If you know the name and date but not the certificate number, you can still obtain the certificate from the County Bureau of Vital Statistics, for an additional fee. It is also possible to order certificates online through the company VitalChek, at www.vitalchek.com.

The Family History Library in Salt Lake City, Utah, has microfilmed Cook County marriage certificates from 1871 to 1920. You can borrow the microfilm from any Family History Center for a fee. Cook County marriage certificates for the years 1871 to 1900 are also available on microfilm, at the Illinois Regional Archives Depository in Chicago.

Indexes

If you do not know the date of your ancestor's marriage, you can search for his or her record in a marriage index. The following marriage indexes provide access to Cook County records.

The Illinois Statewide Marriage Index: Cook County Marriages 1833–95

The Illinois State Archives has created a statewide index to marriages, which is available online at www.cyberdriveillinois.com/departments/archives/marriage.html. The overall span of years statewide is 1763–1900. The years for Cook County will be 1833 to 1900. Currently volunteers have entered marriages 1833 to September 1895 for Cook County.

The 1871–95 entries index civil marriage records held by the county clerk; the pre-1871 entries are taken from *Sam Fink's Index* (described more fully a little later in this chapter)

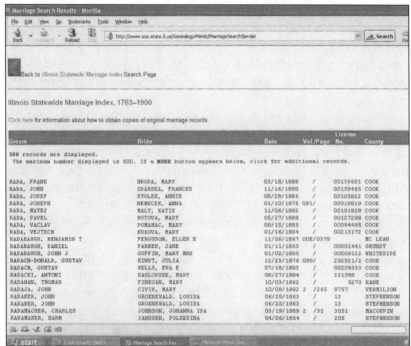

Illustration 5.3: If you're not sure of the way your ancestor spelled his or her surname, you can enter a partial name in the Illinois Statewide Marriage Index, 1763–1900, *and see all the potential matches. These are the results for a search on "Rad." Screen shot courtesy of the Illinois State Archives.*

and refer to newspaper notices.

The index is searchable by bride or groom. There are many spelling errors in the index, so if you come up empty, try variations on the name. Also, note that you can enter in partial names: entering "Rad" will pull up Rada, Radabaugh, Radach, and so on (see Illustration 5.3).

The marriage index will indicate the date and the place of marriage. For the entries that refer to a certificate, the certificate number is listed. For entries taken from *Sam Fink's Index* (indicated by the word *FINK*), only a date is provided. This indicates that one of the newspapers indexed by Fink had a marriage notice on that date.

The Cook County Marriage Index 1871–1916

The Family History Library in Salt Lake City holds a microfilmed marriage index from Cook County that covers the years 1871 to 1916 for grooms and 1878 to 1916 for brides. (Women were not indexed until 1878.) This marriage index is available at some of the suburban Family History Centers and can be loaned to the Newberry Library or any Family History Center around the country for a fee.

Marriage Records After 1916

Besides the two marriage indexes discussed, the Illinois Department of Public Health can verify the facts of a marriage that took place from 1962 to the present for a fee. Forms are available from the IDPH Web site (www.idph.state. il.us/vitalrecords), by phone, or by fax. If your ancestor's marriage falls outside the scope of these resources, you may have to try other methods to find information, as discussed in the following sections.

Newspapers

Before the 1960s, newspapers such as the *Chicago Tribune* and the *Chicago Daily News* typically did not run detailed marriage notices as they do now. However, prominent marriages were sometimes described in the newspaper, and some newspapers occasionally printed lists of recently issued marriage certificates. Because these notices and listings were fairly infrequent, searching for them without a precise date of marriage is unlikely to be fruitful.

There are two newspaper databases that might be worth searching for marriage notices, even if you don't have a date. *The Chicago Tribune Historical Archive* from NewsBank, currently available at the Chicago Historical Society, indexes parts of the *Tribune* going back to the mid-1800s. ProQuest Information and Learning Company is building a complete full-text digital version of the *Tribune*. The company has completed 1890 to 1946 (available at Arlington Heights Memorial Library, Skokie Public Library, and other libraries).

MARRIED.

In this city on the 21st ult., by Rev. Lewis Raymond, Mr. WM. VLIET, to Miss MARY JANE HOAGLAND, all of Milwaukee, Wis.

On the 1st of August, by the same, Mr. JOHN W. BENT to Miss JEANETTE BUCHANAN, all of this City.

Illustration 5.4: Here's an example of a nineteenth-century newspaper marriage notice found by using Sam Fink's Index. *The notice gives the name of the minister, the place of the marriage, and the residences of the bride and groom. It's important to know that the dates in the index are the dates of the newspaper notice, not when the marriage took place.* Source: *Chicago Evening Journal,* August 4, 1853, Page 3, Column 1, Harold Washington Library Center.

Plans are to complete 1849 to 1889 and 1947 to 1984 by 2006. These databases allow you to search large amounts of text instantaneously and are a powerful tool for genealogists.

Sam Fink's Index, 1833–1871

Sam Fink's Index was compiled by a Chicago researcher, and it provides access to pre-Fire newspaper listings going back as far as 1833. The index is available on microfilm at the Newberry Library and IRAD in Chicago, and it can be borrowed for a fee through the Family History Library in Salt Lake City. Marriages are listed alphabetically, followed by the date and a symbol indicating a particular newspaper (see Illustration 5.4). In the front of the index is a list of the newspapers that correlate to the symbols. While the index is a useful tool, remember that very few marriages were noted in the newspaper at that time, and so the index describes only a small percentage of pre-Fire marriages.

❑ Strategy No. 2:
Church Marriage Records

Christian churches typically record marriages, and sometimes these records are more detailed than civil records. Illustration 5.5 is the marriage register entry from Our Lady of Vilna Church for Konstantin/Constantine Petrauskis and Mary Kavlak/Kaulakis, whose civil marriage record is shown in the beginning of this chapter. It is in Latin, and somewhat difficult to read, but very informative. It shows where the bride and the groom were born (Lithuania for both), the names of the parents of both parties, and the names of several witnesses. The Archdiocesan Archives can provide a translation in certificate form (see Illustration 5.6) in exchange for a donation.

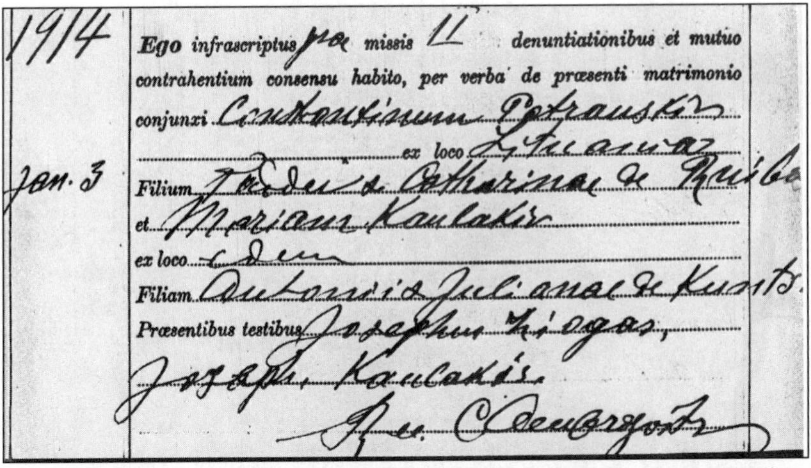

Illustration 5.5: The religious record for the 1914 marriage of Constantine Petrauskis and Mary Kaulakis is in Latin. Notice that Mary's surname appears as Kaulakis, not Kavlak as in Illustration 5.1. Kavlak may have been the Americanized version that she used with non-Lithuanians. Courtesy of Archdiocese of Chicago's Joseph Cardinal Bernardin Archives and Records Center.

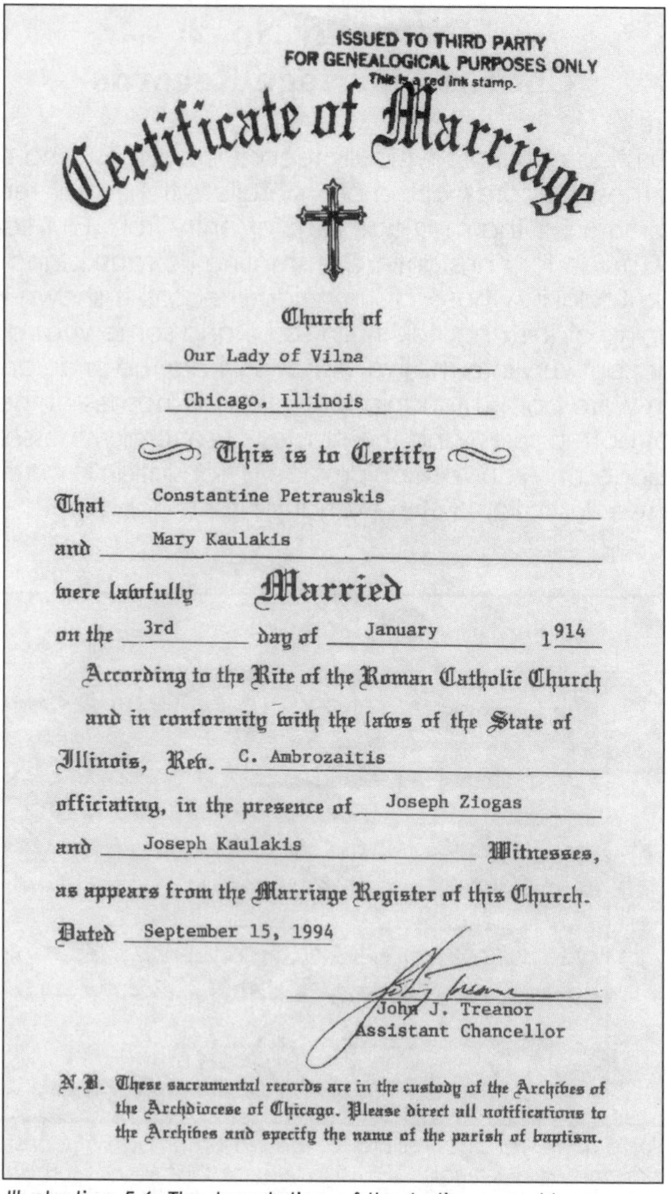

ISSUED TO THIRD PARTY
FOR GENEALOGICAL PURPOSES ONLY
This is a red ink stamp.

Certificate of Marriage

Church of
Our Lady of Vilna
Chicago, Illinois

This is to Certify

That Constantine Petrauskis
and Mary Kaulakis
were lawfully **Married**
on the 3rd day of January 1914
According to the Rite of the Roman Catholic Church
and in conformity with the laws of the State of
Illinois, Rev. C. Ambrozaitis
officiating, in the presence of Joseph Ziogas
and Joseph Kaulakis Witnesses,
as appears from the Marriage Register of this Church.
Dated September 15, 1994

John J. Treanor
Assistant Chancellor

N.B. These sacramental records are in the custody of the Archives of the Archdiocese of Chicago. Please direct all notifications to the Archives and specify the name of the parish of baptism.

Illustration 5.6: The translation of the Latin record leaves out the parents' names and the birthplaces of the bride and groom. Courtesy of Archdiocese of Chicago's Joseph Cardinal Bernardin Archives and Records Center.

Finding Church Records

The hard part is determining which church your ancestors were married at. If your ancestors were Polish and Roman Catholic, you are in luck—there is an online index to marriages in Polish parishes to 1915. This index is available on the Web site of the Polish Genealogical Society of America (www.pgsa. org). If your ancestors have a different background, you will need to do a bit more research to find the church they belonged to.

Finding Catholic Church Records

To determine which Catholic church your ancestors may have attended, find your ancestors' address in a city directory or in the census for the time period when they were married. Once you have an address, check the book *Locations of Chicago Roman Catholic Churches, 1850–1990* by Jack Bochar (Czech and Slovak American Genealogy Society of Illinois, 1998). This will give an idea of which Catholic churches were near your ancestors' home in a particular period. Remember that many Catholic churches had a particular ethnic identity; so, for example, if your ancestors were Italian, you should look for a nearby Italian church. Once you have settled on a church, you can search the church records at the Archives of the Roman Catholic Archdiocese of Chicago or borrow the records through a Family History Center.

Finding Other Church Records

If you don't know which denomination your ancestors belonged to or which church they attended, you might look for clues in other records. If you can locate an obituary of a close relative of the bride or groom, it might indicate the church where the funeral services were held. If a family held funerals at a particular church, it is worth checking to see if they also held weddings there. On the Newberry Library Web site (www.newberry.org), there is a lengthy guide to Chicago church records held by the Newberry, the Family History Library, and several other repositories.

❑ Strategy No. 3:
Unindexed Marriage Records

There are many hidden sources of marriage information. These sources are not indexed as marriage records because the information appears in entirely different types of records, such as court records, federal government records, and military records. Try the types of records discussed below for clues to marriage dates, marriage places, maiden names, and married names.

Divorce and Probate Records

Oddly, Cook County divorce records are easier to locate than marriage records for most years. Divorce records are held by the Cook County Circuit Court Archives and are indexed for the years 1871 to 1986. (See description in Chapter 14, "What to Expect at Chicago-Area Research Facilities.") If you are searching for a marriage that may have ended in divorce, check the divorce index for either the husband or wife. Divorce records provide the date and place of marriage in the bill of complaint and divorce decree. Probate records can also shed light on marriages. In probate cases, potential claimants to an estate are described in the proof of heirship; this would typically include the spouse or former spouse of the deceased. Probate records are kept at the Circuit Court Archives, which also holds indexes to the records from 1871 to the present.

Children's Social Security Applications

If you find an individual in the *Social Security Death Index*, you can request a copy of his or her original Social Security application (see example Illustration 2.3). The application asks for the full name of the applicant's father and the maiden name of the applicant's mother. While it doesn't give specific information about the parents' marriage, discovering the mother's maiden name can help with the search for marriage records.

Civil War Pension Records

If you are searching for marriage records in the late 1800s or early 1900s, consider whether the male was in the Civil War. Veterans received a pension that passed to their widows after their death, so pension records often contain marriage information.

Illustration 5.7 shows a pension claim filed by the children of an Illinois Civil War soldier named Valentine Felty. As part of the application, they filed a copy of their parents' marriage certificate from White County, Illinois (see Illustration 5.8).

The first step in finding the pension record is to check whether the husband fought in the war. One way is to consult *The Roster of Union Soldiers* (Wilmington, North Carolina: Broadfoot Publishing Co., 1997) at the Newberry Library. Another source for information about service in the Civil War is the Civil War veterans database available on the Illinois State Archives Web site, www.sos.state.il.us/GenealogyMWeb/civilwar.html. Either of these sources will tell what unit the veteran served in. Once you know the unit, you can request a pension record from the National Archives in Washington, D.C. Request forms are available at the Newberry Library and the National Archives—Great Lakes.

To increase your chances of success, you might search the index of Civil War pension records. The index is available on microfilm at the National Archives—Great Lakes and is also available as a database on Ancestry.com (subscription Web site).

Using Census Indexes to Search for Married Women

Let's say you are searching for the sister of your great-grandfather. You find her as a child on the 1910 U.S. census. She is 15 years old and living with your great-grandfather and their parents. However, in the 1920 census, she is nowhere to be found. It is reasonable to guess that she was married, but she does not appear in any census index, and searches of church records prove fruitless. Should you give up?

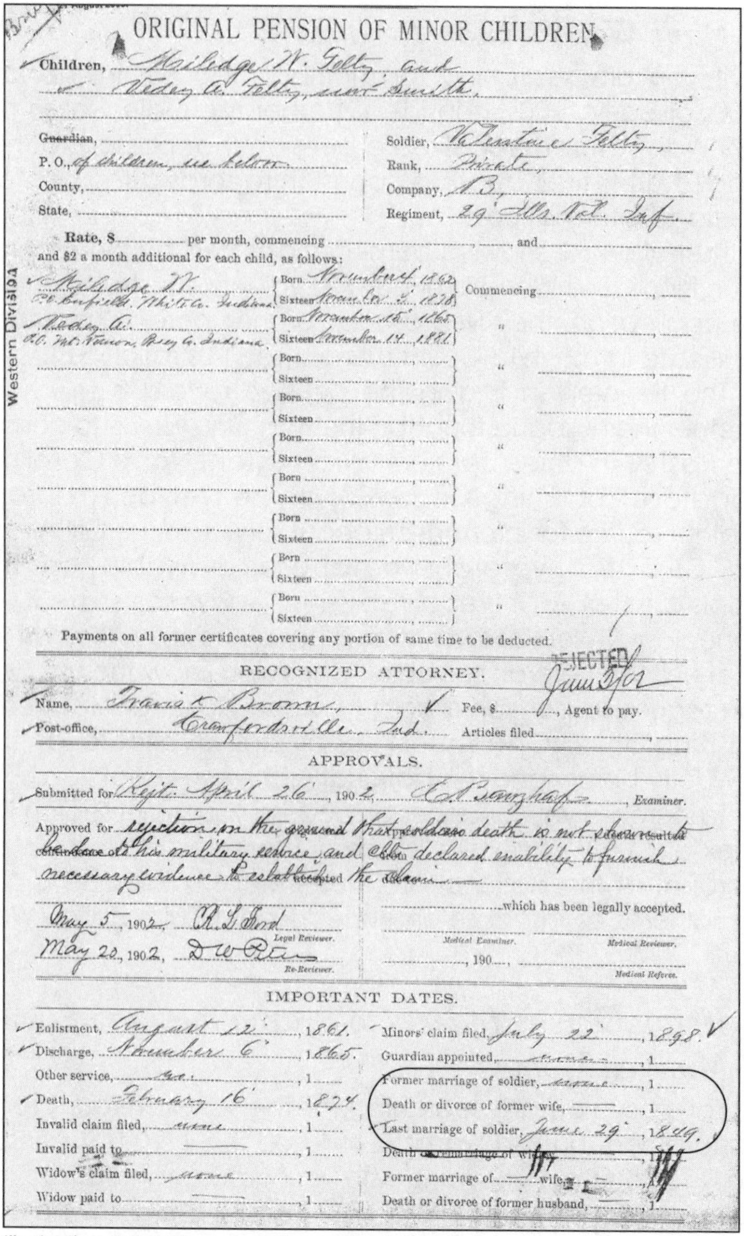

ORIGINAL PENSION OF MINOR CHILDREN.

Children, Miledge N. Felty and Vedey A. Felty, now Smith.

Guardian,	Soldier, Valentine Felty
P. O., of children see below	Rank, Private
County,	Company, B
State,	Regiment, 29 Ills Vol. Inf.

Rate, $........ per month, commencing ...., ..., and ....
and $2 a month additional for each child, as follows:

Miledge N. P.O. Enfield, White Co. Indiana	Born November 4, 1862; Sixteen November 4, 1878	Commencing ....
Vedey A. P.O. Mt. Vernon, Posey Co. Indiana	Born November 14, 1865; Sixteen November 14, 1881	"
	Born ....; Sixteen	"
	Born ....; Sixteen	"
	Born ....; Sixteen	"
	Born ....; Sixteen	"
	Born ....; Sixteen	"
	Born ....; Sixteen	"
	Born ....; Sixteen	"

Payments on all former certificates covering any portion of same time to be deducted.

REJECTED June 5/02

RECOGNIZED ATTORNEY.

Name, Travis & Brown, Fee, $........, Agent to pay.
Post-office, Crawfordsville, Ind. Articles filed ....

APPROVALS.

Submitted for Rejection April 26, 1902, C. A. Branzhaf, *Examiner.*

Approved for rejection on the ground that soldier's death is not shown to be due to his military service and also declared inability to furnish necessary evidence to establish the claim

.... which has been legally accepted.

May 5, 1902, C. R. L. Bond, *Legal Reviewer.*
May 20, 1902, D. W. Peter, *Re-Reviewer.*

Medical Examiner. *Medical Reviewer.* ...., 190..., *Medical Referee.*

IMPORTANT DATES.

Enlistment, August 12, 1861.	Minors' claim filed, July 22, 1898.
Discharge, November 6, 1865.	Guardian appointed, none, 1
Other service, no, 1	Former marriage of soldier, none, 1
Death, February 16, 1874.	Death or divorce of former wife, ——, 1
Invalid claim filed, none, 1	Last marriage of soldier, June 29, 1849.
Invalid paid to ——, 1	Death or remarriage of wife, 1
Widow's claim filed, none, 1	Former marriage of .... wife, 1
Widow paid to ——, 1	Death or divorce of former husband, ——, 1

Western Division

Illustration 5.7: Military pension records can lead you to your ancestor's marriage date. Courtesy of Jeanne Larzalere Bloom.

Of course not—genealogists never give up. There is a long-shot method of searching online census indexes for a married woman that occasionally provides results. Try searching an online index to the first census where you cannot find your great-grandaunt under her maiden name. In the case of the hypothetical example here, that would be the 1920 census. Since you don't know her married name, leave the "last name" search field blank, but fill in the other fields: her first name, year of birth, and place of birth and where you suspect she was living in 1920. This will bring back a list of women who match these categories, which you can browse for potential matches.

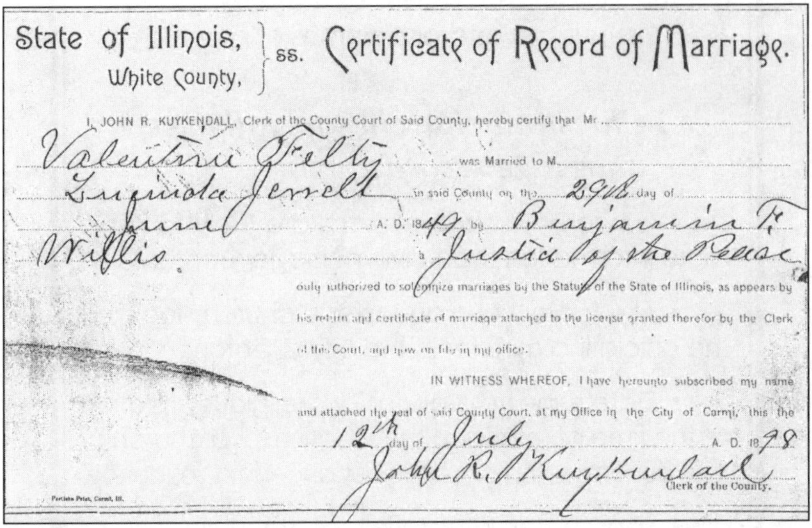
State of Illinois, White County, } ss. Certificate of Record of Marriage.

I, JOHN R. KUYKENDALL, Clerk of the County Court of Said County, hereby certify that Mr Valentine Felty was Married to M Lucinda Jerrett in said County on the 29th day of June A. D. 1849 by Benjamin F. Willis a Justice of the Peace duly authorized to solemnize marriages by the Statute of the State of Illinois, as appears by his return and certificate of marriage attached to the license granted therefor by the Clerk of this Court, and now on file in my office.

IN WITNESS WHEREOF, I have hereunto subscribed my name and attached the seal of said County Court, at my Office in the City of Carmi, this the 12th day of July A. D. 1898

John R. Kuykendall
Clerk of the County.

Perkins Print, Carmi, Ill.

Illustration 5.8: In 1898, the White County court clerk supplied a duplicate of Valentine Felty's marriage record, based on the return made by the justice of the peace in 1849, and on file in the clerk's office. Courtesy of Jeanne Larzalere Bloom.

When (and Who) Did My Ancestor Marry?

Points to Remember

❑ *Be aware of limitations of civil marriage records:*

• There are no Cook County records prior to the Chicago Fire (1871).

• There is a 50-year confidentiality rule for applications and certificates.

• License applications didn't give any more information about the applicants than what was found on the marriage certificate until the twentieth century (1920s: birth dates; 1962: street addresses; 1968: birthplaces and also names of parents).

❑ *Christian churches usually keep marriage records:*

• Church marriage records are likely to have more information than civil marriage records.

• To locate your ancestor's church, look up the officiating minister in the city directory.

• Determine your ancestor's religious affiliation at the time of marriage and search for a church of that denomination close to your ancestor's residence.

• Search for obituaries of your ancestor's parents, siblings, and other close relatives—if funerals were held at a particular church, weddings may also have been held there.

When (and Who) Did My Ancestor Marry?

❑ *Unindexed marriage records can appear in entirely different types of records, such as:*

• Divorce records give the date and place of marriage in the bill of complaint and divorce decree.

• Probate records give proof of heirship, often naming spouse(s) of the deceased.

• Children's Social Security applications give the mother's maiden name.

• Civil War pension records often contain a copy of the marriage certificate or an affidavit of marriage date and place.

• U. S. census online indexes help cast a net for married names of female ancestors.

6 Where Did My Ancestor Live?

Places and dates are the building blocks of genealogy. Where you'll search for records depends on where your ancestor lived. Further, you don't want to pass up a record about your ancestor because you mistakenly think it's the wrong street name or address. Finding an address may help you find other relatives of your ancestor; people usually lived near other relations. An immigrant likely settled with members of the same ethnic group in enclaves like Maxwell Street, Chinatown, and Ukrainian Village. As they prospered, immigrants generally moved to less crowded areas, such as Douglas Park and Jefferson Park.

Once you know the correct address, you can look at maps and figure out the closest place of worship for your ancestor; that's key in obtaining religious records, which are especially important if government vital records do not exist. You can also visit the address and see if the residence is still standing, look for old photographs, or read up on the history of the neighborhood.

❏ Strategy No. 1: Sources for Addresses

If you are trying to track down your ancestor's address, there are many sources you can check, including:

- city directories

- telephone books (keep in mind that many families could not afford phone service until after World War II—they would use a neighbor's phone or public phones at a drugstore or tavern)

- U.S. census (starting in 1880 for cities)

- vital records

- obituaries and death notices

- school records

- employment records

- pension, Social Security, Railroad Retirement Board applications

    - World War I and World War II draft registrations

    - certificate of mailing petition in probate cases

    - old letters

    - fly leaves of your ancestor's books

- almost any type of record where you can look up your ancestor by name

A Word About Annexations

Many Chicago neighborhoods today were once part of separate towns or villages. Hyde Park, Lake View, and Austin are three examples. An ancestor who worked in Chicago and lived in another town will only have his work address listed in the Chicago city directory (see Illustration 7.3). Finding local records of a town now part of Chicago can be difficult, as many were lost in the transition from one government to another. The Illinois Regional Archives Depository (IRAD) at Northeastern Illinois University has the best collection, and historical societies may hold additional sources. The Sulzer Regional Library of the Chicago Public Library (4455 N. Lincoln Avenue, Chicago) has a Neighborhood History Research Collection focusing on the North and Northwest Sides of the city. Special Collections at the Harold Washington Library Center does the same for West and South Side neighborhoods.

First Thing to Know: Address Changes

The year 1909 is a date you should etch in your mind if you're doing Chicago research. That is when all the residential streets in Chicago were renumbered.

Prior to 1909, the city was composed of three divisions: the North Division, the South Division, and the West Division. Each had its own numbering system based on its proximity to the Chicago River and its branches. As you can imagine, it was terribly confusing. A gentleman named Edward P. Brennan came up with the system we have today, which uses the downtown intersection of State Street and Madison Street as the 0–0 points (State for east–west numbers, Madison for north–south numbers). In his system, every 800 numbers equals a mile, so you can easily calculate the location of any address. (There are a few exceptions as you go south of the Loop.)

The residential areas of the North, South, and West Divisions were renumbered on September 1, 1909. The central business district—the Loop and South Loop—changed over on April 1, 1911. (For a fuller explanation of Brennan's innovation, see "Street Numbering Changes" by Gerrit E. Van Wissink in *Streetwise Chicago*.)

What this means to you is that you need to convert any pre-1909 address you find in your research. It's especially important if you want to see the property, as you could be miles away from the actual address.

Both the 1909 and 1910 Chicago city directories published conversion tables for residential areas in the front of the books. There are also separate guides to new and old house numbers. Directories and/or guides are available at the Newberry Library, the Chicago Historical Society, the Municipal Reference Library of Harold Washington Library Center, and the Richard J. Daley Library of University of Illinois at Chicago. The Chicago Historical Society has put the residential (1909) conversion table online at www.chsmedia.org/househistory/1909snc/start.pdf. The Loop–South Loop (1911) conversion tables are also online at www.chsmedia.org/househistory/1911snc/start.pdf. (Adobe Reader software is required to view both tables. The files are quite large and take much time to load and work with.) Another online source is the POINTers in Person Web site (www.rootsweb.com/~itappcnc/pipcnstreet.htm), with a useful page on how to mathematically calculate new addresses from old addresses, as well as a link to a database containing coordinates and changed street names.

To convert a pre-1909 address from the conversion tables:

1. Find the street name. Numbered streets are spelled out and listed alphabetically, so Twenty-Fifth Street comes before Twenty-First Street.

2. Once you find the street name, look for the "Old" column in either odd or even, depending on the number. Be sure you're in the correct column. If you can't find the old number, look for the closest one—the old number may have been part of a multi-unit apartment building. You can then verify the nearest cross street by looking at the "Street and Avenue Guide" in the front of the 1909 or 1910 directory. Another possibility is that nothing existed at that address in 1909.

If you can't find the street name, there are two possibilities. One is that many streets on the South Side of Chicago kept the same numbering, so they were eliminated from the conversion tables. Another is that the street name may have been something different in 1909. For example, I was researching the history of a house at 1940 N. Honore Street. I wanted to know what the address was prior to 1909. I looked in the guide to new and old house numbers, but the new numbers for Honore Street only go up to 1510 (see Illustration 6.2). I researched the street name in the compilation "Chicago Streets" (see discussion later this chapter) and learned it had previously been named Girard Street. I looked under Girard in the conversion tables in the "New" column and there it was (see Illustration 6.3).

Address Changes in Cook County Suburbs

Towns outside of Chicago generally use railroad tracks as the baselines for numbering. As towns grew, the numbering may have needed adjustment, especially if nearby areas were annexed. Consult histories of the town and the local historical society. Fire insurance maps will often show old and new house numbers (see discussion later in this chapter).

Second Thing to Know: Street Name Changes

There have been many changes to street names over the history of Chicago. Some were changed because of duplication with areas incorporated into the city, such as Beverly and Rogers Park. Some were changed to honor famous figures: 22nd Street, for example, was renamed Cermak Road to commemorate Mayor Anton Cermak, who died from a bullet fired at President Franklin D. Roosevelt. And some, I'm sure, were changed because they were just plain goofy: Fake Street, Purple Street, and Swell Street are some of my favorites.

How to Find Street Name Changes

"Chicago Streets," a compilation by William Martin and updated by John McNalis, can help you find street name changes. It is available at the Newberry Library and IRAD. The Chicago Historical Society has posted it online at www. chsmedia.org/househistory/nameChanges/start.pdf. (Adobe Reader software is required for viewing the file.)

Look up the name alphabetically. A dash in front of it means the name has changed; the coordinates of the new name are given. There can be four or more listings of streets with the same name, and the only way you can tell which new name is yours is to work with the coordinates. Having a date for the name change would simplify things, but "Chicago Streets" doesn't state when the change was made.

If you have many listings with the same name, first determine the direction of the name you have by looking in the city directory. Say you found ancestors living at an address in the 1900 census. Go to the 1900 city directory and look in the "Street and Avenue Guide." It will state what division the street is in, the direction it runs, and its beginning and ending points. Check to see which cross street is the closest to the address.

Returning to "Chicago Streets," you can eliminate some of

NEW AND OLD HOUSE NUMBERS 67

North Halsted St.

Odd Nos.

New	Old
23	50 S
25	48 S
27	46 S
29	44 S
31	42 S
33	40 S
35	38 S
37	36 S
41	34 S
107	24 S
109	22 S
121	16 S
123	14 S
125	12 S
127	10 S
159	9
161	11
163	13
165	15
171	21
173	23
175	25
177	27
179	29
181	31
213	43
231	59
301	63
315	75
409	127
411	129
419	135
421	139
423	141
441	151
443	153
445	155
447	157
449	159
451	161
453	163
455	165
457	167
459	169
501	183
507	187
509	191
511	193
513	195
515	197
517	203
523	207
805	and
911	River
923	375
931	401
1001	403
1013	421
1129	465
1153	481
1155	483
1209	499
1211	501
1213	503
1215	505
1219	507
1221	509
1223	511
1225	513
1229	515
1231	517
1233	519
1235	521
1239	523
1241	525
1301	527
1303	529
1305	531
1309	533
1311	535
1313	537
1315	539
1319	541
1325	545
1327	547
1331	549
1333	551
1335	553
1337	555
1339	557
1343	559
1401	561
1403	563
1405	565
1407	567
1413	569
1417	571
1419	573
1421	575
1423	577
1425	579
1429	581

Even Nos.

New	Old
12	61 S
14	59 S
16	57 S
18	55 S
20	53 S
22	51 S
24	49 S
28	47 S
30	45 S
32	43 S
34	41 S
42	33 S
112	21 S
114	19 S
116	17 S
120	15 S
122	13 S
124	11 S
154	8
156	10
160	12
162	14
164	16
166	18
168	20
172	22
174	26
176	26½
178	28
206	38
208	40
210	46
212	50
216	46
222	50
224	52
234	80
300	62
302	64
306	66
308	68
408	130
412	132
414	134
416	136
418	138
446	158
448	160
450	162
452	164
454	166
456	168
458	170
460	172
462	174
464	176
466	178
468	180
470	182
516	200
518	202
520	204
522	206
524	208
526	210
528	212
600	218
604	220
606	222
608	224
610	226
612	228
614	230
616	232
618	234
620	236
622	238
624	240
626	242
628	244
630	246
666	270
688	288
692	294
678	280
682	284
700	296
702	294
708	298
716	300
724	306
866	360
884	364
904	380
914	384
918	386
920	388
926	394
930	396
1012	416
1014	418
1018	424

Odd Nos.

New	Old
1419	597
1459	603
1461	605
1465	609
1469	611
1473	615
1475	615
1501	619
1509	629
1511	631
1515	633
1517	635
1519	637
1523	639
1531	647
1535	651
1537	653
1551	659
1555	657
1559	661
1563	663
1565	665
1623	695
1625	697
1629	699
1631	701
1633	703
1635	705
1641	709
1643	711
1645	713
1647	715
1649	717
1653	719
1655	721
1657	723
1659	725
1661	727
1665	729
1701	731
1703	733
1705	735
1707	737
1711	739
1713	741
1715	743
1717	745
1721	747
1723	749
1725	751
1727	753
1729	755
1733	757
1815	769
1817	771
1819	773
1823	775
1825	777
1829	781
1831	785
1835	785
1839	789
1841	791
1845	795
1847	799
1849	799
1853	801
1855	803
1857	805
1863	809
1865	813
1867	815
1871	817
1901	823
1903	825
1905	827
1907	829
1911	831
1913	833
1915	835
1921	839
1923	841
1925	843
1945	859
1947	859
1949	861
1951	863
1955	865
1959	867
1961	869
1963	871
1967	875
1969	877
1971	879
1973	881
2001	885
2003	887
2005	889
2007	891
2011	893
2013	895
2015	897
2017	901

Even Nos.

New	Old
1216	502
1218	504
1224	508
1226	510
1230	514
1234	516
1236	518
1244	524
1300	526
1302	528
1308	534
1328	548
1330	550
1332	552
1342	560
1400	562
1404	564
1406	566
1408	568
1412	570
1414	572
1416	574
1418	576
1420	578
1426	582
1430	584
1432	586
1440	588
1472	612
1500	614
1510	618
1522	632
1526	634
1528	636
1530	638
1532	640
1534	642
1536	644
1538	646
1568	668
1612	686
1616	692
1618	"
1624	696
1626	698
1628	700
1630	702
1632	704
1636	706
1638	708
1640	710
1642	712
1644	714
1646	716
1650	718
1654	720
1656	722
1660	726
1700	732
1704	734
1706	736
1708	738
1710	740
1712	742
1714	744
1718	746
1720	748
1722	750
1724	752
1726	754
1730	756
1732	758
1800	760
1804	762
1806	764
1808	766
1810	768
1814	770
1816	772
1818	774
1820	776
1824	778
1826	780
1828	782
1830	784
1834	786
1836	788
1838	790
1840	792
1844	794
1846	796
1848	798
1852	800
1854	802
1856	804
1858	806
1862	808
1864	810
1866	812
1868	814
1870	816
1874	818
1900	821

Odd Nos.

New	Old
2053	929
2055	931
2059	933
2101	935
2103	937
2105	939
2107	941
2111	943
2113	945
2117	949
2119	951
2123	953
2125	955
2127	957
2129	959
2131	961
2139	967
2143	971
2147	973
2149	975
2151	977
2153	979
2155	981
2159	983
2201	985
2209	991
2211	995
2213	997
2215	999
2217	1001
2221	1005
2227	1007
2229	1009
2233	1011
2235	1013-5
2237	1017
2239	1019
2243	1021
2245	1023
2247	1025
2251	1027
2253	1033
2259	1039
2309	1045
2311	1045
2315	1047
2317	1049
2319	1053
2321	1055
2323	1057
2325	1059
2327	1061
2329	1063
2335	1069
2343	1073
2345	1075
2349	1081
2351	1083
2405	1100
2407	1102
2409	1104
2411	1106
2413	1108
2417	1112
2419	1114
2423	1118
2425	1120
2427	1122
2429	1124
2433	1128
2435	1130
2437	1132
2439	1134
2441	1138
2445	1140
2447	1142
2449	1142
2451	1148
2453	"
2455	1150
2457	1152
2459	1154
2463	1156
2465	1160
2501	1162
2503	1164
2507	1166
2509	1170
2511	1172
2515	1174
2517	1176
2519	1178
2521	1180
2523	1182
2531	1192
2533	1194
2535	1196
2545	1206
2549	1208
2551	1210
2553	1212
2555	1214

Even Nos.

New	Old
1926	814
1928	816
1930	818
1934	850
1936	852
1938	854
1942	856
1944	858
1946	860
1948	862
1956	868
1958	870
1962	872
1964	874
1966	876
1970	880
1972	882
2000	886
2002	888
2004	890
2008	892
2010	894
2012	896
2014	898
2018	900
2020	902
2022	904
2024	906
2028	908
2030	910
2032	912
2034	914
2038	916
2040	918
2042	920
2044	922
2048	924
2052	930
2056	932
2058	934
2100	936
2102	940
2108	944
2110	946
2112	948
2116	950
2118	952
2120	954
2122	956
2126	958
2128	960
2130	962
2132	964
2136	966
2138	968
2140	970
2142	972
2146	974
2148	976
2150	978
2154	980
2156	982
2158	984
2200	986
2202	990
2206	992
2208	994
2210	996
2214	1000
2218	1002
2220	1004
2222	1006
2224	1008
2228	1010
2230	1012
2232	1014
2234	1016
2238	1018
2240	1020
2242	1022
2248	1026
2250	1028
2252	1030
2256	1038
2304	1042
2306	"
2312	1048
2314	"
2318	1056
2320	1060
2328	1064
2332	1070
2346	"
2348	"
2416	1109
2418	1111
2420	1115
2422	1117
2424	1119
2426	1121
2430	1125
2432	1127

Odd Nos.

New	Old
2619	1244
2625	1252
2629	1256
2631	1258
2633	1260
2647	1272
2649	1274
2653	1280
2659	1288
2663	1290
2673	1300
2683	1308
2701	1318
2703	1320
2707	1324
2709	1326
2713	1330
2717	1332
2719	1334
2721	1336
2723	1340
2733	1348
2735	1350
2737	1352
2801	1362
2807	1368
2809	1368
2811	1370
2813	1372
2815	1374
2817	1376
2819	1378
2821	1380
2825	1382
2829	1390
2831	1392
2837	1400
2839	1402
2841	1402½
2843	1404
2845	1406
2849	1408
2909	1434
2917	1444
2919	1446
2921	1448
2931	1458
2939	1464
2941	1468
2943	1470
2945	1472
2949	1474
3015	1508
3017	1510
3023	1516
3025	1518
3109	1556
3111	1558
3113	1560
3115	1562
3117	"
3123	1572
3127	1574
	1576
3133	1580
3137	1584
3145	1592
3153	1600
3155	1602
3159	1606
3161	1608
3169	1614
3201	1624
3203	1626
3209	1632
3211	1634
3215	1638
3219	1642
3223	1644
3225	1646
3227	1650
3233	1652
3239	1664
3241	1666
3243	1668
3245	1670
3247	1672
3251	1674
3253	1676
3255	1678
3257	1680
3323	1714
3325	"
3335	1724
3337	1726
3355	1746
3359	1748
3401	1756
3403	1758
3407	1760
3409	1762
3411	1766
3413	1768

Even Nos.

New	Old
2522	1183
2524	1185
2534	1195
2536	1197
2538	1201
2540	1203
2542	1205
2546	1207
2548	1209
2550	1211
2552	1213
2554	1215
2558	1217
2600	1229
2602	1231
2606	1233
2608	1235
2610	1237
2612	1239
2616	1241
2618	1245
2620	1247
2622	1249
2626	1251
2628	1253
2630	1257
2632	1261
2636	1263
2638	1265
2640	1267
2646	1271
2648	1273
2650	1275
2652	1279
2656	1283
2658	1285
2660	1287
2666	1295
2672	1299
2676	1305
2678	1307
2686	1313
2700	1317
2704	1319
2706	1321
2708	1323
2710	1325
2714	1327
2718	1335
2722	1337
2726	1339
2728	1341
2730	1343
2732	1347
2734	1349
2736	1351
2816	1375
2820	1377
2824	1383
2834	1395
2838	1397
2846	1405
2852	1413
2856	1415
2904	1431
2908	1433
2910	1435
2912	1439
2914	1441
2938	1465
2942	1467
2950	1475
2952	1477
2954	1479
2956	1481
2958	1483
3010	1511
3032	1525
3036	1529
3056	1549
3160	1607
3164	1611
3210	1633
3212	1635
3216	1639
3220	1643
3238	1661
3242	1665
3248	1671
3250	1673
3254	1679
3258	1681
3300	1683
3304	1695
3306	1697
3310	1699
3312	1701
3314	1703
3316	1705
3320	1709
3322	1711
3324	1713
3342	1731

Odd Nos.

New	Old
3443	1800
3447	1801
3451	1806
3455	1812
3513	1834
3515	1836
3517	1838
3519	1840
3521	1842
3523	1844
3527	1846
3535	1856
3537	1858
3539	1860
3541	1862
3543	1864
3547	1866
3549	1868
3551	1872
3601	1890
3605	1894
3607	1896
3619	1910
3621	1912
3623	1916
3625	"
3655	1942
3657	1944
3659	1946
3701	1956
3703	1958
3705	1960
3707	1962
3709	1964
3711	1966
3713	1968
3715	1970
3723	1976
3727	1980
3729	1982
3731	1982½
3733	1984
3735	"
3737	1988
3739	1990
3741	1992
3743	1994
3745	1996
3747	1998
3749	2000
3751	2002
3753	2004
3755	2006
3801	2030
3809	2040

Even Nos.

New	Old
3424	1782
3434	1789
3438	1793
3442	1795
3444	1799
3504	1827
3506	1829
3512	1833
3520	1841
3522	1843
3526	1849
3530	1851
3532	1853
3534	1859
3542	1863
3544	1865
3548	1871
3550	1875
3552	1877
3554	1879
3556	1879½
3558	1881
3600	1893
3602	1895
3608	1897
3626	1917
3628	"
3644	1937
3648	1941
3654	1943
3656	1945
3700	1955
3702	1957
3704	1959
3706	1961
3708	1963
3710	1967
3716	1971
3718	1973
3720	1975
3752	2007
3754	2009
3764	2021
3800	2031

South Halsted St.

New	Old
13	78
15	80
"	80½
17	82
19	82
21	84
23	86
25	88
27	90
29	90½
31	92
33	94
35	96
37	98
39	98½
41	100
101	102
103	104
105	106
107	108
109	110
111	112
113	114
115	116
117	118
123	120
125	122
127	124
131	126
133	128
135	130
137	132
139	134
201	136
203	138
205	140
207	142
211	144
213	146
215	148
217	150
223	154
227	156
229	192
231	160

New	Old
6	73
8	"
10	75
12	77
14	79
16	81
22	85
24	87
26	89
30	91
32	93
34	95
38	99
100	101
102	103
104	107
106	109
110	111
112	113
114	115
116	"
118	117
216	147
122	121
126	123
128	125
130	127
132	129
134	129½
136	131
138	133
200	135
202	137
204	137½
206	139
208	141
210	143
212	145
216	147
218	149
220	151
222	153
226	155
228	157

Illustration 6.1: To convert the old address of 1014 N. Halsted, first find the listing for North Halsted Street. Then look in the "Old" column under even numbers. New address is 2232 N. Halsted. Source: Plan of Re-Numbering City of Chicago: table showing new and old house numbers, August 1909.

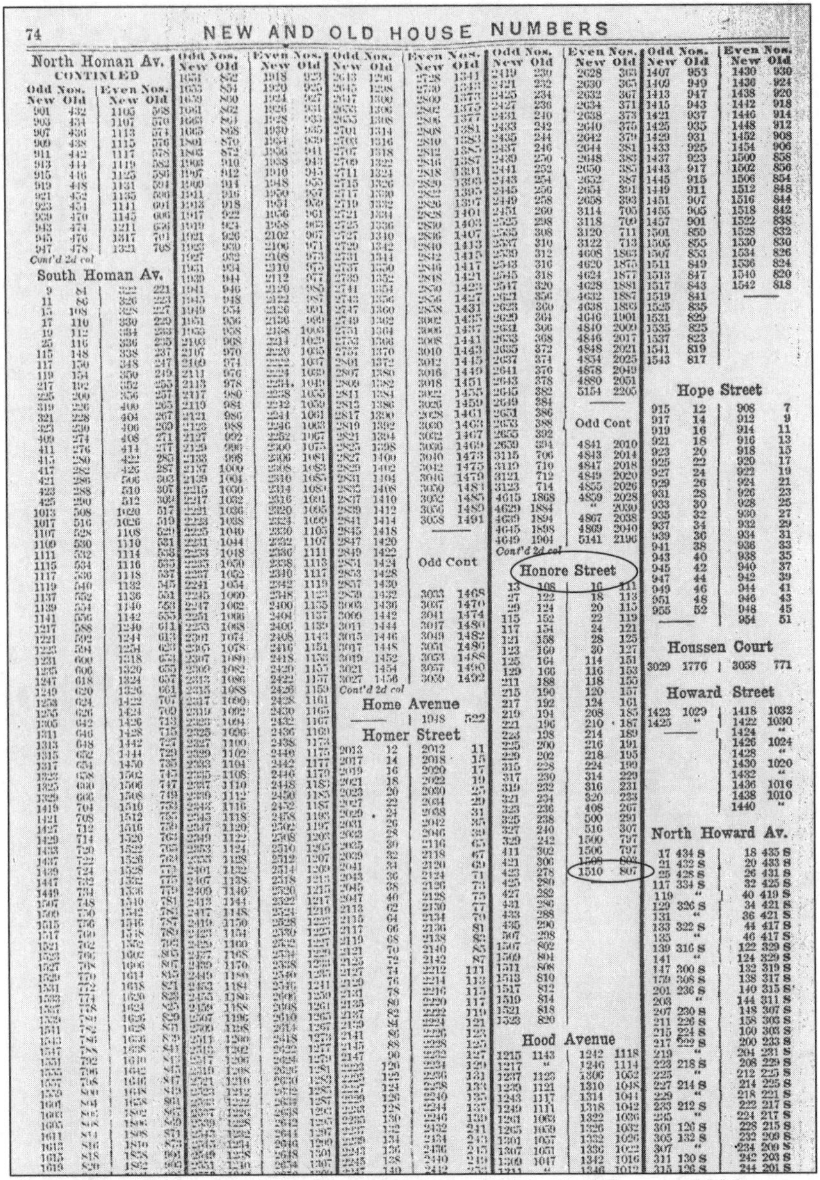

74 NEW AND OLD HOUSE NUMBERS

Odd Nos. New	Odd Nos. Old	Even Nos. New	Even Nos. Old
1407	953	1430	930
1409	949	1436	924
1413	947	1438	920
1415	943	1442	918
1421	937	1446	914
1425	935	1448	912
1429	931	1452	908
1433	925	1454	906
1437	923	1500	858
1443	917	1502	856
1445	915	1506	854
1449	911	1512	848
1451	907	1516	844
1455	905	1518	842
1457	901	1522	838
1501	859	1528	832
1505	855	1530	830
1507	853	1534	826
1511	849	1536	824
1513	847	1540	820
1517	843	1542	818
1519	841		
1525	835		
1531	829		
1535	825		
1537	823		
1541	819		
1543	817		

Honore Street

13	108	16	111
27	122	18	113
29	124	20	115
115	152	22	119
117	154	24	121
121	158	28	125
123	160	30	127
125	164	114	151
129	166	116	153
211	188	118	155
215	190	120	157
217	192	124	161
219	194	208	185
221	196	210	187
223	198	214	189
225	200	216	191
229	202	218	195
315	228	224	199
317	230	314	229
319	232	316	231
321	234	320	233
323	236	408	267
325	238	500	291
327	240	516	307
329	242	1500	797
411	302	1506	797
421	306	1508	803
423	278	1510	807
425	280		
427	282		
431	286		
433	288		
435	290		
507	298		
1507	802		
1509	804		
1511	808		
1513	810		
1517	812		
1519	814		
1521	818		
1523	820		

Hood Avenue

1215	1143	1242	1118
1217	"	1246	1114
1237	1123	1306	1052
1239	1121	1310	1048
1243	1117	1314	1044
1249	1111	1318	1042
1261	1063	1322	1036
1265	1059	1326	1032
1301	1057	1332	1026
1307	1051	1336	1022
1309	1047	1342	1016
1311	"	1346	1012

Hope Street

915	12	908	7
917	14	912	9
919	16	914	11
921	18	916	13
923	20	918	15
925	22	920	17
927	24	922	19
929	26	924	21
931	28	926	23
933	30	928	25
935	32	930	27
937	34	932	29
939	36	934	31
941	38	936	33
943	40	938	35
945	42	940	37
947	44	942	39
949	46	944	41
951	48	946	43
955	52	948	45
		954	51

Houssen Court

3029	1776	3058	771

Howard Street

1423	1029	1418	1032
1425	"	1422	1030
		1424	"
		1426	1024
		1428	"
		1430	1020
		1432	"
		1436	1016
		1438	1010
		1440	"

North Howard Av.

17	434 S	18	435 S
21	432 S	20	433 S
25	428 S	26	431 S
117	334 S	32	425 S
119	"	40	419 S
129	326 S	34	421 S
131	"	36	421 S
133	322 S	44	417 S
135	"	46	417 S
139	316 S	122	329 S
141	"	124	329 S
147	300 S	132	319 S
159	308 S	138	317 S
201	236 S	140	315 S
203	"	144	311 S
207	230 S	148	307 S
211	226 S	158	303 S
215	224 S	160	303 S
217	222 S	200	233 S
219	"	204	231 S
223	218 S	208	229 S
225	"	212	225 S
227	214 S	214	225 S
229	"	218	221 S
233	212 S	222	217 S
235	"	224	217 S
301	126 S	228	215 S
305	132 S	232	209 S
307	"	234	209 S
311	130 S	242	203 S
315	126 S	244	201 S

Illustration 6.2: Here is the puzzlement—I want to find the pre-1909 address of 1940 N. Honore Street, but the new numbers stop at 1510 N. Honore. Source: Plan of Re-Numbering City of Chicago: table showing new and old house numbers, August 1909.

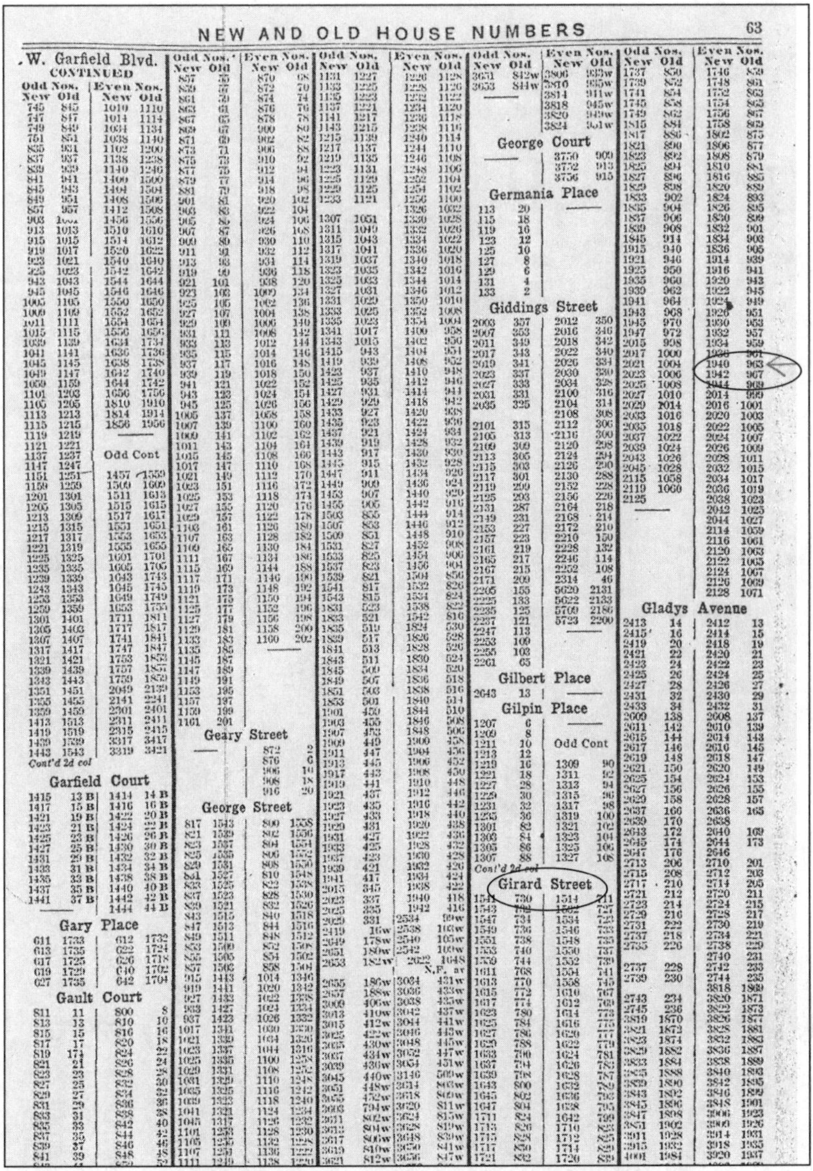

NEW AND OLD HOUSE NUMBERS 63

W. Garfield Blvd.
CONTINUED

Odd Nos. New	Old	Even Nos. New	Old
745	845	1010	1110
747	847	1014	1114
749	849	1034	1134
751	851	1038	1140
835	931	1102	1200
837	937	1138	1238
839	939	1140	1246
841	941	1400	1500
845	943	1404	1504
849	951	1408	1506
857	957	1412	1508
903	[illegible]	1456	1556
913	1013	1510	1610
915	1015	1514	1612
919	1017	1520	1622
923	1021	1540	1640
925	1023	1542	1642
943	1043	1544	1644
945	1045	1546	1646
1005	1105	1550	1650
1009	1109	1552	1652
1011	1111	1554	1654
1015	1115	1556	1656
1039	1139	1634	1734
1041	1141	1636	1736
1045	1145	1638	1738
1049	1147	1642	1740
1059	1159	1644	1742
1101	1203	1656	1756
1105	1205	1810	1910
1113	1213	1814	1914
1115	1215	1856	1956
1119	1219		
1121	1221		
1137	1237		
1147	1247		
1151	1251		
1159	1259		
1201	1301		
1205	1305		
1213	1309		
1215	1315		
1217	1317		
1221	1319		
1225	1325		
1235	1335		
1239	1339		
1243	1343		
1253	1353		
1259	1359		
1301	1401		
1305	1403		
1307	1407		
1317	1417		
1321	1421		
1339	1439		
1343	1443		
1351	1451		
1355	1455		
1359	1459		
1413	1513		
1419	1519		
1439	1539		
1443	1543		

Cont'd 2d col

Odd Cont

New	Old
1457	1559
1509	1609
1511	1613
1515	1615
1517	1617
1551	1651
1553	1653
1555	1655
1601	1701
1605	1705
1643	1743
1645	1745
1649	1749
1653	1755
1711	1811
1717	1817
1741	1841
1747	1847
1753	1853
1757	1857
1759	1859
2049	2139
2141	2241
2301	2401
2311	2411
2315	2415
3317	3417
3319	3421

Garfield Court

Odd New	Old	Even New	Old
1415	13 B	1414	14 B
1417	15 B	1416	16 B
1421	19 B	1422	20 B
1423	21 B	1424	22 B
1425	23 B	1426	26 B
1427	25 B	1430	30 B
1431	29 B	1432	32 B
1433	31 B	1434	34 B
1435	33 B	1438	38 B
1437	35 B	1440	40 B
1441	37 B	1442	42 B
		1444	44 B

Gary Place

Odd New	Old	Even New	Old
611	1733	612	1732
613	1735	622	1724
617	1725	626	1718
619	1729	640	1702
627	1735	642	1704

Gault Court

Odd New	Old	Even New	Old
811	11	800	8
813	13	810	10
815	15	816	16
817	17	820	18
819	17½	824	22
821	21	826	24
823	23	828	28
827	25	832	30
829	27	834	32
831	29	836	36
833	31	838	38
835	33	842	40
837	35	844	42
839	37	846	46
841	39	848	48

Odd Nos. New	Old	Even Nos. New	Old
857	55	870	68
859	57	872	70
861	59	874	74
863	61	876	76
867	65	878	78
869	67	900	80
871	69	902	82
873	71	906	88
875	73	910	92
877	75	912	94
879	77	914	96
881	79	918	98
901	81	920	102
903	83	922	104
905	85	924	106
907	87	926	108
909	89	930	110
911	91	932	112
913	93	934	114
919	99	936	118
921	101	938	120
923	103	1000	134
925	105	1002	136
927	107	1004	138
929	109	1006	140
931	111	1008	142
933	113	1012	144
935	115	1014	146
937	117	1016	148
939	119	1018	150
941	121	1022	152
943	123	1024	154
945	125	1026	156
1005	137	1058	158
1007	139	1100	160
1009	141	1102	162
1011	143	1104	164
1015	145	1108	166
1017	147	1110	168
1021	149	1112	170
1023	151	1116	172
1025	153	1118	174
1027	155	1120	176
1029	157	1122	178
1103	161	1126	180
1107	163	1128	182
1109	165	1130	184
1111	167	1134	186
1115	169	1144	188
1117	171	1146	190
1119	173	1148	192
1121	175	1150	194
1125	177	1152	196
1127	179	1156	198
1129	181	1158	200
1133	183	1160	202
1135	185		
1145	187		
1147	189		
1149	191		
1153	195		
1157	197		
1159	199		
1161	201		

Geary Street

Odd New	Old	Even New	Old
		872	2
		876	6
		906	16
		908	18
		916	20

George Street

Odd New	Old	Even New	Old
817	1543	800	1558
821	1539	802	1556
823	1537	804	1554
825	1535	806	1552
829	1531	808	1550
831	1527	810	1548
833	1525	822	1538
837	1523	828	1530
839	1521	832	1526
843	1515	840	1518
847	1513	844	1516
849	1511	848	1512
853	1509	852	1508
855	1505	854	1502
857	1503	858	1504
915	1443	1014	1346
919	1441	1020	1342
927	1433	1022	1338
933	1427	1024	1334
937	1423	1026	1332
1017	1341	1030	1330
1021	1339	1034	1326
1023	1337	1044	1316
1025	1335	1100	1258
1029	1331	1108	1252
1031	1329	1110	1248
1035	1325	1116	1242
1039	1323	1118	1240
1041	1321	1124	1234
1045	1317	1126	1232
1101	1253	1128	1230
1105	1235	1132	1228
1107	1251	1136	1222
1111	1249	1138	1220

Odd Nos. New	Old	Even Nos. New	Old
1131	1227	1226	1128
1133	1225	1228	1126
1135	1223	1232	1122
1137	1221	1234	1120
1141	1217	1236	1118
1143	1215	1238	1116
1215	1139	1240	1114
1217	1137	1244	1110
1219	1135	1246	1108
1223	1131	1248	1106
1225	1129	1252	1104
1229	1125	1254	1102
1233	1121	1256	1100
1307	1051	1326	1032
1311	1049	1330	1028
1315	1043	1332	1026
1317	1041	1334	1022
1319	1037	1336	1020
1323	1035	1340	1018
1325	1033	1342	1016
1327	1031	1344	1014
1331	1029	1346	1012
1333	1025	1350	1010
1335	1023	1352	1008
1341	1017	1354	1004
1343	1015	1400	958
1415	943	1402	956
1419	939	1404	954
1423	937	1408	952
1425	935	1410	948
1427	931	1412	946
1429	929	1414	944
1433	927	1418	942
1435	923	1420	938
1437	921	1422	936
1439	919	1424	934
1443	917	1428	932
1445	915	1430	930
1447	911	1432	928
1449	909	1434	926
1453	907	1436	924
1455	905	1440	920
1503	855	1442	916
1507	853	1444	914
1509	851	1446	912
1531	827	1448	910
1533	825	1452	908
1537	823	1454	906
1539	821	1456	904
1541	817	1504	856
1543	815	1532	826
1831	523	1534	824
1833	521	1538	822
1835	519	1542	816
1839	517	1824	530
1841	513	1826	528
1843	511	1828	526
1845	509	1830	524
1849	507	1834	520
1851	503	1836	518
1853	501	1838	516
1901	459	1840	514
1903	455	1844	510
1907	453	1846	508
1909	449	1848	506
1911	447	1900	458
1913	445	1904	456
1917	443	1906	452
1919	441	1908	450
1921	437	1910	448
1923	435	1912	446
1927	433	1916	442
1929	431	1918	440
1931	427	1920	438
1933	425	1922	436
1937	423	1928	432
1939	421	1930	428
1941	417	1932	426
2015	345	1934	424
2023	337	1938	422
2025	335	1940	418
2029	331	1942	416
2419	16w	2534	99w
2649	178w	2538	103w
2651	180w	2540	105w
2653	182w	2542	109w
		2622	1648 N.F. av
2655	186w	3034	431w
2657	188w	3036	433w
3009	406w	3038	435w
3013	410w	3042	437w
3015	412w	3044	441w
3025	422w	3046	443w
3035	430w	3048	445w
3037	434w	3052	447w
3039	436w	3054	451w
3045	440w	3146	509w
3051	448w	3614	803w
3055	452w	3618	809w
3603	794w	3620	811w
3611	802w	3624	815w
3613	804w	3628	819w
3617	806w	3648	839w
3619	810w	3650	841w
3621	812w	3656	847w

Odd Nos. New	Old	Even Nos. New	Old
3651	842w	3806	933w
3653	844w	3810	935w
		3814	941w
		3818	945w
		3820	949w
		3824	951w

George Court

Odd New	Old	Even New	Old
		3750	909
		3752	913
		3756	915

Germania Place

Odd New	Old	Even New	Old
113	20		
115	18		
119	16		
123	12		
125	10		
127	8		
129	6		
131	4		
133	2		

Giddings Street

Odd New	Old	Even New	Old
2003	357	2012	350
2007	353	2016	346
2011	349	2018	342
2017	343	2022	340
2019	341	2026	334
2023	337	2030	330
2027	333	2034	328
2031	331	2100	316
2035	325	2104	314
		2108	308
2101	315	2112	306
2105	313	2116	300
2109	309	2120	298
2113	305	2124	294
2115	303	2126	290
2117	301	2130	288
2119	299	2152	228
2125	293	2156	226
2131	287	2164	218
2149	231	2168	214
2153	227	2172	210
2157	223	2210	150
2161	219	2228	132
2165	217	2246	114
2167	215	2252	108
2171	209	2314	46
2205	155	5620	2131
2225	133	5622	2133
2235	125	5709	2186
2237	121	5723	2200
2247	113		
2253	109		
2255	103		
2261	65		

Gilbert Place

Odd New	Old	Even New	Old
2643	13		

Gilpin Place

Odd New	Old	Odd Cont New	Old
1207	6		
1209	8		
1211	10		
1213	12		
1219	16	1309	90
1221	18	1311	92
1227	28	1313	94
1229	30	1315	96
1231	32	1317	98
1235	36	1319	100
1301	82	1321	102
1303	84	1323	104
1305	86	1325	106
1307	88	1327	108

Cont'd 2d col

Girard Street

Odd New	Old	Even New	Old
1541	730	1514	711
1543	732	[illegible]	727
1547	734	1534	723
1549	736	1546	733
1551	738	1548	735
1553	740	1550	737
1559	744	1552	739
1611	768	1554	741
1613	770	1558	745
1615	772	1610	767
1617	774	1612	769
1623	780	1614	773
1625	784	1616	775
1627	786	1620	777
1629	788	1622	779
1633	790	1624	781
1637	794	1626	783
1639	798	1628	787
1643	800	1632	789
1645	802	1636	793
1647	804	1638	795
1711	824	1642	799
1713	826	1710	823
1715	828	1712	825
1717	830	1714	829
1721	832	1720	831

Odd Nos. New	Old	Even Nos. New	Old
1737	850	1746	859
1739	852	1748	861
1741	854	1752	863
1745	858	1754	865
1749	862	1756	867
1815	884	1758	869
1817	886	1802	875
1821	890	1806	877
1823	892	1808	879
1825	894	1810	881
1827	896	1816	885
1829	898	1820	889
1833	902	1824	893
1835	904	1826	895
1837	906	1830	899
1839	908	1832	901
1845	914	1834	903
1915	940	1836	905
1921	946	1914	939
1925	950	1916	941
1935	960	1920	943
1939	962	1922	945
1941	964	1924	949
1943	968	1926	951
1945	970	1930	953
1947	972	1932	957
2015	998	1934	959
2017	1000	1936	961
2021	1004	1940	963
2023	1006	1942	967
2025	1008	1944	969
2027	1010	2014	999
2029	1014	2016	1001
2033	1016	2020	1003
2035	1018	2022	1005
2037	1022	2024	1007
2039	1024	2026	1009
2043	1026	2028	1011
2045	1028	2032	1015
2115	1058	2034	1017
2119	1060	2036	1019
2125		2038	1023
		2042	1025
		2044	1027
		2114	1059
		2116	1061
		2120	1063
		2122	1065
		2124	1067
		2126	1069
		2128	1071

Gladys Avenue

Odd New	Old	Even New	Old
2413	14	2412	13
2415	16	2414	15
2419	20	2418	19
2421	22	2420	21
2423	24	2422	23
2425	26	2424	25
2427	28	2426	27
2431	32	2430	29
2433	34	2432	31
2609	138	2608	137
2611	142	2610	139
2615	144	2614	143
2617	146	2616	145
2619	148	2618	147
2621	150	2620	149
2625	154	2624	153
2627	156	2626	155
2629	158	2628	157
2637	166	2636	165
2639	170	2638	
2643	172	2640	169
2645	174	2644	173
2647	176	2646	
2713	206	2710	201
2715	208	2712	203
2717	210	2714	205
2721	212	2720	211
2723	214	2724	215
2729	216	2728	217
2731	222	2730	219
2737	218	2734	221
2735	226	2738	229
		2740	231
2737	228	2742	233
2739	230	2744	235
		3818	1869
2743	234	3820	1871
2745	236	3822	1873
3819	1870	3826	1877
3821	1872	3828	1881
3823	1874	3832	1883
3829	1882	3836	1887
3833	1884	3838	1889
3835	1888	3840	1893
3839	1890	3842	1895
3843	1892	3846	1899
3845	1896	3848	1901
3847	1898	3906	1923
3851	1902	3910	1926
3911	1928	3914	1931
3915	1932	3918	1935
4001	1984	3920	1937

Illustration 6.3: Puzzle solved—I learned that Honore Street was known as Girard Street when the conversion tables were published. I went to the listing of Girard Street and found the new numbers going up through 2128. My old address of 1940 N. Honore, therefore, was previously known as 963 N. Girard.

1909 DIRECTORY 1909

CHANGES IN STREET NAMES SINCE 1905.

OLD NAME.	NEW NAME.	LOCATION.
Armour av.	Grove av.	Garfield boul. to 65th.
Avenue K.	Ewing av.	69th to Hyde Lake.
B.	Garfield ct.	Southport av. to Dominick.
Benson	Loomis	31st to 33d.
Bernard	Trumbull av.	Foster av. to Balmoral av.
Bissell	Bincher.	Wellington to Barry av.
Bissell	Oak pl.	Belmont av. to School.
Broom.	Hartland ct.	Grand av. to W. Ohio.
Bryson.	Potomac av.	50th av. to Franklin av.
Buena Park ter.	Buena ter.	Evanston av. to Hazel av.
Central boul.	Normal av.	71st to 81st.
Central ct.	Franklin boul.	Garfield Park to Garfield Park.
Centre.	136th pl.	South Water st. to Randolph.
Charles pl.	Lomax pl.	O. & W. I. R. R. to Indiana av.
Christiana pl.	Phinney av.	5th av. to Franklin.
Clarence.	Fillmore	Western av. to Ravenswood Park
Clay av.	Argyle.	44th av. e. ½ blk.
Cottage Grove av.	Frances pl.	Carmen av. to Catalpa av.
Coventry.	Beny pl.	100d to Milwaukee av.
Crosby.	Grace.	North av. to Clybourn pl.
Custom House ct.	Federal.	Division to Vedder.
Cutler.	W. steuaw av.	Jackson boul. to 15th.
Dayton.	Reta.	Adams to Jackson boul.
Dayton.	Soult.	Cornelia av. to Addison.
Devon av.	Lafayette av.	Wellington to Barry av.
Dreyer.	Marshfield av.	Garfield boul. to 63d.
Dudley.	Winchester av.	Belmont av. to Lake Michigan.
Dunning.	Greenwood ter.	45th to 71st.
Eberly av.	St. Louis av.	North av. to Webster av.
Egleston av.	Canal	Lawrence av. to 72d av.
Emerald.	Kammerling av.	95th to 100d.
Evanston av.	Robert av.	80th av. to Central av. (dale av.)
Evanston av.	Lloyd av. rd	3162 av. to Pratt av.
Fayette ct.	Throop.	Bonaparte to Lyman.
Fifty-first.	Hyde Park boul.	Harrison to Oregon av.
Follansbee.	D-twin terrace.	Lake Michigan to Drexel Square.
Forest.	Paulina	Morse av. to Rogers av.
Forty-third ct.	Lowell av.	North av. to Argyle.
Fremont.	Hazel av.	Buena av. to Wellington.
Fremont.	Mildred av.	Cornelia av. to Graceland av.
Frink.	Fulton.	44th av. ne. to 52d av.

OLD NAME.	NEW NAME.	LOCATION.
Goldsmith av.	Normal av.	75th to 76th.
Hedges st.	Edgecomb pl.	Evanston av. to Clarendon av.
Holcomb av.	Avondale av	44th av. to Lawrence av.
Hough st.	Sait.	Archer av. to N. ¼ blk.
Hoyne ct.	Hoyne av.	Alr-s av. to North av.
Humboldt N.	Richmond N.	Diversey av. to Montrose av.
Humboldt S.	Richmond S.	Jackson boul. to 33d.
Jackson Park av.	Stony Is. and av.	56th to 59th.
Jasper.	Cornell av.	59th av. to Murray.
Kline av.	Sheridan rd.	Diversey boul. to Belmont av.
Lake View av.	Hamilton ct.	Webster av. to Fullerton av.
Larrabee.	51st av.	Madison to Colorado av.
Ledyard av.	Bensen.	31st to 33d.
McCallum.	Cortez.	Willow av. to Central av.
Nelson.	King pl.	Ashland boul. to North.
Noble.	Barry av.	Western av. to Halsted.
North Shore Drive.	Sheridan rd	Belmont av. to Grace.
Ogden front.	Lincoln av.	Wells to Cl. rk.
Olga.	Waveland ct.	Waveland av. to Grace.
Owasco.	Kensington av.	47th av. to Central av.
Pacific.	Gladys av.	Lake Calumet to Michigan av.
Pacific av.	Furmans	Sanford to Gratt.
Pensacola av.	Palmer pl.	Jackson boul. to Taylor.
Pine.	Reed pl.	Sacramento av. to Kedzie av.
Pullman av.	Lincoln Park boul	Perry to Clark.
Ridgeland av.	Cottage Grove av.	North Water to Oak.
River.	East End av.	103d to 115th.
Seipp av.	135th	Anthony av. to 83d.
72d pl.	East End av.	Dolton av. to Calumet av.
Shefield av.	Patrick pl.	69th to 93d.
Sherman av.	Sheridan rd.	I. C. R. R. to Greenwood av.
62d pl.	Manistee av.	Foster av. to Devon av.
Southwest boul.	Englewood av.	118th to 128th.
34th pl	M. rshal boul	Wentworth av. to Halsted.
Touhy av.	Douglas pl.	Douglas Park av. to Rhodes av.
Trusdell av.	Kenilworth av.	Ridge av. to the Lake.
Vernon Park pl.	Monroe av.	18th av. to Devon av.
Weed ct.	Oregon av	Centre av. to Loomis.
West ct.	Weed.	Clybourn av. n.e. ½ blk.
Wingert av.	Cambridge av.	Belmont av. ½ blk.
Woollacott	Myrtle av.	73d av. to Winter.
	California terrace	N. Halsted e. ¼ blk.

Illustration 6.4: Just some of the street name changes in a four-year period. Notice there were three Fremont Streets and two Bissell Streets at one time. It pays to proceed carefully in your research! Source: Lakeside City Directory of Chicago, 1909.

the listings because they are the wrong direction. You can zero in on the remaining ones and see which hook up to a known cross street.

The Chicago Street Name File is another way to do this. It's a wooden card file in the sixth-floor Chicago Room at Harold Washington Library Center. It gives the origin of street names as well as the date of the name changes, per City Council ordinances. You may have to spend time cross-referencing, as sometimes only portions of streets were changed.

Fire insurance maps (see discussion later in this chapter) usually show the old street name in parentheses. By comparing different years of maps, you can get an idea of when the name changed.

Street Name Changes in Cook County Suburbs

The local historical society or public library is your best source of information. Often they have files for each street, which may contain clippings about former names. Consult histories of the towns and old maps, including fire insurance maps.

❑ Strategy No. 2:
Sources for Photographs

You can see where your ancestor lived from the comfort of your own computer. The Cook County Assessor's Web site has recent color photos of all property in the county, residential and commercial. Go to www.cookcountyassessor. com/search/search.asp and select "Search by Address." Type in the current address, street name, and city. On the "Property Search Results" screen, click on "View Image" to see the photo. Click on "Property Index Number" to get more details, such as square footage and number of bathrooms. The site gives an age for the building, but take it with a shaker of salt; I have consistently found the ages to be off base, and I do not know the basis of their information.

If you click on "Images" on the search engine Google (www.google.com) and type in something like "Halsted Street Chicago," you'll get an interesting array of photos from Web sites—some old, most new. Please respect the site owners' copyrights and ask permission if you want to publish the photo in your family history.

Images from the *Chicago Daily News* from 1902 to 1933 are posted online. You can search by street name or owner's name. You can purchase copies from the owner, the Chicago Historical Society. The URL is http://memory.loc.gov/ammem/ndlpcoop/ichihtml/cdnhome.html.

For an additional source of old photographs, go in person to the Chicago Historical Society, which maintains "street files" of photographs. "Street files" are file folders of street scenes. One set of files, "Ready Prints," is in open-shelf cabinets, arranged by street name. Another, more extensive set must be paged by filling out a call slip specifying the street name and block. Historical societies for Chicago neighborhoods and suburbs often have street files as well. You usually can purchase reproductions of any photo you find.

❑ Strategy No. 3: Fire Insurance Maps

Besides photographs, fire insurance maps give you much information. This type of map lets you see a footprint of your ancestor's house and workplace. It also shows you the neighborhood—the schools, places of worship, shops, factories. You can see the changes over time, because the maps were updated periodically as the neighborhoods developed.

Fire insurance maps help insurance companies rate buildings according to the degree of fire risk. Surveyors made notes on construction materials, building usage, and types of fire prevention measures utilized (fire alarms, fire escapes, and so on). Such maps are not unique to Chicago—the earliest one was done in 1790 for Charleston, South Carolina, and many cities and towns across the United States have been mapped. You can access them in either of two ways. Large bound atlases show color coding for the construction materials (pink = brick, yellow = frame, and so on). Microfilm or digital format is in black and white but is easier for making copies (most places don't permit copying of the bound atlases).

Finding Fire Insurance Maps

The Chicago Historical Society has many bound atlases, mostly for Chicago but also for a handful for suburbs and other parts of Illinois. A guide to finding the right one for the address you're interested in is in a binder at every table in the CHS Research Center. You will also have online access to digitized versions of Chicago and suburban maps at the Research Center.

The Richard J. Daley Library at the University of Illinois at Chicago has a microfilmed set for Chicago and Cook County towns. There's an excellent guide showing exactly what each map covers. A few early bound atlases reside in Special Collections. The Harold Washington Library Center has the same microfilmed set and provides map guides.

IRAD allows you to make color copies of its atlases. However, IRAD's collection is not as useful for older genealogical research because the maps, dating from 1916 to 1950, were periodically updated with corrections pasted over the previous information. The last update was in 1972, so you can see what was there at that time but not before.

The Map and Geography Library at the University of Illinois at Urbana–Champaign has an extensive collection, both in atlas and on microfilm. Color copies and scans can be made from the atlases. Library holdings are listed at www.library. uiuc.edu/max/sanb-chi.shtml.

Environmental Data Resources bought the library of the Sanborn Map Company, the largest maker of fire insurance maps. For a fee, EDR will do a search for the current address you give them and provide copies of the maps they have (up to 15), either as electronic files or prints or both (black and

Illustration 6.5: Detail of an 1886 fire insurance map of Chicago showing three blocks on the Near North Side bounded by Chicago Avenue on the north, Erie Street on the south, Market Street (now Orleans Street) on the west, and Franklin Street on the east.

In this small area lie three churches: Grace Lutheran, St. Paul's German Lutheran, and Norwegian–Danish Lutheran. Children living here would attend the Huron Street Elementary School. Their parents might work at one of the manufacturing firms on the west side of Market Street making wagons, pool tables, or vinegar. Once you locate your ancestor's home or workplace, the map tells you the lot dimensions, the footprint of the building, what it's made of (though you'll need a color version to tell that), whether there was water service, and if the street was paved. It's almost as good as going back in time yourself. Source: *Robinson's Atlas of Chicago, 1886, Volume 3, Plate 7 and index map to Volume 3.*

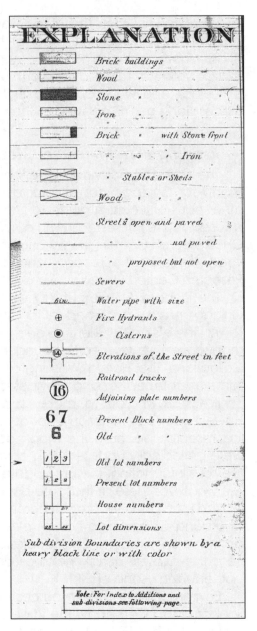

EXPLANATION

Brick buildings
Wood "
Stone "
Iron "
Brick " with Stone front
" " Iron
" Stables or Sheds
Wood " " "
Streets open and paved
" not paved
" proposed but not open
Sewers
6in. Water pipe with size
⊕ Fire Hydrants
◉ " Cisterns
⑭ Elevations of the Street in feet
Railroad tracks
⑯ Adjoining plate numbers
6 7 Present Block numbers
6 Old " "
1 2 3 Old lot numbers
1 2 3 Present lot numbers
House numbers
Lot dimensions

Subdivision Boundaries are shown by a heavy black line or with color

Note: For Index to Additions and sub-divisions see following page.

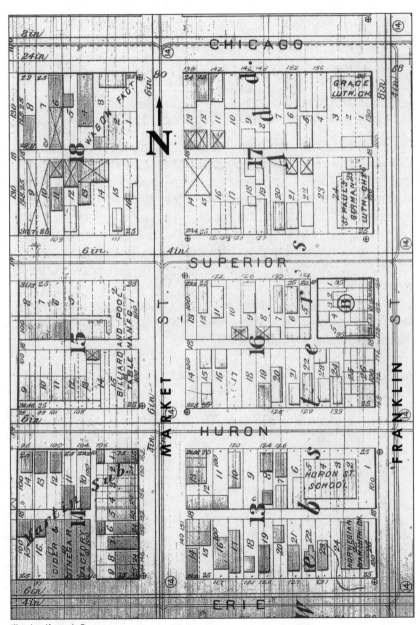

Illustration 6.5

white only). Contact:

Environmental Data Resources
440 Wheelers Farms Road
Milford, CT 06460
800/352-0050 (Customer Service)
www.edrnet.com/reports/historical.html

The Library of Congress Photoduplication Service can supply you, for a fee, with photocopies, color transparencies, prints, and digital images of any fire insurance map dated before September 19, 1906, in its collection. You need to provide information from the book *Fire Insurance Maps in the Library of Congress* (Washington, D.C.: Library of Congress, 1981), available at the Newberry Library and the Richard J. Daley Library, among others. The information you'll need to provide includes the entry number, city name, edition date, and plate number or street location desired. If you happen to be in Washington, you are welcome to take a digital camera to the Geography and Map Division. Contact:

Library of Congress
Photoduplication Service
101 Independence Avenue SE
Washington, DC 20540-4570
202/707-5640
www.loc.gov/preserv/pds
photoduplication@loc.gov

Where Did My Ancestor Live?

Points to Remember

❏ *There are many sources you can check to locate the address of your ancestor, including city directories, school records, draft registrations, and old letters, to name a few.*

❏ *Many Chicago neighborhoods were once separate towns or villages:*

• Look for local preannexation records; they may have more information about your ancestor.

❏ *Convert any pre-1909 Chicago addresses:*

• Use printed or online conversion tables. Start with the street name, then look for the old address in "Even" or "Odd" columns. If the street name isn't there, it could have changed.

(Continued next page)

Where Did My Ancestor Live?

❑*Watch for street name changes
in Chicago:*

• Consult the Martin and McNalis compilation "Chicago Streets" or the Chicago Street Name File. Narrow down multiple possibilities by referencing the "Street & Avenue Guide" in city directories for the direction and cross streets of the street you want. Fire insurance maps usually show the old name in parentheses.

❑*Find address and street name
changes in Cook County suburbs:*

• Ask at the local historical society and public library, or check fire insurance maps.

❑*View online images of your
ancestor's house or street:*

• Cook County Assessor's Web site (www.cookcountyassessor.com/search/search.asp)

• Google "Images" search (www.google.com)

• *Chicago Daily News* photos from 1901 to 1933 (http://memory.loc.gov/ammem/ndlpcoop/ichihtml/cdnhome.html

7 What Occupation Did My Ancestor Have?

Knowing your ancestor's job can lead you to discovering records and information you couldn't get any other way—for example, accidents on the job, participation in strikes, and wages and salaries. You'll have more insight into your ancestor's life—and the life of his or her family—when you learn that your great-grandfather worked in the meatpacking industry or Aunt Sophie took in washing after her husband died. If you know an ancestor made airplane engines during World War II or ran a tavern during Prohibition, you have a link to national events.

❑ Strategy No. 1: City Directories

The easiest way to find your ancestor's profession is to look in city directories. These are like phone books—people are listed alphabetically by surname—but are better because they give the occupation and work address in addition to the name and home address. Directory publishers sent canvassers door-to-door to ask about residents. But because businesses were the primary users of city directories, residents of poorer neighborhoods might not be covered.

You can consult Chicago city directories on microfilm at the Harold Washington Library Center, the Chicago Historical Society, the Newberry Library, and the University of Illinois at Chicago's Richard J. Daley Library. You can also get them on loan for a fee through Family History Centers affiliated with the Church of Jesus Christ of Latter-day Saints. The available years are 1839, 1843 to 1846, 1848 to 1857, 1859 to 1917, 1923, and 1928–29 (final edition published).

The Chicago Historical Society and the Newberry Library have good collections of suburban Cook County directories. Also check the historical society in the town of interest. The years available will vary by town.

Tips for Directory Information:

• You won't find your ancestors in the Chicago city directory unless they lived or worked in the city. If they lived in a suburb, only the name of the town will be listed, not the complete address.

• Women are generally listed in the Chicago city directories only if they were widows or if they were employed outside the home (as a seamstress, a teacher, a secretary, and so on). In Illustration 7.1, there are three Annie Jennings, each the widow of a different man. Suburban directories, such as for Evanston, may list the wife's name following her husband's.

• Chicago telephone directories sometimes list occupations. You might be surprised to know that Chicago phone books are available from 1878 onward. The early ones list physicians, undertakers, and workers in other occupations for whom having a phone was important.

• If you can't find your ancestor in the city directory for a particular year, be sure to look at the page in the front titled "Names too late for classification" or "Removals, changes, etc." This is an alphabetical list of changes obtained too close to the publication date for the printer to typeset in the body of the directory.

• If your ancestor's name does not appear under its proper spelling, try looking under phonetic spellings of the name. Ethnic names may have gotten quite garbled from an English-speaking canvasser writing down what a foreign speaker said in an accent.

• Some immigrants may not show up in a directory because they were afraid they would be called up for military service if they answered a stranger's questions. Keep checking other years—you can usually find your ancestor in at least one directory.

• If the city directory lists only a home address and no occupation, this may mean the person had no fixed work location, such as a bricklayer who went to different job sites. It could also mean the person worked out of the house or was retired.

Illustration 7.1: This column from the 1909 Chicago city directory lists people having occupations ranging from candlemaker (Michael Jenniches) to traffic manager (Charles A. Jennings). You will find a key to the abbreviations used at the front of the alphabetical listings; for example, "lab" = laborer, "clk" = clerk, and "com trav" = commercial traveler (what we now call a traveling salesman). Source: Lakeside Directory of City of Chicago, 1909, Newberry Library.

JENNEY, MUNDIE & JENSEN (William B Mundie and E C Jensen) architects 1401 New York Life bldg tel Randolph-3024 and Automatic-2701
Jenniches George H clk h rear 192, 24th pl
  Michael candlemkr h rear 192, 24th pl
Jenning Margaret wid Frederick h 13762 Leyden av
  Theodore P h 588 Lasalle av
Jennings Abiline W wid Edgar C h 3235 Dover
  Agatha A Miss teacher h 898 S Central Park av
  Agnes H h 6558 Ross av
  Agnes J dressmkr 222 Palmer pl
  Albert A dairy traffic agt 62, 2 Sherman h 821 W Jackson boul
  Albert R furn rooms 232 Ontario
  Alfred clk 715, 205 Lasalle h 5127 Wabash av
  Alfred J buyer 200 State h 169 Lake View av
  Alma Mrs h 288 Illinois
  Alma B Mrs milliner h 103 N 52d av
  Andrew F salesman h 453 W Lake
  Anna M Miss clk 925, 144 Vanburen h 6558 Ross av
  Annie wid James h 38 Sibley
  Annie wid Robert h 569, 27th
  Annie wid William h 962 N Kedzie av
  Anthony com trav h 353 W 61st
  Arthur printer News h 75 Park av
  Arthur A clk h 821 W Jackson boul
  Arthur E lab h 922, 36th
  Arthur J chief clk 1228, 9 Jackson boul h 2402 N 42d ct
  Arthur T M collr 157 Michigan av h 2112 Michigan av
  August jr porter h 3438 Wabash av
  August H lab h 22 N Ada
  Augustus janitor bds 3438 Wabash av
  A Miss clk 402 Central sta h 218 Oak
  Benjamin clk Hamilton nat bank h 157 Union
  Benjamin lab h 296 Clark
  Benjamin F coachman h 534, 50th
  Bert teaming bds 4233 Wabash av
  Bridget wid Michael W h 6558 Ross av
  Bridget wid William h 26 W 19th
  Bros (John and Thomas Jennings) saloon 196 N Wells
  Bros Mnfg Co (The) Arthur R Oughton mngr; silver plateware 806, 42 Madison
  Caleb S elev bldr h 816 Leland av
  Celia E wid George h 5916 Union av
  Charles clk 7801 Vincennes rd h 7040 Justine
  Charles A traffic mngr 1106, 143 Dearborn h 2485 N Hermitage av
  Charles D draftsman h 209 S Howard av
  Charles E chief clk 204, 169 Jackson boul h 2384 N 40th av
  Charles E clk PO h 6932 Vernon av
  Charles E ins broker h 6129 Woodlawn av

1909 DIRECTORY

"*The Best, the Cheapest.*"

CELEBRATED
SILK UMBRELLAS.
PALMER HOUSE, CHICAGO

OSGOOD

Algernon S capitalist 801, 101 Washington
   bds Sherman house
Alice F Miss teacher h 1815 Surf
Art Colortype Co 165 and 167 Adams
A M & Son (Albert M and Albert T Osgood)
   lumber 766 W Adams
Charles A mngr 259 Wabash av h Austin
Charles V com trav h 287½ Lincoln av
Clarence B com trav 128 Franklin h 724
   Flournoy
Co Edwin S Osgood pres; Charles J Whipple
   sec; engravers 167 Adams
Edwin stationer C & NW Ry 56 Kinzie h
   Oak Park
Edwin S pres Osgood co 167 Adams h Austin
Eliza wid John B h 287½ Lincoln av
Ervin E 1163 The Rookery h 48 Scott
Everett W ins solcr 405, 171 LaSalle h Win-
   netka
Frank D dept mngr 216 Monroe h 2554 N
   Paulina
Frank G saloon 9235 Commercial av
Frederick C agt 1328 Monadnock blk h 2728
   Wabash av
Frederick F salesman 216 Monroe h 635
   Walnut
Frederick S v pres Osgood co 167 Adams h
   Austin
George engraver bds 238 Dearborn av
George B clk 231 Franklin h 766 W Adams
Harry S clk h 766 W Adams
Henry R clk 1 W Washington h 430 W
   Drexel boul
Henry D lumber W 22d sw cor Fisk h
Hiram J switchman h 2724 N 46th av
Howard C h 2257 South Park av
Howard C Mrs dre smkr 2257 South Park
   Surf
James S insp 1107, 109 Randolph h
John D com trav 221 Adams h 272 S L

Illustration 7.2: The 1899 Chicago city directory shows Edwin Osgood working for the Chicago and North Western Railroad at 56 Kinzie [Street]. Because he lived outside the city (in Oak Park), the directory publisher did not feel obliged to give a complete home address. Notice also that when no city is given, the assumption is that the address is in Chicago. Source: Lakeside Directory of City of Chicago, 1899, Newberry Library.

1005 Lake Street
Telephone 45.

Jas. W. Carter

==COAL==

Staple Dry Goods at lowest Prices

OAK PARK.

Oak Park Times, R L Rowe, editor...........................131 Marion st
Oaks, K, mgr, Chicago Vaccine Stables...............122 Marion st
Oaks, Martha B miss, sec'y Chicago Vaccine Stables...122 Marion st
OAKS, W. W., prop. Avenue Pharmacy............**122 Marion st**
Ober, Frank W, editor, 705 Association bldg.......117 S Kenilworth av
O'Brien, Clara M miss, compositor, E O Vaile............416 Marion st
O'Connor, C J, Chicago city collector's office...........1020 S Boulevard
O'Connor, D, prin Coleman School...................................1020 S Boulevard
O'Connor, J J, attorney 1407 Title & Trust bldg........1020 S Boulevard
O'Connor, M J, clerk County bldg....................................1020 S Boulevard
O'Connor, Mary M miss, 1407 Title & Trust bldg......1020 S Boulevard
O'Connor, Nellie miss, stenographer Probate Court...1020 S Boulevard
O'Connor, Teresa miss, Hanchett Paper Co.............1020 S Boulevard
O'Laughlin, James, stone quarry, Bellewood............115 S Austin av
Olcese, _____..251 Clinton av
Olcutt, Chas, painter...134 Holley ct
Olds, A F Dr, veterinarian..425 S Euclid av
Olds, C May miss...425 S Euclid av
Olson, Ada miss..1225 Washington av
Olson, Geo, express, 125 Lake st..Harlem
Olson, Peter A, machinist...710 N Lombard av
Onthank, J, station agt..............................C & N-W Ry station, Austin av
Onthank, Margaret mrs, station agt.........C & N-W Ry station, Austin av

THE AVENUE PHARMACY **W. W. OAKS, Proprietor.**
E. L. MEAD, R. Ph.
116 North Oak Park Av.

Oriel, F H, salesman, 232-4 Monroe st...........................124 S Boulevard
O'Rourke, E J, motorman C & P St Ry..............................322 Highland av
Orr, George H, American Hotel Register Co, 189 LaSalle st.431 N Groveav
Orth, Andreas, Forest Home Cemetery.............................913 Belleforte av
Orth, Andrew, lumberman..940 Belleforte av
Orth, Fred, with Beriard & Moreney Mill Co...................913 Belleforte av
Orton, Ester M mrs...The Kenton
Osborne, Geo, with Farson, Leach & Co.........................519 Randolph av
Osborne, Louisa mrs...519 Randolph st
Osborne, M mrs, boarding..1017 Lake st, flat G
Osgood, Edwin, with C & N-W Ry Co........................**305 N Euclid av**
Ott, J W..316 N Euclid av
Outhet, Elizabeth miss...215 Lake st
Overstreet, H T, transfer, 42 River st..............................120 W Ontario st
Owen, Edwin, Harlem Library...355 N Boulevard
Owen, E A miss, telegraph operator 103 Marion st......234 S Boulevard
Owen, E H...314 S Boulevard
Owen, E G, clerk Penn. Co...218 Wesley av
Owen, Geo, pressman E O Vaile...Austin
Owen, Geo H, contr agt Penn. Co, 4 Sherman st........318 Wesley av
Owen, Helen E miss, operator W U Tel Co, 103 Marion st.214 S Boulevard
Owen, Ira J, mandolinist..110 Maple av
Owen, Susie O miss...314 S Boulevard
Owen, W P, deputy assessor Cicero................................218 Wesley av
Owen, W R, vessel owner, 35 Metropolitan blk............110 Maple av

WHERE do you get your Creams and Ices? We get ours at A. BURGESS,' 140 Lake St.

AVENUE DRY GOODS STORE. 107 OAK PARK AV.

Illustration 7.3: To find Edwin's home street address, you would look in the 1899 Oak Park directory (shown here, bottom arrow). It confirms his place of employment but does not give the Chicago work address, unlike the listing for George Orr, for example (top arrow), who worked at 189 LaSalle Street. It's assumed you know that LaSalle Street is in Chicago. Source: Oak Park Directory, 1899, The Historical Society of Oak Park and River Forest.

❏ Strategy No. 2: U.S. Census

The U.S. census is a great tool for tracking down occupational information. Here's what you can find out:

• 1940–2000: For privacy reasons, these censuses will not be released until 72 years have passed. You can obtain information for a fee if you prove you are an heir of the person and the person is deceased. Request Form B6–600 from the following:

Personal Census Search Unit
U.S. Census Bureau
P.O. Box 1545
Jeffersonville, IN 47131
812/218-3046
fax: 812/288-3371

• 1960–2000: These censuses did not ask questions about occupation.

• 1950: This census lists employment status, hours worked in week, occupation, industry, and class of worker.

• 1940: This census lists employment status, whether a person was in private or non-emergency government work, or in public emergency work (WPA, CCC, for example); if in private work, did the person work the past week; if seeking work or on public emergency work, the duration of unemployment; the number of weeks worked last year, income last year, occupation, industry, and class of worker.

• 1930: This census lists occupation, industry, class of worker (wage worker, employer, self-employed), and whether a person was at work the previous day or last regular working day.

• 1920: This census lists occupation, industry, and class of worker (wage worker, employer, self-employed).

• 1910: This census lists occupation, industry, class of worker (wage worker, employer, self-employed), and whether a per-

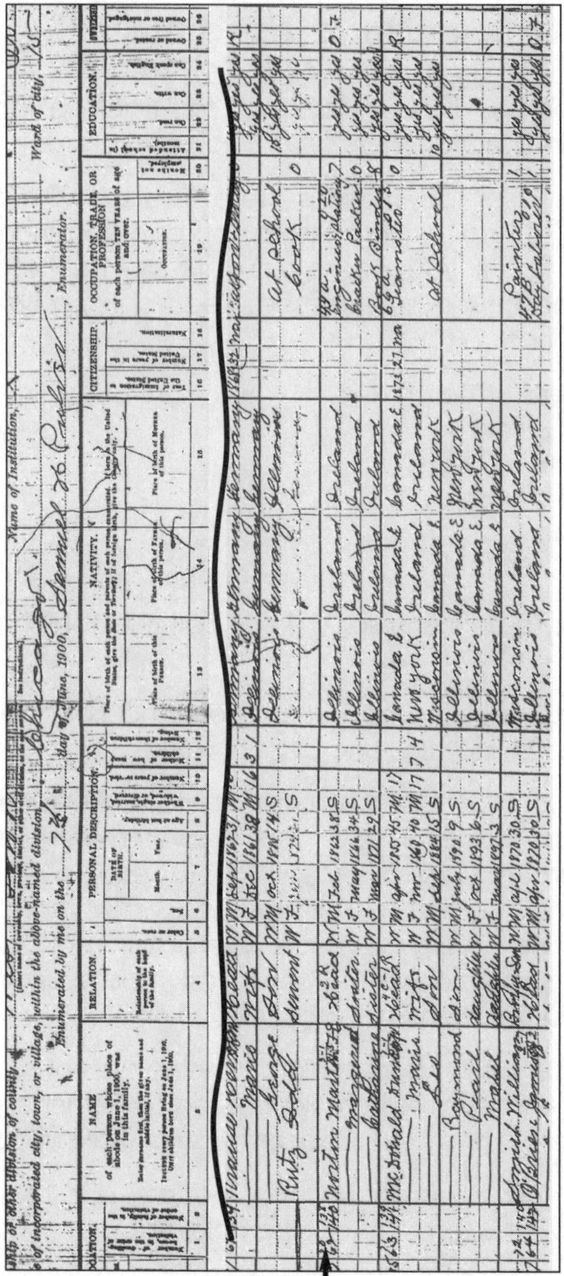

Illustration 7.4: In studying the Norton family, the 1900 census reveals that Martin is an engineer (the specific type could be plating or stationary), out of work for seven months; Catherine (written "Catharine") is a bookbinder, out of work for eight months; and Margaret (written "Margeret") is a cracker packer, without any unemployment. She must have been the main source of income for that year. Source: 1900 U.S. Census, Reel 264, ED 481, Sheet 8, Lines 75–77.

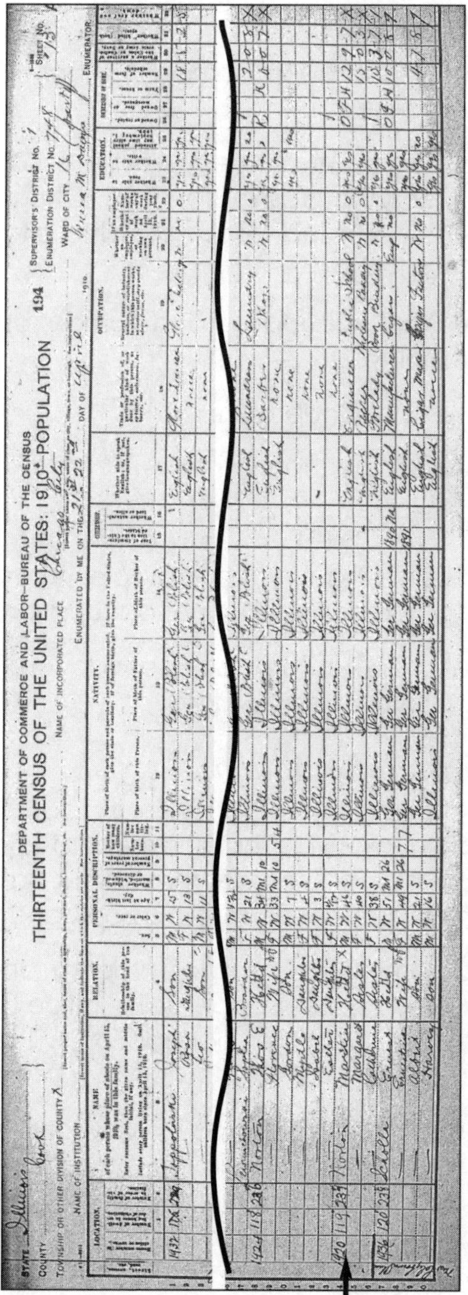

Illustration 7.5: In 1910 all three were in the same line of work, but we get more information: Martin is an engineer at a public school. Margaret is a packer at a wholesale bakery, and Catherine is a forelady at the bookbindery. Source: 1910 U.S. Census, Reel 258, ED 748, Sheet 13A. Family Visitation #239.

son was out of work on April 15, 1910.

• 1900: This census lists occupation and number of months a person was not employed.

• 1890: This census was virtually destroyed in a 1921 fire at the Bureau of the Census in Washington, D.C. One microfilm reel of fragments was compiled, which included a few Illinois counties but not Cook.

• 1880: This census lists occupation and number of months a person was not employed.

• 1870: This census lists occupation.

• 1860: This census lists occupation.

• 1850: This census lists occupation.

• 1840: This census lists industry (for example, mining, commerce, navigation of the ocean) but not occupation.

• 1830: Chicago was not incorporated as a town until 1833, so there is no 1830 Chicago census data.

Tips for Census Information:

• "Keeping house" or "none" is often indicated in the space for occupation for wives. That just means they did not work outside the home. For income, they might have sewn clothing, watched children, given music lessons, and the like.

• Teenage and sometimes younger children often had occupations of messenger, newspaper seller, office boy, and so forth. Otherwise the space for occupation will read "at school" or will be blank.

• For U.S. censuses from 1850 to 1880, if your ancestor was a farmer, look for more information in the *agricultural schedules*. These are separate compilations that tell you about things such as how many acres were owned, what types of crops were raised, and how many livestock died that year.

• For U.S. censuses from 1850 to 1880, if your ancestor was

a manufacturer (for example, a shoemaker, a miller, or a worker in a similar small business), look for more information in the *manufacturing schedules*. These separate compilations tell you about things such as location, number of employees, and annual production.

See Chapter 10 ("Nuts and Bolts of the U.S. Census") for more information on finding your ancestor in the census.

❑ Strategy No. 3: State Census

If you had early ancestors in Chicago or elsewhere in Cook County, you may be able to find some occupational information in the Illinois state census. Illinois took censuses every five years starting in 1820 and ending in 1865 (except for 1850 and 1860, when the federal censuses were used). All of these named the head of household only; the others in the household were merely counted in age groups by sex. Here's what you can find out:

• 1865: This census lists type and valuation of products of manufacturing establishments (for example, blacksmith, cooper) and valuations of livestock, crops, and other agricultural products. Cook County is not indexed, but volunteers at the Illinois State Archives are working on it. The returns for Cook County are available on microfilm at the Newberry Library, Northern Illinois University, Southern Illinois University, the University of Illinois at Urbana–Champaign, the Illinois State Library, the C. E. Brehm Memorial Public Library District (Mt. Vernon, Illinois), and the Allen County Public Library (Fort Wayne, Indiana). The writing is faint and hard to read.

• 1855: This census lists type and valuation of products of manufacturing establishments (for example, tinshop, saddlery), valuations of livestock and coal mine products, and pounds of wool produced. It occasionally lists the occupation of head of household. An index for Cook County is available on microfilm at the Newberry Library and the Illinois State Archives and on the Internet at Ancestry.com (subscription

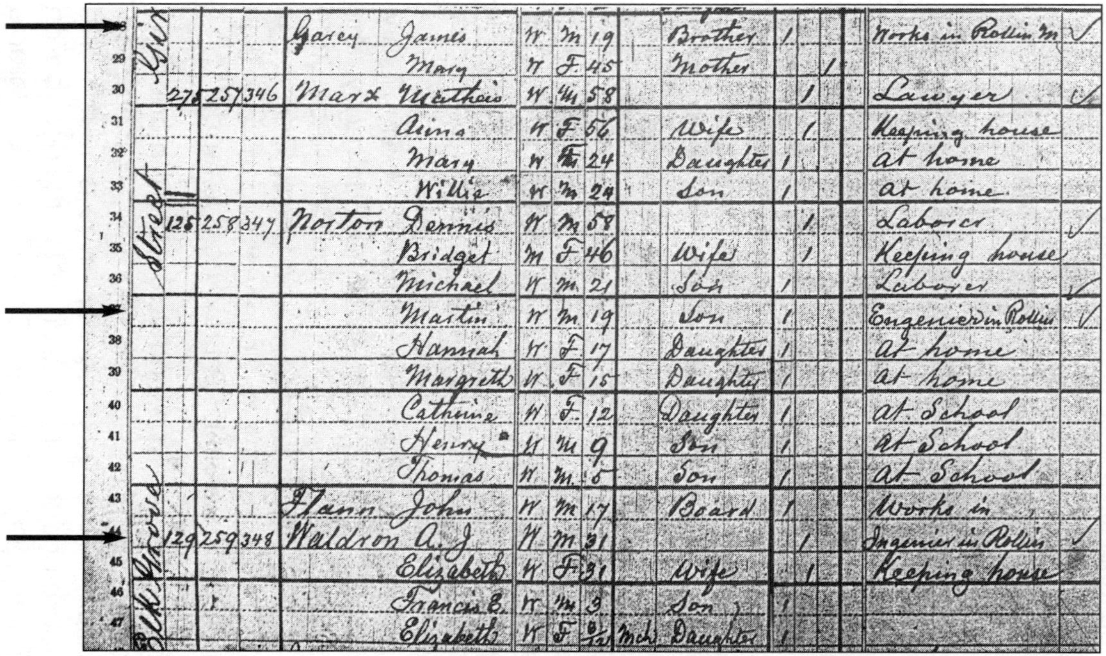

28				Garey	James	W	M	19	Brother	Works in Rollin M
29					Mary	W	F	45	Mother	
30	275	257	346	Marx	Mathias	W	M	58		Lawyer
31					Anna	W	F	56	Wife	Keeping house
32					Mary	W	F	24	Daughter	at home
33					Willie	W	M	24	Son	at home
34	125	258	347	Norton	Dennis	W	M	58		Laborer
35					Bridget	W	F	46	Wife	Keeping house
36					Michael	W	M	21	Son	Laborer
37					Martin	W	M	19	Son	Engenier in Rollin
38					Hannah	W	F	17	Daughter	at home
39					Margreth	W	F	15	Daughter	at home
40					Cathrine	W	F	12	Daughter	at School
41					Henry	W	M	9	Son	at School
42					Thomas	W	M	5	Son	at School
43				Flann	John	W	M	17	Board	Works in
44	129	259	348	Waldron	A. J.	W	M	31		Ingenier in Rollin
45					Elizabeth	W	F	31	Wife	Keeping house
46					Francis E.	W	M	3	Son	
47					Elizabeth	W	F	[illegible]	Daughter	

Illustration 7.6: You won't get the name of the company your ancestor worked for from the U.S. census, but sometimes you can figure it out. When researching the Dennis Norton family, I found a city directory listing for 1868 stating, "Norton, Dennis, roller, Chicago Rolling Mill Co. r. 537 Elston rd." In the 1880 census, his son Martin is "Engenier in Rollin" and neighbor A.J. Waldron is "Ingenier in Rollin." Another neighbor, James Garey , "Works in Rollin M." Source: 1880 U.S. Census, Reel 196, ED 155, Sheet 36, Lines 28–44.

Illustration 7.7: Looking at an 1886 map for 537 Elston, I noticed that the North Chicago Rolling Mill Co. (highlighted on map) was a few blocks away and concluded that it must have been the workplace for many in the neighborhood. Source: Robinson's Atlas of the City of Chicago, 1886, Volume 4, Plate 25.

Web site), in the database "Illinois Census, 1810–90." The Ancestry site is available free at the Newberry Library, the Arlington Heights Memorial Library, the Elmhurst Public Library, and other libraries. The returns for Cook County are on microfilm at the Newberry Library, Northern Illinois University, the Illinois State Library, the C. E. Brehm Memorial Public Library District (Mt. Vernon, Illinois), and the Allen County Public Library (Fort Wayne, Indiana). They have been poorly reproduced and are hard to read.

• 1845: No returns for Cook County survive.

• 1840: This census lists type and number of manufacturing establishments (for example, sawmill, gristmill). No information about agriculture was recorded. An index for Cook County is on the Internet at Ancestry.com (subscription Web site), in the database "Illinois Census, 1810–90." The Ancestry site is available free at the Newberry Library, the Arlington Heights Memorial Library, the Elmhurst Public Library, and other libraries. Another index is at the Illinois State Archives (*Name Index To Early Illinois Records*). The returns for Cook County are available on microfilm at the Illinois State Archives and the Illinois State Library.

• 1835: No returns for Cook County survive.

• 1830: Cook County was not formed until 1831. Inhabitants were part of Putnam County, and those returns have not survived.

• 1825: Returns for the county that Cook was part of have not survived.

• 1820: No occupational information was recorded.

❑ Strategy No. 4: Sources for Teachers

Hooray for bureaucracy! The Chicago Board of Education generated a wealth of material about teachers. You may find similar tools from the boards of education in Cook County towns. Since these materials were created with taxpayer

Appendix.   153

NAMES OF
TEACHERS EMPLOYED,
MAY, 1891.

Names in Small Capitals indicate Principals of Schools and Special Teachers; names in Italics, Assistants to Principals and Head Assistants; and names in German Text, Teachers of German.

NAME.	SCHOOL.	RESIDENCE.
Abbott, Mary A... ......Headley...............		62 Gault Place.
Accola, Emma.......Lake View. Nos. 4 and 6..1330 Wellington Street		
Adams, Alice E..........Clarke... ....501 Ogden Avenue.		
Adams, Alice M..........Webster...............		3816 Johnson Place.
ADAMS, CARRIE G........Goodrich............		398 Washington Boul.
Adams, Elizabeth........Shurtleff... ....6952 Dickey Street.		
Adams, Elvira H ....Armour Street........Oak Park, Ill.		
Adams, Kittie E..........Cooper...............476 Center Avenue.		
Adams, Maggie C........Longfellow...........476 Center Avenue.		
Adams, Mary C..........Lake View No. 1.... ..Evanston, Ill.		
Adams, Mary T..........Rogers................476 Center Avenue.		
Adams, Mattie J........ Polk Street..........486 W. Taylor Street.		
Adams, Minnie V........D. S. Wentworth.....7036 Winter Street.		
Adams, Nettie R........ .Haven... ....2104 Michigan Avenue.		
Adams, Sophia B........King................422 S. Oakley Avenue.		
Adams, Victoria A.......Jefferson High........Irving Park, Ill.		
Addy, Alice E ....Cornell...............5312 Madison Avenue.		
Addy, Mary S... ....Ward...... ....2949 La Salle Street.		
Abler, Hannah...........Harrison............41 E. 13th Street.		
Adolf, Mattie..........Andersenville Branch.18 Winthrop Place.		
Ahern, Alma E........ ..Throop............2953 Butler Street.		
Ahern, Ellen ....Hoffman Av. Branch..797 N. Western Av.		
Ahern, Mary...........Boulevard............797 N. Western Av.		
Ahern, Mary...........Healy...............625 53rd Street.		
Aiken, Lois M...........Ogden................73 N. State Street.		
Aimer, Helen...........Calhoun............1346 Jackson Street.		
Aitchison, Jessie D......J. N. Thorp ....378 Escanaba Avenue.		

Illustration 7.8: Want to know where your teacher–ancestor worked and lived? Check Board of Education records. Source: Chicago Board of Education, *36th Annual School Report for Year Ending June 30, 1890,* Newberry Library.

money, they are public records.

The Chicago Board of Education *Directory* provides the names and addresses of teachers and board members from 1897 to 1930. From 1930 to 1954, only the names of principals, assistant principals, and superintendents are listed. The Municipal Reference Library at Harold Washington Library Center has years 1897 to 1954. The Newberry Library holds 1895 to 1896, 1900 to 1909, and 1928 to 1929.

The Chicago Board of Education *Annual Report* lists the workplaces of teachers in the nineteenth century, in addition to their names and addresses. The *Annual Reports* include photos of new schools and interior shots of classrooms, giving insight into education methods of the time. You'll find the years 1867 to 1925 at the Municipal Reference Library at Harold Washington Library Center. The Newberry Library holds 1859 to 1870, 1872 to 1915, and 1918.

Finally, the *Chicago Board of Education Proceedings* give budgets for each school and the salaries of the personnel. It also lists teachers on maternity leave, those who were transferred, and those injured on the job. You'll have to dig through these massive volumes because they have no name index. Information is organized by school or school district. Years 1871/2 to 1917/8 are at the Newberry Library, while 1922/23 to the present are at the Municipal Reference Library at Harold Washington Library Center. The University of Illinois at Chicago's Richard J. Daley Library has 1960/1 to 1971/2.

❑ Strategy No. 5:
Sources for City Workers (Chicago)

As one of the largest cities in America, Chicago hired employees in a broad spectrum of occupations to provide service to residents. The quote below makes this clear:

> No college has a curriculum as extensive as that of the Public Service of this city.
>
> The field covered includes employees in the fol-lowing groups: Architecture, Bacteriology, Chemistry, Engineering, . . . Accounting, Statistics, Horticulture,

Library Science, Pharmacology, Medicine, Dentistry, Nursing, Pathology, Transportation inspection, Electrical inspection, Food inspection, Inspectors of weights and measures, Inspectors of buildings, construction and of meters, the street cleaning and repair service, the skilled trades, the unskilled labor service as well as the Police and Fire and Clerical service. (Source: *31st Annual Report Civil Service Commission City of Chicago—Year 1925*, pages 12–13, Municipal Reference Library, Harold Washington Library Center.)

The wide range of occupations and the steady nature of the work means there's a good possibility your ancestor may have worked for the city at some point. The *Annual Report* of the Civil Service Commission from 1896 to 1925 and 1940 lists appointments, retirements, resignations, suspensions, transfers, and leaves of absence. Each has an "Index to Minutes" (a name index). You may find a reference to a female ancestor who changed her name upon marriage. The 1925 edition, for example, noted that Elizabeth Barnes, Division Chief, Public Library, was now Elizabeth Lipkau. The "Alphabetical List of Positions in the Service of the City of Chicago" in the back of the reports gives the job title and salary range. The Municipal Reference Library at Harold Washington Library Center is where you'll find these volumes. Because of their fragility, photocopying is not permitted.

At the Illinois Regional Archives Depository at Northeastern University, you can look at the Civil Service *Promotional Registers* for 1895 to 1950. These are listings of applicants who took tests to be hired or promoted during those years. It includes their scores and their dates of hiring or promotion. There is no master index; you'll have go through each year to find your ancestor.

You may find references to aldermen and department heads in the *Chicago City Council Proceedings* (1861–present), *City Manual* (1908–16), and *Mayor's Messages and*

Municipal Reports (1880–96), all at the Municipal Reference Library at Harold Washington Library Center. The *City Manual*, for instance, explains the duties of the department heads and lists the names of those working under them. There is a table of contents but no name index.

If an ancestor was a firefighter, check the *Report of the Fire Marshal* (1871–1930) at the Municipal Reference Library at Harold Washington Library Center. Rosters of the fire companies are listed; the ones through 1882 provide the employee's country of birth and/or former occupation. Most volumes list retirements, deaths, and awards for heroism.

Another good source is the Fire Museum of Greater Chicago, a fledgling institution with all sorts of information on past firefighters, the firehouses they were assigned to, and the fire equipment they used. The museum's archives include photographs, books, journals, and periodicals. The museum is currently housed in temporary quarters with limited hours. It plans to move to a historic fire station soon. Contact:

Fire Museum of Greater Chicago
P.O. Box 4914
Chicago, IL 60680
773/777-4511
fax: 877/865-6295
firemuseum@hotmail.com

❑ Strategy No. 6:
Sources for Railroad Workers

With Chicago being the transportation crossroads of the country, chances are good your ancestor worked for one of the many railroads that used the city as a hub. For information about your ancestor's service from 1936 onward, contact:

Railroad Retirement Board
844 N. Rush Street
Chicago, IL 60611
www.rrb.gov/geneal.html

PENSIONER'S RECORD. -3436

No. *1704* Name *Gillingham, George H.*

Division or Department *2u P Dept - Chi Shops*

Occupation when Pensioned *Foreman Paint Shop -*

Age when Pensioned, Years *70* Months *-*

Length of Service, Years *44* Months *6*

Average Monthly Pay for last ten years, $ *105.13*

Amount of Monthly Allowance, $ *46.78* *42.70* 1932 x 8.07

Date Pension Was Allowed, Mo. *Oct* Day *29* Year *1917*

Date Pension began, Month *Nov* Day *1* Year *1917*

Address when pensioned *605 N. Grove Av - Oak Park, Ill*

Present Address

Where Check is sent *as above*

~~Date of Death~~ or discontinuance, Mo. *Aug.* Day *17* Year *1936*

DECEASED

Total Amount of Pension Received, $ *9,455.68*

(OVER)

Illustration 7.9a: Pensioner's record for George H. Gillingham shows that he worked for the railroad most of his life, from age 26 to age 70. He started out as a painter and rose to foreman of the paint shop, which according to his obituary, handled locomotives exclusively. His average monthly pay was $105.13, entitling him to a pension of $46.78. This amount was nearly cut in half in the Depression. Courtesy of Craig Pfannkuche, Genealogical Archivist, Chicago and North Western Historical Society. (Record continues next page.)

For earlier employees, check city directories or the census to find the name of the railroad, then look to see if there is an archive for that company.

For instance, there is a Chicago and North Western Historical Society, which has employment records. Contact:

Craig Pfannkuche
8612 Memory Trail
Wonder Lake, IL 60097
815/653-9459
craig@pfannkuche.com

The South Suburban Genealogical and Historical Society holds the employment records of the Pullman Car Works

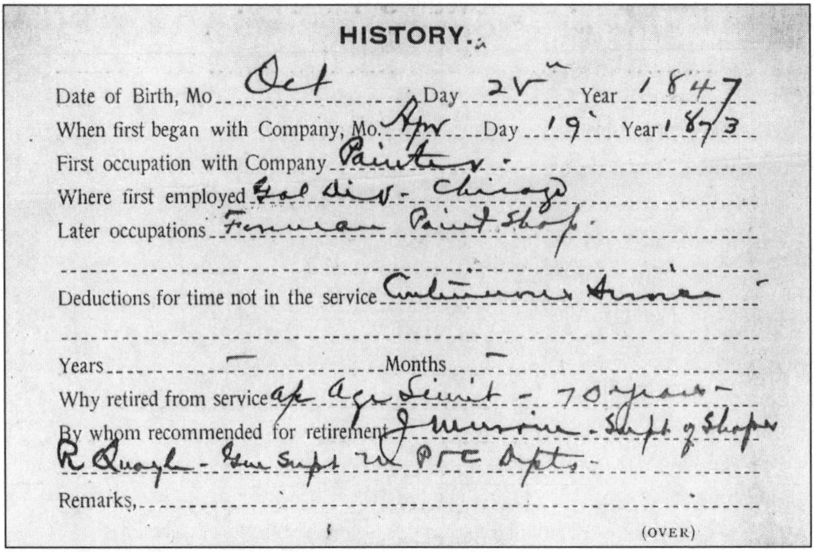

HISTORY.

Date of Birth, Mo. _Oct_ _____ Day _2ᵛ_ Year _1847_

When first began with Company, Mo. _Apr_ Day _19_ Year _1873_

First occupation with Company _Painter_ -

Where first employed _Sal div - Chicago_

Later occupations _Foreman Paint Shop._

Deductions for time not in the service _Continuous service_ -

---

Years _____ Months _____

Why retired from service _age Age Limit - 70 years -_

By whom recommended for retirement _J menroin - Supt of Shops_
R Quayle - Gen Supt M P E Dpts -

Remarks, _____

(OVER)

Illustration 7.9b

(approximately 200,000 employees who manufactured the sleeping cars, dining cars, and so forth). Searches are free; there is a fee for each file ordered. Contact:

South Suburban Genealogical and Historical Society
3000 W. 170th Place
Hazel Crest, IL 60429-1174
708/335-3340
www.rootsweb.com/~ssghs
ssghs@usa.net

The Newberry Library holds employment records for Pullman Company employees—those who worked the train runs, such as porters, maids, and dining car attendants. A guide to the Pullman Company archives is posted on the Newberry Library Web site, www.newberry.org. Go to "Collections Descriptions," then "American History," then "Railroads." The Newberry also holds archives of the Illinois Central and Burlington Northern Railroads, but these are largely business records and contain very little employment information.

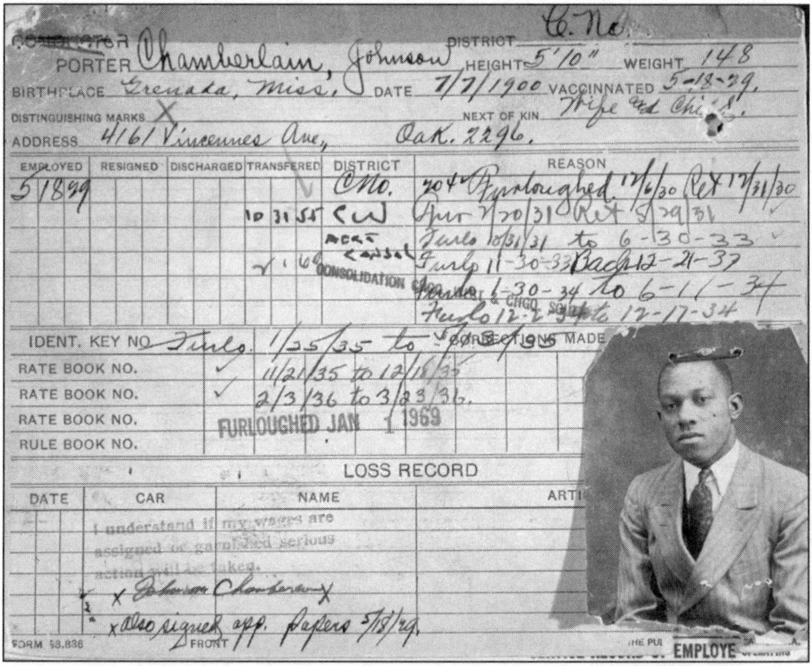

PORTER Chamberlain, Johnson DISTRICT C. No.
HEIGHT 5'10" WEIGHT 148
BIRTHPLACE Grenada, Miss. DATE 7/7/1900 VACCINNATED 5-18-29
DISTINGUISHING MARKS X NEXT OF KIN Wife and Child
ADDRESS 4161 Vincennes Ave, Oak. 2296.

EMPLOYED	RESIGNED	DISCHARGED	TRANSFERED	DISTRICT	REASON
5/18/29				C. No.	Furloughed 12/6/30 Ret 12/31/30
			10 31 55	C W	Fur 7/20/31 Ret 8/29/31
					Furlo 10/31/31 to 6-30-33
					Furlo 11-30-33 Back 12-21-37
				CONSOLIDATION	Furlo 1-30-34 to 6-11-34
					Furlo 12-2-34 to 12-17-34

IDENT. KEY NO. Furlo 1/25/35 to ... CORRECTIONS MADE
RATE BOOK NO. 11/21/35 to 12/18/35
RATE BOOK NO. 2/3/36 to 3/23/36.
RATE BOOK NO. FURLOUGHED JAN 1 1969
RULE BOOK NO.

LOSS RECORD

DATE	CAR	NAME	ARTI...
		I understand if my wages are assigned or garnisheed serious action will be taken.	
		x Johnson Chamberlain x	
		x Also signed app. papers 5/18/29.	

FORM 58.836 FRONT
... EMPLOYE ...

Illustration 7.10: The front of Johnson Chamberlain's employment record summarizes his 40-year career as a porter, from a hire date of May 18, 1929, to the final furlough, January 1, 1969. Of special importance to genealogists is his exact birth date and birthplace, and a photo taken probably shortly after hiring. Source: Chamberlain, Johnson—Employee Service Record. Pullman Company Archives, Case Pullman 06/02/03, Box 216, the Newberry Library.

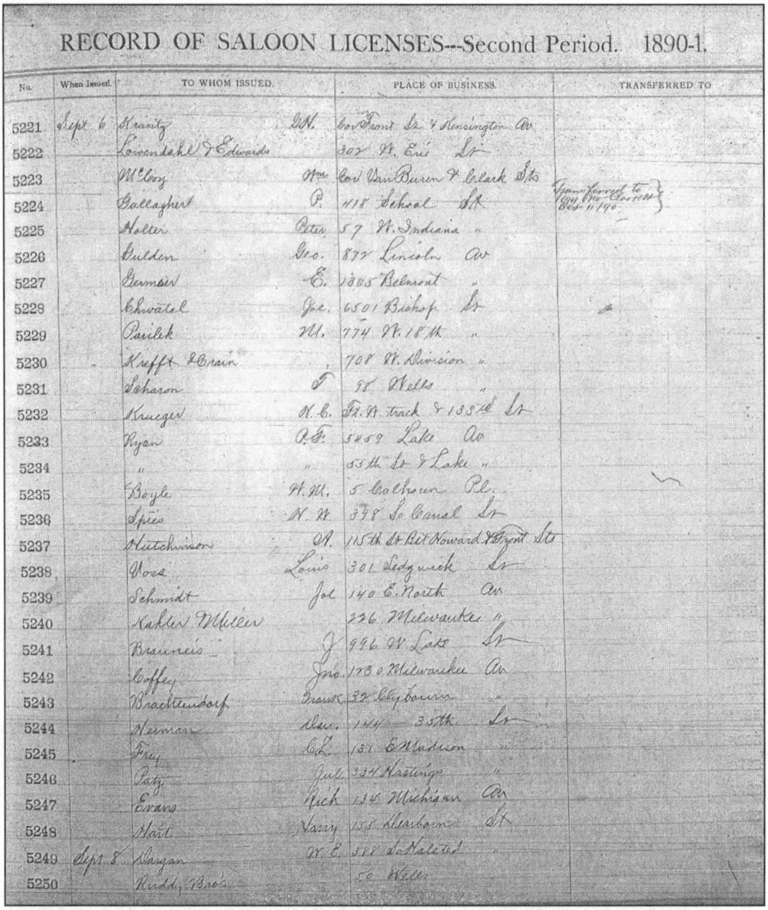

Illustration 7.11: Did your ancestor operate a drinking establishment? You can verify that and learn where it was located by consulting saloon license records. You may even find a note about the business moving to another location, as in number 5224.
Source: Chicago: Saloon License Record 7/0035/01, Illinois Regional Archives Depository at Northeastern Illinois University.

❑ Strategy No. 7:
Sources for Professionals

You can usually find information on ancestors who worked in professions that required specialized education and licensing: physicians, nurses, lawyers, engineers, accountants, architects, undertakers, and the like.

First, check directories specific to that profession. The American Medical Association, for example, came out with *Directory of Deceased American Physicians*, 1804–1929, available at the Newberry Library and other libraries. Entries summarize the information found in the AMA's master files. There were directories done at different points in time for lawyers and other professions, especially in the period between 1880 and 1930. The Chicago Historical Society and the Newberry Library have good collections of these historical directories.

Next, check for licensing. It might have been required by the state. Check Record Group 208.00 in the *Descriptive Inventory of the Archives of the State of Illinois* for holdings on accountants, barbers, plumbers, and many more. It's online at www.sos.state.il.us/departments/archives/di/208__002.htm. (Note: There is a double-length underscore in this URL.) Many cities also had requirements. Chicago, for example, had saloonkeepers and peddlers buy licenses, and you can see lists of those who paid at the Illinois Regional Archives Depository.

Finding school records is trickier. Many medical schools dissolved in the 1890s and early 1900s, and no one kept the records. Architects did not have formal courses of study in the nineteenth century; they learned by working for established practitioners. At other schools you must prove the student is deceased before accessing the records. Follow the trail of the school to the present to determine if the records from the time period you seek are available and what restrictions apply.

What Occupation Did My Ancestor Have?

Points to Remember

❏ *Tips for searching city directories:*

• Chicago city directories end with the 1928–29 edition. Use phone books after that. The limitations of phone books are that they won't list occupations as consistently and won't cover as many people.

• Women appear in Chicago city directories only if they were widows or employed outside the home.

• If you can't find your ancestor in the directory, try the following:
—Check for alternate/phonetic spellings.
—Check the front section "Names too late for classification" or "Removals, changes, etc."
—Check other years.

• Suburban city directories give the home address for those who worked in Chicago.

❏ *Tips for further information in the U.S. census:*

• If your ancestor was a farmer from 1850 to 1880, look for the U.S. agricultural schedules, which tell you about the number of acres owned, the type of crops grown, livestock losses, and more.

What Occupation Did My Ancestor Have?

• If your ancestor had a small business making goods from 1850 to 1880, look for U.S. manufacturing schedules, which tell you about the number of employees, annual production, and more.

• Occupational information (on deceased individuals only) for 1940 and 1950 is available for a fee from the Census Bureau.

❏ *Tips for finding information on professionals:*

• Check directories of specific professions.

• Check for state license records (Record Group 208.00 in the Illinois StateArchives, www.sos.state.il.us/departments/archives/di/208__002.htm; note double-length underscore).

• Check for city license records (Chicago and suburbs).

• Check records of trade or professional schools (are records extant? what is access policy?).

8 When Did My Ancestor Die and Where Is My Ancestor Buried?

Answering the question of when your ancestor died is the best way to learn where he or she is buried. Determining a burial place can be done without a death date, but it is quite time-consuming. Cook County is the second-largest county in the United States, and there is no master index to all the cemeteries.

❏ Strategy No. 1:
Determine the Death Date

Your first step should be to look among family papers for a death certificate, funeral program, remembrance card, newspaper clipping, or listing in the family Bible. If you don't have these, proceed to the general kinds of death indexes discussed in Chapter 12, "Nuts and Bolts of Birth and Death Records."

There are two specialized death indexes you can try if your ancestor does not show up in general death indexes. One is the *Chicago Police Department Homicide Record Index, 1870–1930*. It is posted on the Web site of the Illinois Regional Archives Depository (IRAD) at Northeastern Illinois University (www.sos.state.il.us/departments/archives/homicide. html). Search by victim's name; the index gives the event date, the names of other persons involved, and the volume and page number of the record. With this information you can request a copy from the archives, or go in person and view it. An expanded transcription of the Chicago Police Department records went online June 2004 at http://homicide. northwestern.edu. The record usually contains the place of the assault, the date of death if later than the assault, and the manner of death. It may also contain notes on the assailant's arrest, conviction, and sentencing. Pursue any leads that the homicide record gives you, such as court cases and newspaper accounts.

The other specialized death index (also compiled by IRAD) is the *Cook County Coroner's Inquest Record Index, 1872–1911*. It is available at www.sos.state.il.us/departments/ archives/cookinqt.html. You can search it by the name of the deceased.

Inquests are held for anyone dying accidentally or suspiciously, such as someone who collapsed in the street, was found in the river, or was hit by a street car. If you see

---

Inquest No. 2434.

Inquest on Louise Rayner at No. 84 West Division Street in the City of Chicago Cook County on the 26th day of January 1876.

Verdict:

That the said Louise Rayner, now lying dead at No. 84 West Division St. in the City of Chicago County of Cook and State of Illinois, came to her death on the 23rd day of January 1876, from exhaustion. And, we, the Jury, find that the death could have been prevented by the timely and judicious use of instruments and we therefore believe that Dr. Robert L. Adison who was called in due time, has been guilty of gross neglect and Malpractice.

John A. Rolf (foreman)	Valentine Roesohs	DeForest Petine
John Schultz	Charles Koch	John Simpson
Jacob Schaffner	P. Larsen	F. J. Hoffman
Ignatz Pais	Andrew Anderson	C. Sinning

Witnesses   Dr. Robert L. Adison No. 128 West Erie Street
                    Gertrude Huntgeburt " 321 Noble " (Midwife)
                    Dr. D.C. Stillians   " 112 Milwaukee Avenue

---

Illustration 8.1: Inquests are held at a place where the body can be examined. In this 1876 case, it was the home where the woman had died. A jury of 12 listened to witnesses and rendered a verdict to the coroner. By the mention of a midwife, you know the case involved childbirth. Source: Cook County Coroner's Inquest Record #2434, Volume 2, page 133.

"The victim of an intoxicated doctor"

"On the 26th, Coroner Dietzch investigated, in No. 84 West Division Str., a Swedish woman's dead body, Mrs. Louisa Rainer (?), who on the past Sunday evening had died in childbirth. The midwife called for a doctor Addison, who lived in No. 128 West Erie Street, who in an intoxicated condition arrived at 9 am, and after he had given the woman some medicine, sat down by the fireplace in a room nearby, without paying her anymore attention.

Until 9 pm that day the woman was lying in bed with terrible pains, when finally the husband called for doctor Stilliams, who delivered the baby, but he came too late and couldn't save the mother or the baby, who both died.

At the postmortem examination, doctor Stilliams certified that when he arrived, the woman's pulse had already stopped; that doctor Addison was so intoxicated that he couldn't give proper answers to the questions he was asked, and that he, the whole time, explained that the woman was "all right," even after she was dead. Other people, who belonged to the family, also verified this evidence, and the jury decided that Mrs. Rainer's cause of death was "malpractice" performed by doctor R.S. Addison, who at the time was intoxicated.

Coroner Dietzsch ordered to arrest the awful man, who was the reason to both the mother's and the baby's deaths, but when this is written (on Sunday), he was still not found. Hopefully he will soon be in the hands of justice, to get his punishment and to warn other quacks.

Mrs. Rainer was 34 years old and had three children from before."

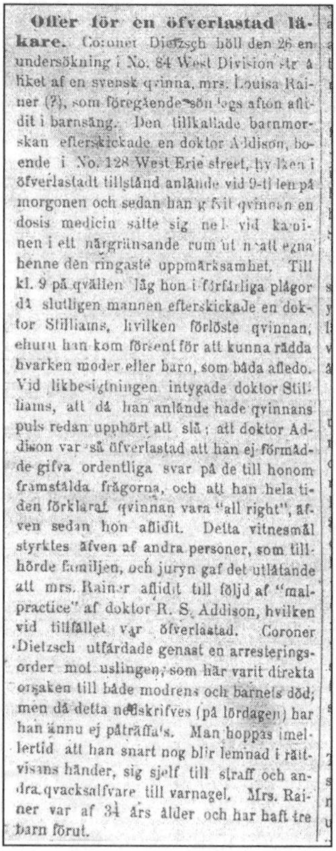

Offer för en öfverlastad läkare. Coronet Dietzsch höll den 26 en undersökning i No. 84 West Division str å liket af en svensk qvinna, mrs. Louisa Rainer (?), som föregående söndags afton aflidit i barnsäng. Den tillkallade barnmorskan efterskickade en doktor Addison, boende i No. 128 West Erie street, hvilken i öfverlastadt tillstånd anlände vid 9-tiden på morgonen och sedan han gifvit qvinnan en dosis medicin satte sig ned vid kaminen i ett närgränsande rum utan att egna henne den ringaste uppmärksamhet. Till kl. 9 på qvällen låg hon i förfärliga plågor då slutligen mannen efterskickade en doktor Stilliams, hvilken förlöste qvinnan, ehuru han kom försent för att kunna rädda hvarken moder eller barn, som båda afledo. Vid likbesigtningen intygade doktor Stilliams, att då han anlände hade qvinnans puls redan upphört att slå; att doktor Addison var så öfverlastad att han ej förmådde gifva ordentliga svar på de till honom framstälda frågorna, och att han hela tiden förklarat qvinnan vara "all right", äfven sedan hon aflidit. Detta vitnesmål styrktes äfven af andra personer, som tillhörde familjen, och juryn gaf det utlåtande att mrs. Rainer aflidit till följd af "malpractice" af doktor R. S. Addison, hvilken vid tillfället var öfverlastad. Coroner Dietzsch utfärdade genast en arresteringsorder mot uslingen, som här varit direkta orsaken till både modrens och barnets död; men då detta nedskrifves (på lördagen) har han ännu ej påträffats. Man hoppas imellertid att han snart nog blir lemnad i rättvisans händer, sig sjelf till straff och andra qvacksalfvare till varnagel. Mrs. Rainer var af 34 års ålder och har haft tre barn förut.

Illustration 8.2: My client had told me that Louise Rayner was Swedish. Sure enough, on page 4 of the February 3, 1876, issue of Svenska Amerikaren, *there appeared this article, which I had translated at North Park University's Center for Scandinavian Studies. Notice the spelling variations in the two doctors' names between the inquest record and the newspaper accounts. You would need to do more research to determine which spellings are correct.* Translation used with permission of Eleanor Baird.

the coroner's signature on a death certificate, look for an inquest file. It is a gold mine of information on the circumstances of the death and the background of the deceased.

Inquest files for 1872 to 1911 are held at IRAD (with some gaps for years 1879 to 1880, and 1888). You can go in person and make copies or request them by mail or phone for a small fee. Files after 1911 are at what is now called the Office of the Medical Examiner. There is a copying fee, but

---

The Drunken Doctor.

Coroner Dietzsch is still occupied in investigating the case of Louisa Rainer, the woman who died in child-birth night before last, through alleged neglect on the part of an alleged drunken physician, Dr. R.S. Addison, of 128 West Erie street. He went to the house about 9 o'clock Monday morning, and after giving her some medicine, he left her and paid no more attention to her. The woman lingered along in great agony until 9 o'clock in the evening, when Dr. Stillians was called in, but he was too late to save her life. She died shortly after he arrived. An undertaker named Kunkel, who has a "coffin concern" on Milwaukee avenue, tried to bury the remains without a permit, but the Superintendent of the Cemetery refused to have the body interred without the permit. This is the second time this fellow Kunkel has tried the same game. It is hoped that he and the Doctor will be brought to justice as they deserve to be.

Illustration 8.3: One of the major dailies gave details about Louise's attempted burial. Its suspicious circumstances apparently triggered the inquest. Source: Chicago Evening Journal, January 26, 1876, page 1, column 8. (See Chapter 11, "Nuts and Bolts of Newspaper Searching," for tips on how to find these types of articles.)

this is money well spent. Contact:

Medical Records Section
Office of the Medical Examiner
2121 W. Harrison Street
Chicago, IL 60612
312/666-0500

When your ancestor is the subject of an inquest, he or she is automatically newsworthy. Go straight to the newspapers for coverage of the death or inquest, using the dates you found in the file. In Illustration 8.1, the date of death was January 23, 1876, and the inquest date was January 26, 1876. Illustrations 8.2 and 8.3 are two of the articles I found.

❏ Strategy No. 2:
Determine the Place of Burial

There are four types of records that provide information on your ancestor's final resting place: death certificates, death notices and obituaries, church records, and cemetery records. You may not find all of them, but you should be able to find at least one.

Death Certificates
The death certificate always states the disposition of the body, whether buried, cremated, or given to medical science. A burial permit is necessary for interment in a lot or mausoleum, and the permit is not issued without the signature of a physician or coroner on the death certificate.

Though they can be expensive and difficult to find, you should always pursue the death certificates of your ancestors. You will learn more than just the place of burial. You'll learn the name of the funeral home or undertaker, which is a potential source of further records. You'll learn the cause of death, important to know for your own medical history. And you'll

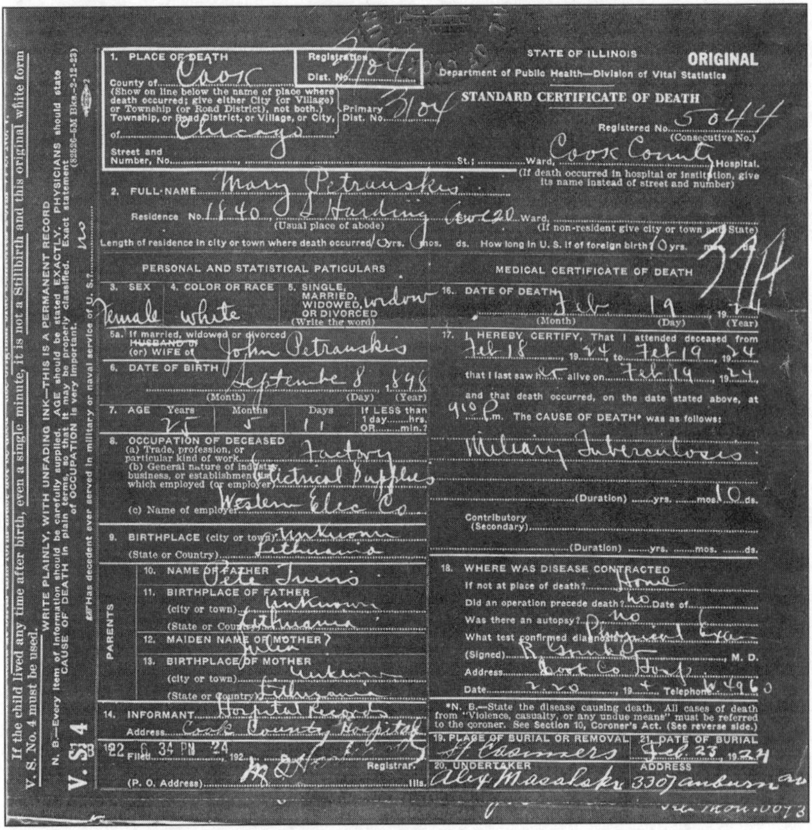
V. S. No. 4 must be used. If the child lived any time after birth, even a single minute, it is not a Stillbirth and this original white form

WRITE PLAINLY, WITH UNFADING INK—THIS IS A PERMANENT RECORD
N. B.—Every item of information should be carefully supplied. AGE should be stated EXACTLY. PHYSICIANS should state CAUSE OF DEATH in plain terms, so that it may be properly classified. Exact statement of OCCUPATION is very important.

STATE OF ILLINOIS
ORIGINAL
Department of Public Health—Division of Vital Statistics
STANDARD CERTIFICATE OF DEATH

1. PLACE OF DEATH
County of Cook
(Show on line below the name of place where death occurred; give either City (or Village) or Township (or Road District), not both.)
Township, or Road District, or Village, or City, of Chicago
Registration Dist. No. 3184
Primary Dist. No. 3104
Registered No. 5044 (Consecutive No.)
Street and Number, No. ..... St.; ..... Ward, Cook County Hospital.
(If death occurred in hospital or institution, give its name instead of street and number)

2. FULL NAME Mary Petrauskis
Residence No. 1840 S Harding Ave 20 Ward.
(Usual place of abode) (If non-resident give city or town and State)
Length of residence in city or town where death occurred 2 yrs. mos. ds. How long in U. S. if of foreign birth 10 yrs.

PERSONAL AND STATISTICAL PATICULARS
3. SEX Female
4. COLOR OR RACE white
5. SINGLE, MARRIED, WIDOWED, OR DIVORCED (Write the word) widow
5a. If married, widowed or divorced HUSBAND OF (or) WIFE of John Petrauskis
6. DATE OF BIRTH September 8, 1848 (Month) (Day) (Year)
7. AGE Years 75 Months 5 Days 11 If LESS than 1 day.....hrs. OR.....min.?
8. OCCUPATION OF DECEASED
(a) Trade, profession, or particular kind of work Factory
(b) General nature of industry, business, or establishment in which employed (or employer) Electrical Supplies
(c) Name of employer Westen Elec Co
9. BIRTHPLACE (city or town) Unknown
(State or Country) Lithuania
PARENTS
10. NAME OF FATHER Pete Turnis
11. BIRTHPLACE OF FATHER (city or town) Unknown
(State or Country) Lithuania
12. MAIDEN NAME OF MOTHER ? Julia
13. BIRTHPLACE OF MOTHER (city or town) Unknown
(State or Country) Lithuania
14. INFORMANT Hospital Records
Address Cook County Hospital
Filed 1922 6 34 PM 24 192.....
Registrar.
(P. O. Address) ..... Ills.

MEDICAL CERTIFICATE OF DEATH
16. DATE OF DEATH Feb 19 1924 (Month) (Day) (Year)
17. I HEREBY CERTIFY, That I attended deceased from Feb 18 1924, to Feb 19 1924
that I last saw her alive on Feb 19 1924,
and that death occurred, on the date stated above, at 910 P.m. The CAUSE OF DEATH* was as follows:
Miliary Tuberculosis
(Duration) .....yrs. .....mos. 10 ds.
Contributory (Secondary)
(Duration) .....yrs. .....mos. .....ds.
18. WHERE WAS DISEASE CONTRACTED
If not at place of death? Home
Did an operation precede death? no Date of
Was there an autopsy? no
What test confirmed diagnosis?
(Signed) ..... M. D.
Address Cook Co Hosp
Date 2 20 1924 Telephone
*N. B.—State the disease causing death. All cases of death from "Violence, casualty, or any undue means" must be referred to the coroner. See Section 10, Coroner's Act. (See reverse side.)
19. PLACE OF BURIAL OR REMOVAL St Casimers
21. DATE OF BURIAL Feb 23 1924
20. UNDERTAKER Alex Masalski
ADDRESS 3307 Auburn av

Has decedent ever served in military or naval service of U. S.? no

V. S. 4

Illustration 8.4: A typical death certificate contains many clues for further avenues of research. Source: Cook County Bureau of Vital Statistics. Courtesy of Walter J. Podrazik.

learn particulars about your ancestors' address, occupation, parentage, and place of birth, which you can compare with other sources you find in your research.

Keep in mind as you search for death certificates that they may not exist. It was not mandatory in Illinois to issue death certificates until 1916, and the Chicago Fire in 1871 destroyed records prior to that time. I have found in my research that death registration from 1871 to 1916 was generally better than birth registration, but still, people slipped through the cracks. If you're not finding a death record in Cook County, consider neighboring counties and states. Try also the out-of-town death index covering Cook County residents who died elsewhere and were shipped back for burial. See Chapter 12 for further information.

The various categories on a death certificate can lead you to a lot of information about your ancestor. To show you how a death certificate can be a jumping-off place for more information, take a look at the example in Illustration 8.4. When I analyzed this document about my husband's grandmother, these are the questions I asked myself (the numbers refer to the categories on the certificate):

2. Residence: Is the house on Harding still standing? Did Mary own or rent? Check property records at the Cook County Recorder of Deeds.

5a. Husband's name: Is John a mistake? Or was it the name Constantine used with English speakers? I will need to search under "John" as well as "Constantine" when looking for his records.

6. Date of birth: How does this date compare with the age given on Mary's marriage certificate and the birth certificates of her children?

9. Birthplace: There is no help here in learning the exact location in Lithuania.

12. Mother's name: The hospital records clerk probably guessed Julia because Mary's daughter was named Julia.

16. Date of death: Check what papers (both English and Lithuanian) were published in 1924. Then search for death notices and obituaries.

19. Place of burial: Go to St. Casimir Lithuanian Cemetery and photograph Mary's headstone. Also look for other relatives.

20. Undertaker: This undertaker was also used for Constantine. Auburn Avenue is not in the current street guide. I learned the name had been changed to Lituanica Avenue

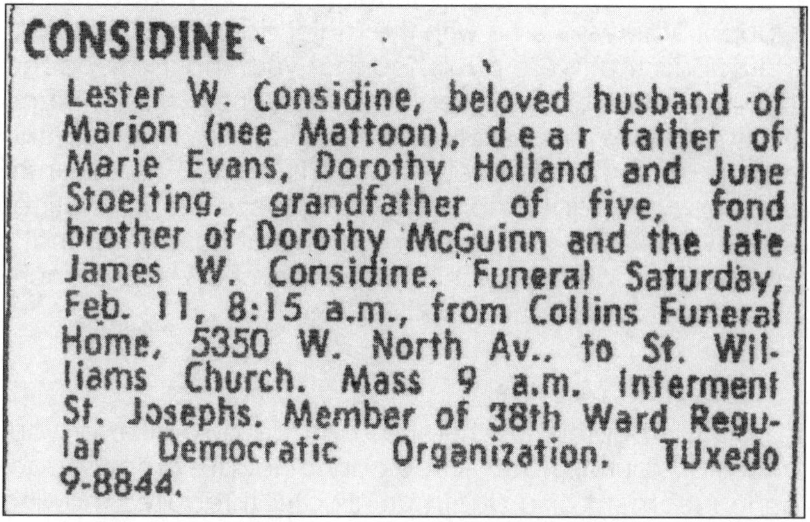

CONSIDINE ·

Lester W. Considine, beloved husband of Marion (nee Mattoon), d e a r father of Marie Evans, Dorothy Holland and June Stoelting, grandfather of five, fond brother of Dorothy McGuinn and the late James W. Considine. Funeral Saturday, Feb. 11, 8:15 a.m., from Collins Funeral Home, 5350 W. North Av., to St. Williams Church. Mass 9 a.m. Interment St. Josephs. Member of 38th Ward Regular Democratic Organization. TUxedo 9-8844.

Illustration 8.5: A typical death notice from a major daily newspaper. The burial took place at St. Joseph's Cemetery. There are two cemeteries by that name in the area, one in River Grove (western Cook County) and one in Hammond, Indiana, east of Chicago. Judging from the far west location of the funeral home, the cemetery in River Grove is meant. The death certificate would give the exact location. Source: *Chicago Daily News*, February 10, 1961, page 31.

by checking the compilation "Chicago Streets" (see Chapter 6, "Where Did My Ancestor Live?"). Labanauskas Funeral Home is now located there; check here for further records.

Death Notices and Obituaries

If you have your ancestor's death date, finding a death notice or an obituary can be a shortcut to learning the place of burial. The difference between a death notice and an obituary is that a death notice generally concentrates on the funeral arrangements, while an obituary usually focuses on the details of a person's life.

Start with the date of death and keep searching for a week. If your ancestor's first language was not English, look at ethnic newspapers first. (See Chapter 16, "Ethnic Resources," for sources, including obituary indexes, by group.) Otherwise, start with the major dailies and check all the papers that were published that year. Tip: Newspapers in the twentieth and twenty-first centuries usually place death notices and obituaries toward the back of the paper, near the classifieds or sports pages. Nineteenth-century newspapers tended to squeeze death notices wherever there was space at the end of a column. That's another reason why Chicago researchers need more newspaper indexing and digitization.

Church Records

Death registers of churches can be a source for your ancestor's burial place, if you cannot locate a newspaper announcement or a death certificate. It requires knowing the religion of your ancestor (not always the one he or she grew up in) and determining which congregation the ancestor belonged to.

Finding the correct church can be simple if your ancestor lived in one place for a long time and perhaps attended the same church he or she was married in. Or you may need to do detective work, based on ethnicity and address at the time of death. Your first step should be Scott Holl's *Guide to Chicago Church and Synagogue Records*, posted on the genealogy section of the Newberry Library's Web site, www.newberry.org, and available at the Newberry's Local and Family History reference desk. It gives locations of archives, denominational Web sites, materials held by the Newberry, and film numbers of records that the Latter-day Saints have microfilmed.

To find religious records in Cook County towns, first determine if the church or synagogue is still in existence. A history of the town can be helpful. Check with the local library or historical society; many histories are also held by the Newberry Library or the Chicago Historical Society. If the place of worship exists, call or write the office administrator to learn the

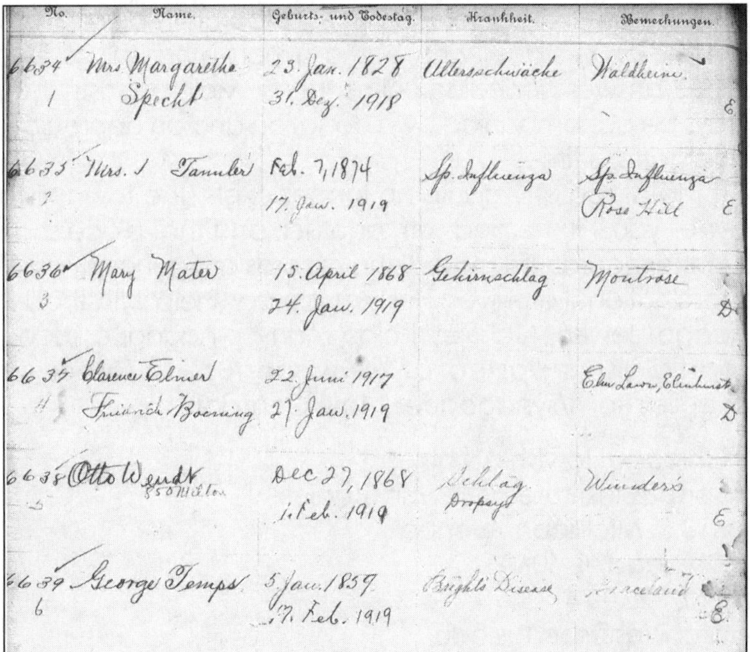

No.	Name.	Geburts- und Todestag.	Krankheit.	Bemerkungen.
6634 1	Mrs. Margaretha Specht	23. Jan. 1828 31. Dez. 1918	Altersschwäche	Waldheim E
6635 2	Mrs. J Tannler	Feb. 7, 1874 17. Jan. 1919	Sp. Influenza	Sp. Influenza Rose Hill E
6636 3	Mary Mater	15. April 1868 24. Jan. 1919	Gehirnschlag	Montrose D
6637 4	Clarence Elmer Friedrich Boening	22. Juni 1917 27. Jan. 1919		Elm Lawn, Elmhurst D
6638 5	Otto Wendt 850 Milton	Dec 27, 1868 1. Feb. 1919	Schlag Dropsy	Wunders E
6639 6	George Temps	5. Jan. 1859 17. Feb. 1919	Bright's Disease	Graceland E
6640 7	Alexander Eilert	9. Jan. 1837 25. Feb. 1919	Nephritis	Graceland E
6641 8	Mrs. Frank Warnecke	12. April 1876 Feb. 28 1919	Herzschlag	Wunders D
6642 9	Mrs. Marie Luehring	10. Nov. 1843 1. März 1919	Schlag	Wunders D+E
6643 10	Edna Gertrude Haberle	April 30, 1886 March 22, 1919	Pneumonia.	Rose Hill

Illustration 8.6: This example of a burial register from a German Lutheran church is written in a mixture of German and English. The column heading translations from left to right are "Name," "Birth and Death Day," "Illness," and "Remarks." The cemetery is given in the last column. Waldheim and Wunders are traditionally German cemeteries. Source: Deaths 1888–1937, First St. Paul's Evangelical Lutheran Church, Chicago, Illinois, Microfilm 1077, Reel 3, Newberry Library. Used with permission of Asa Carter, President, First St. Paul's.

research policy. If possible, do your research in person rather than rely on a staffer who has a million other things to do besides answer genealogical requests. Mail requests should always be accompanied by a donation and an appreciation of the staffer's time.

If the place of worship no longer exists, the town history may tell you if it merged with another, and that place should have the records. If it closed, the records are generally sent to denominational archives; Holl's guide can help with that. The Chicago Jewish Archives holds many synagogue records. A partial list is posted at www.spertus.edu/asher_cja/cja_collections/synagogues.html. Contact:

Chicago Jewish Archives
Spertus Institute of Jewish Studies
618 S. Michigan Avenue
Chicago, IL 60605
312/322-1741
archives@spertus.edu

Cemetery Records

For ease of use, I've divided this discussion into three parts: finding a burial when you know the cemetery, finding a burial when you don't know the cemetery, and finding cemetery records in general.

When You Know the Cemetery

Finding your ancestor's grave is fairly straightforward when you have the name of the cemetery from family papers or a death notice. Go to the cemetery office to get the location and a map. Then go to the designated section and start looking. It is helpful to take along a whisk broom or snow brush to clear dirt and leaves from flush markers. If you go with someone else, genealogists Mary and Walter Sand recommend wearing whistles to signal each other across open fields. Give yourself plenty of time—don't go half an hour before the gates close. If there are caretakers living on the grounds, please don't bother them. They won't be able to answer your questions anyway, as the records are in the cemetery office.

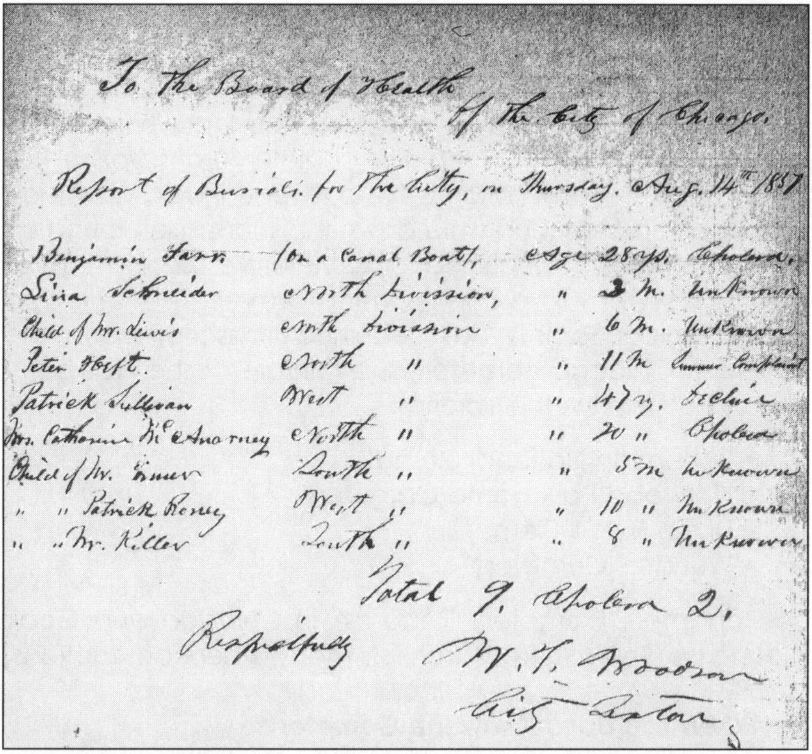

To the Board of Health
of the City of Chicago.

Report of Burials for the City, on Thursday. Aug. 14th 1851

Benjamin Farr	(On a Canal Boat),	Age 28 ys.	Cholera.
Lina Schneider	North Division,	" 3 m.	Unknown
Child of Mr. Lewis	North Division	" 6 m.	Unknown
Peter Hoeft.	North "	" 11 m	Summer Complaint
Patrick Sullivan	West "	" 47 y.	Decline
Mrs. Catharine McAnarney	North "	" 20 "	Cholera
Child of Mr. Timer	South "	" 5 m	Unknown
" " Patrick Roney	West "	" 10 "	Unknown
" " Mr. Keller	South "	" 8 "	Unknown

Total 9. Cholera 2.

Respectfully
W. T. Wooden
City Sexton

Illustration 8.7: Nineteenth-century cemetery records are particularly useful because of spotty death registration. This example from the Chicago City Cemetery gives the names of the deceased, the division of the city they died in, their age, and the cause of death. Source: "City Sexton's Report on Interments," 1851/52 0821A 08/14, *Chicago City Council Proceedings Files, 1833–1871*, Roll 30CF46, IRAD.

You may run into cases of illegible or nonexistent tombstones. You'll just have to do the best you can, by process of elimination and further checking with the office about surrounding graves, to determine that this is your ancestor's resting place. Another surprise you may encounter is a *term grave*. This is a grave that, in effect, was leased by the family. When the family stopped paying on it, the marker was turned over and another body buried on top. Term graves were most often used for children and stillbirths, but adults were also interred in them. If your ancestor is in a term grave, the cemetery can give you the location, but it will have another person's tombstone on it.

Old, filled cemeteries may no longer have a cemetery office. To locate a grave, check with a local historical or genealogical society to see if a cemetery *transcription* has been done. A transcription is like a reverse index. Volunteers walk the cemetery and write down the information found on the tombstones. In published form, there are usually maps or a survey system to aid in locating graves. The Chicago Genealogical Society has published transcriptions of the following Chicago cemeteries, available at the Newberry Library and many other libraries:

- Bohemian National Cemetery
- Norwood Park Home Cemetery
- Union Ridge Cemetery
- Wunders Cemetery

The chapter "Cemetery Records" in *Chicago and Cook County: A Guide to Research* lists many other transcriptions.

When You Don't Know the Cemetery

Be prepared for a long hunt. What you'll have to do is determine which cemeteries were in existence at the time of your ancestor's death. Look in a city directory or phone book for that year. Zero in on the ones that correspond to your ancestor's religion, ethnicity, and residence. For example, a South Side Irish resident could likely be in Holy Sepulchre or Mount Olivet on 111th Street. There is an excellent list of the cemeteries favored by different groups in Helen Sclair's article "Ethnic Cemeteries" in the book *Ethnic Chicago* (see "Beginner's Bookshelf").

If you don't find your ancestor in the most likely group of cemeteries, check the remaining ones. Some of them may have closed, and the bodies moved to another cemetery. Such was the case with the Chicago City Cemetery, located at Clark Street and North Avenue, where the Chicago Historical Society is now. It was in operation from about 1857 to 1865. The city could not get clear title to the land

and decided to vacate it. The land eventually became part of Lincoln Park. Records of burials and lot holders in the City Cemetery appear in the *Chicago City Council Proceedings Files, 1833–1871.* They are held at IRAD, and there is an index on IRAD's Web site (www.sos.state.il.us/departments/archives/chicago_proceedings/proceedings_intro.html) and in print at many libraries. The index is not by name but by type of file. You want to look at "City Sexton's Report on Interments" and "City Sexton's Report on Cemetery Lots Sold" (titles vary slightly). Most of these reports are from the 1850s.

Finding Cemetery Records in General

The first place to try is the cemetery office. Some places, such as Rosehill and Oak Woods, charge a small fee for genealogical queries. Always try to get a photocopy or printout of the information on file, rather than having the clerk write it out for you. That way you avoid a possible misreading by the clerk and you have a copy of the original for your files.

Records vary from index cards to ledgers to schematics of family plots. Be sure to get everything that pertains to your ancestors. Being polite and patient will get you a lot farther than being demanding.

The 42 Catholic cemeteries of the Archdiocese of Chicago can provide the date of burial, the age at the time of death (if available), and the burial location within the cemetery. "Normally no other information is available or provided to the public," states the Archdiocese's Web site. You can print a request form from the Web site and bring it with you or mail it to the cemetery office. Parish cemeteries do not have offices, so the request must go to the administration office. Addresses and the form are at www.cathcemchgo.org (go to "Information," then "Interments").

Another place for cemetery records is the Family History Library, which makes its microfilms available for a fee to Family History Centers affiliated with the Church of Jesus Christ of Latter-day Saints, as well as to certain libraries, such as the Newberry Library. These records of Chicago cemeteries have been microfilmed:

- Graceland Cemetery, 1860–66
- Mount Olivet Cemetery, c. 1931–88
- St. Benedict Cemetery, 1885–1989
- St. Boniface Cemetery, 1864–1987
- St. Casimir Lithuanian Cemetery, c. 1903–88
- St. Gabriel Cemetery, c. 1953–80
- St. Henry Cemetery, 1864–1987

The Newberry Library holds microfilm of the following records:

- Forest Home Cemetery, 1877–1980 (Forest Park)
- Waldheim Cemetery, 1873–1967 (Forest Park)
- Wunders Cemetery, 1867–1944 (Chicago)

Considering Loretto Szucs lists more than 200 cemeteries in the metropolitan Chicago area, that's a very small percentage of records that have been preserved. It's similar to the newspaper indexing situation—the overwhelming nature of the task scares off anyone thinking of attempting it.

Lastly, check for societies that offer cemetery lookups. The Chicago Genealogical Society will search for Bohemian National Cemetery burials from 1888 to 1892 (there is a small fee for nonmembers). The society's index is online at www.chgogs.org/bncintro.html. The South Suburban Genealogical and Historical Society has a master index to 93 cemeteries in southern Cook County and northern Will County. There is no fee to see if a name appears in the index, but a fee applies for photocopies and processing of hits. Details are at the society's Web site, www.rootsweb.com/~ssghs/cemetery.htm.

Where Did My Ancestor Die and Where Is My Ancestor Buried?

Points to Remember

❏ *Searching for death notices/ obituaries:*

1. Get date of death (or date of publication from an obituary or newspaper index). Don't search without it!

2. Look for both death notices and obituaries, often there are more details in one kind than another.

3. Start with the date of death and keep searching for a week.

4. Search *all* the newspapers published that year: major dailies, ethnic papers, neighborhood weeklies.

5. Look near the classifieds in twentieth-century newspapers. Look at all pages in nineteenth-century newspapers.

❏ *Finding burial place — when you know the cemetery:*

• Get location and map from cemetery office (if no office, hunt for cemetery transcription).

• Give yourself plenty of time.

• Take tools for clearing off grave markers.

• Don't bother the caretakers.

Where Did My Ancestor Die and Where Is My Ancestor Buried?

❏ *Finding burial place —*
when you don't know the cemetery:

• Look in city directory or phone book to see which cemeteries existed that year.

• Make a list of most likely ones based on ancestor's religion, ethnicity, and residence; search those first.

• If ancestor is not there, pursue all other cemeteries in operation that year. You may have to trace where bodies were moved from closed cemeteries, such as the Chicago City Cemetery.

❏ *Finding cemetery records*
in general:

• Try the cemetery office first.

• See if records have been microfilmed.

• Check for societies offering cemetery lookups.

9 When Did My Ancestor Come to America?

The reality of being a citizen of the United States is that if you go back far enough, you're going to find your family came here from another country. The question is, when? And what port or border crossing did they come through? What ship or transportation did they use? What drove them to leave their homeland?

That last question is best answered through the homework you do in the beginning—talking to relatives and looking for letters and journals. The other questions are answered by examining secondary source material, primarily government documents.

Because this is a book for beginners, I'm not going to talk about colonial records and tracing your ancestor back to the Mayflower. Chicago and Cook County did not exist until the 1830s. I'm not going to talk about finding slave ancestors and what country in Africa they came from. That is not a task for beginners; it is highly challenging and most of the records are outside Illinois. Lastly, I'm not going to cover Native Americans, because they came thousands of years ago and were here when the Europeans "discovered" them.

What I will talk about are strategies to find the date, the place, and the method by which your ancestor came to the United States.

❏ Strategy No. 1: U.S. Census

The 1900, 1910, 1920, and 1930 censuses asked questions about immigration and *naturalization* (becoming a U.S. citizen if foreign born). Your ancestor's answers can be valuable clues, but don't take them as gospel. People didn't have to show proof of what they said. The census taker would come to the door, say in 1920, and ask, "When did you come to this country, Mrs. Olson?" and she'd say something like, "Ya, I come ven I was little girl, 40 years ago," and the census taker would subtract 40 years from 1920 and write down "1880." So you see how loose that date can be. Add in communication problems with immigrants, fears immigrants had in answering government questions, and responses by uninformed members of the household, and you know to be skeptical about the responses. Don't go flying off to passenger lists for the year given. Use it as an initial starting point only and test it against other evidence you uncover.

These are the specifics of what was asked on the different census schedules:

• 1930: year of immigration, whether naturalized, ability to speak English

• 1920: year of immigration, whether naturalized, year of naturalization, ability to speak English

• 1910: year of immigration, whether naturalized, whether able to speak English, or if not, language spoken

• 1900: year of immigration, number of years in the United States, naturalization status, ability to speak English

The 1940 census asked about citizenship status, and the 1950 census asked people whether they were naturalized. These censuses will not be released until 2012 and 2022, respectively, for privacy reasons. You can obtain the information if you prove you are an heir of the person and that the person is deceased. There is a fee. Request Form B6–600 from:

Personal Census Search Unit
U.S. Census Bureau
P.O. Box 1545
Jeffersonville, IN 47131
812/218-3046
fax: 812/288-3371

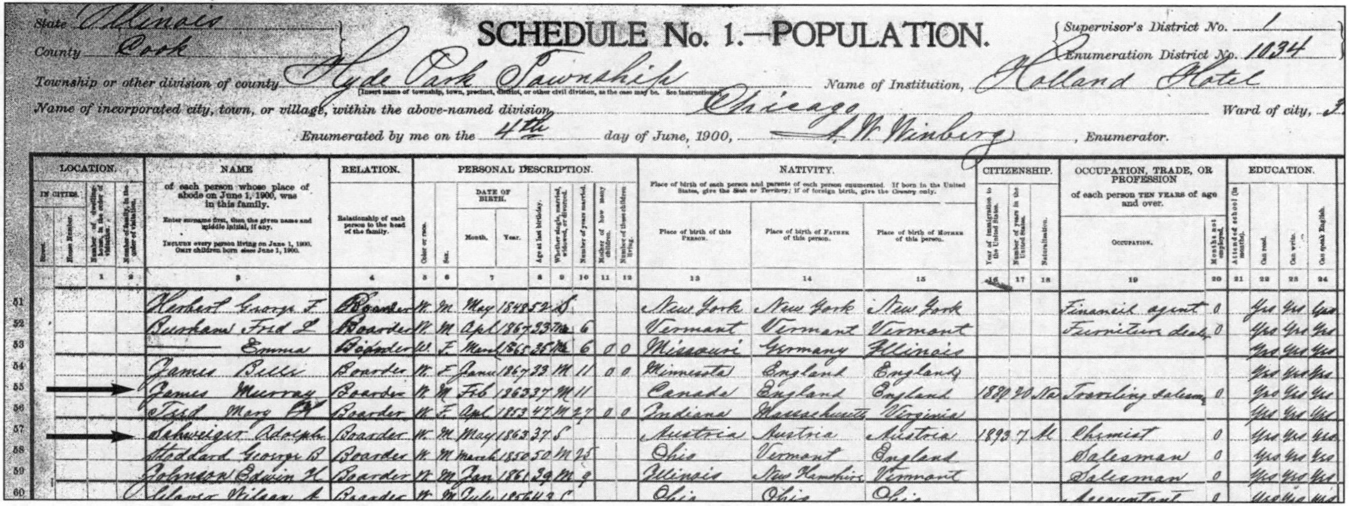

SCHEDULE No. 1.—POPULATION.

State: Illinois
County: Cook
Township or other division of county: Hyde Park Township
Name of Institution: Holland Hotel
Name of incorporated city, town, or village, within the above-named division: Chicago
Supervisor's District No. 1
Enumeration District No. 1034
Enumerated by me on the 4th day of June, 1900, A. W. Winberg, Enumerator.

Line	Name	Relation	Color	Sex	Month	Year	Age	Marital	Yrs married	Mother of	Living	Birthplace	Father	Mother	Yr. immig.	Yrs in U.S.	Naturalization	Occupation	Months not employed	Read	Write	Speak English
51	Herbert George F.	Boarder	W	M	May	1848	52	S				New York	New York	New York				Financil agent	0	Yes	Yes	Yes
52	Burham Fred L	Boarder	W	M	Apl	1867	33	Wd	6			Vermont	Vermont	Vermont				Furniture deal	0	Yes	Yes	Yes
53	Emma	Boarder	W	F	March	1865	35	Wd	6	0	0	Missouri	Germany	Illinois						Yes	Yes	Yes
54	James Belle	Boarder	W	F	June	1867	33	M	11	0	0	Minnesota	England	England						Yes	Yes	Yes
55	James Murray	Boarder	W	M	Feb	1863	37	M	11			Canada	England	England	1880	20	Na	Traveling salesm	0	Yes	Yes	Yes
56	Tisd Mary	Boarder	W	F	Apl	1853	47	M	27	0	0	Indiana	Massachusetts	Virginia						Yes	Yes	Yes
57	Schweiger Adolph	Boarder	W	M	May	1863	37	S				Austria	Austria	Austria	1893	7	Al	Chemist	0	Yes	Yes	Yes
58	Stoddard George B	Boarder	W	M	March	1850	50	M	25			Ohio	Vermont	England				Salesman	0	Yes	Yes	Yes
59	Johnson Edwin H	Boarder	W	M	Jan	1861	39	M	9			Illinois	New Hampshire	Vermont				Salesman	0	Yes	Yes	Yes
60		Boarder	W	M	July							Ohio	Ohio	Ohio				Accountant	0			

Illustration 9.1: According to the answers he gave in the 1900 census, Murray James was born in Canada and immigrated in 1880. Therefore he had lived in the United States for 20 years. The abbreviation "Na" or "NA" means "naturalized."

Adolph Schweiger came from Austria in 1893, he says. That makes seven years in the United States. The abbreviation "Al" or "AL" means "alien," someone who is not a U.S. citizen.

You may also see the abbreviation "Pa" or "PA." It does not mean "Pennsylvania"; it means the first citizenship papers have been filed. A waiting period, which has varied in U.S. history, takes place between filing a foreigner's Declaration of Intention to become a citizen and being able to take the oath of citizenship. If you see "Nr" or "NR," it means "not reported"—the census taker was not able to get an answer. Source: 1900 U.S. Census, Reel 287, ED 1034, Sheet 3B, Lines 55 and 57.

The five most recent censuses (1960, 1970, 1980, 1990, and 2000) did not ask questions about immigration or citizenship. Censuses prior to 1900 did not ask about those topics either, except for the 1820 and 1830 ones, which tallied foreigners who were not naturalized. The Illinois state census, taken 1820, 1825, 1830, 1835, 1840, 1845, 1855, and 1865, did not ask any questions pertaining to immigration and naturalization.

You'll want to find your ancestor in as many of the 1900–30 censuses as pertain. Chapter 10 ("Nuts and Bolts of the U.S. Census") tells you how to do that by name or address.

❑ Strategy No. 2: Death Certificates

At various points in Cook County history, the standard death certificate form asked questions about the deceased's length of residence in the city, state, and United States. Knowing the approximate date of arrival can be a starting point for your research in passenger records and naturalizations.

As with census answers, be leery of what you find on a death certificate. A grieving relative of the deceased—someone who was focused more on emotions and funeral arrangements than filling forms out accurately—often provides the information. Or the informant could be someone who didn't know the deceased at all, such as a hospital records clerk. Always cross-check the length of residence given in other sources, such as city directories or property records, before spending months following a false trail.

❑ Strategy No. 3: Late Nineteenth-Century Voter Registrations

If your ancestor was in Cook County in the 1880s or early 1890s, you may be in luck. There is a microfilmed set of voter registration records that gives the length of residence in the precinct, county, and state and the date, place, and court of naturalization. This set is called *Record and Index of Persons*

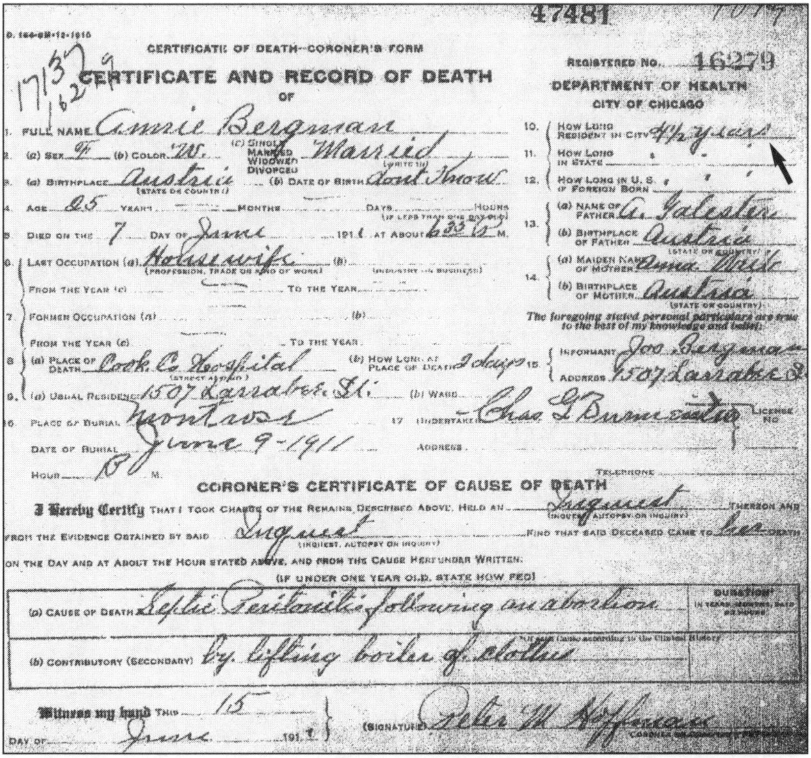

47481

CERTIFICATE OF DEATH—CORONER'S FORM

CERTIFICATE AND RECORD OF DEATH OF

REGISTERED NO. 16279

DEPARTMENT OF HEALTH CITY OF CHICAGO

1. FULL NAME Annie Bergman
2. (a) SEX F (b) COLOR W. (c) SINGLE, MARRIED, WIDOWED, DIVORCED Married (WRITE IN)
3. (a) BIRTHPLACE Austria (STATE OR COUNTRY) (b) DATE OF BIRTH dont know
4. AGE 25 YEARS — MONTHS DAYS HOURS (IF LESS THAN ONE DAY OLD)
5. DIED ON THE 7 DAY OF June 1911 AT ABOUT 6:35 P. M.
6. LAST OCCUPATION (a) Housewife (PROFESSION, TRADE OR KIND OF WORK) (b) (INDUSTRY OR BUSINESS) FROM THE YEAR (c) TO THE YEAR
7. FORMER OCCUPATION (a) (b) FROM THE YEAR (c) TO THE YEAR
8. (a) PLACE OF DEATH Cook Co Hospital (STREET ADDRESS) (b) HOW LONG AT PLACE OF DEATH 2 days
9. (a) USUAL RESIDENCE 1507 Larrabee St. (b) WARD
10. HOW LONG RESIDENT IN CITY 4½ years
11. HOW LONG IN STATE " "
12. HOW LONG IN U. S. IF FOREIGN BORN " "
13. (a) NAME OF FATHER A. Galester (b) BIRTHPLACE OF FATHER Austria (STATE OR COUNTRY)
14. (a) MAIDEN NAME OF MOTHER Anna Weisz (b) BIRTHPLACE OF MOTHER Austria (STATE OR COUNTRY)

The foregoing stated personal particulars are true to the best of my knowledge and belief:

15. INFORMANT Jos Bergman ADDRESS 1507 Larrabee St.
16. PLACE OF BURIAL Montrose DATE OF BURIAL June 9-1911 HOUR 10 M.
17. UNDERTAKER Chas G Burmeister LICENSE NO ADDRESS TELEPHONE

CORONER'S CERTIFICATE OF CAUSE OF DEATH

I Hereby Certify THAT I TOOK CHARGE OF THE REMAINS DESCRIBED ABOVE, HELD AN Inquest (INQUEST, AUTOPSY OR INQUIRY) THEREON AND FROM THE EVIDENCE OBTAINED BY SAID Inquest (INQUEST, AUTOPSY OR INQUIRY) FIND THAT SAID DECEASED CAME TO her DEATH ON THE DAY AND AT ABOUT THE HOUR STATED ABOVE, AND FROM THE CAUSE HEREUNDER WRITTEN: (IF UNDER ONE YEAR OLD, STATE HOW FED)

(a) CAUSE OF DEATH Septic Peritonitis following an abortion

(b) CONTRIBUTORY (SECONDARY) by lifting boiler of clothes

Witness my hand THIS 15 DAY OF June 1911 (SIGNATURE) Peter M Hoffman CORONER

Illustration 9.2: The informant for Annie Bergman's death certificate in June 1911 was her husband, Joseph (his relationship to her is not stated on the document, I knew it from other records). Later death certificates note the relationship of the informant to the deceased. Joseph said that she had been in the United States, Illinois, and Chicago four and a half years. Doing the math, that would mean arrival from Austria about January 1907. I searched under her maiden name, Galester, on the Ellis Island Web site and found a likely match, Anna Galestur, arriving in 1902 at age 14. So you can see how the length of residence is only a guide. If you look at line 3, Joseph didn't know—or probably couldn't recall in the stress of the moment—his wife's date of birth. Proceed carefully with death information, and gather as much as you can from all possible avenues (see Chapter 8, "When Did My Ancestor Die and Where Is My Ancestor Buried?"). Source: Cook County Bureau of Vital Statistics.

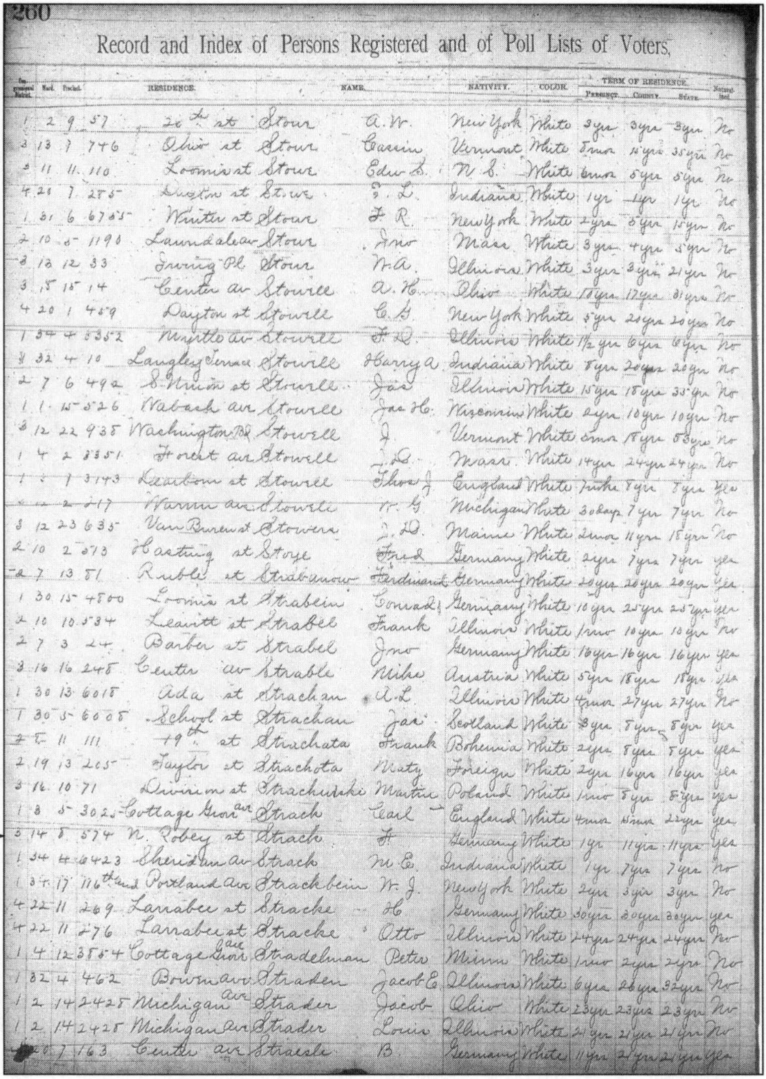

260

Record and Index of Persons Registered and of Poll Lists of Voters,

Congressional District	Ward	Precinct		Residence	Name		Nativity	Color	Term of Residence: Precinct	County	State	Naturalized
1	2	9	57	20th st	Stour	A.W.	New York	White	3 yrs	3 yrs	3 yrs	No
3	13	7	746	Ohio st	Stour	Cassin	Vermont	White	5 mos	15 yrs	35 yrs	No
3	11	11	110	Loomis st	Stour	Edw S.	N.S.	White	6 mos	5 yrs	5 yrs	No
4	21	7	255	Dayton st	Stour	J. L.	Indiana	White	1 yr	1 yr	1 yr	No
1	31	6	6755	Winter st	Stour	F.R.	New York	White	2 yrs	5 yrs	15 yrs	No
2	10	5	1190	Lawndale av	Stour	Jno	Mass	White	3 yrs	4 yrs	5 yrs	No
3	13	12	33	Irving Pl	Stour	W.A.	Illinois	White	3 yrs	3 yrs	21 yrs	No
3	15	15	14	Center av	Stowell	A.H.	Ohio	White	15 yrs	17 yrs	31 yrs	No
4	20	1	459	Dayton st	Stowell	C.S.	New York	White	5 yrs	20 yrs	20 yrs	No
1	34	4	5352	Myrtle av	Stowell	F.D.	Illinois	White	1½ yrs	6 yrs	6 yrs	No
3	32	4	10	Langley Terrace	Stowell	Harry A.	Indiana	White	8 yrs	20 yrs	20 yrs	No
2	7	6	492	S. Union st	Stowell	Jas	Illinois	White	15 yrs	18 yrs	33 yrs	No
1	1	15	526	Wabash av	Stowell	Jas H.	Wisconsin	White	2 yrs	10 yrs	10 yrs	No
3	12	22	935	Washington Bl	Stowell	J.	Vermont	White	2 mos	18 yrs	53 yrs	No
1	4	2	3351	Forest av	Stowell	D.	Mass.	White	14 yrs	24 yrs	24 yrs	No
1	5	7	3143	Dearborn st	Stowell	Thos J.	England	White	7 mos	8 yrs	8 yrs	Yes
		2	217	Warren av	Stowell	W.G.	Michigan	White	30 days	7 yrs	7 yrs	No
3	12	23	635	Van Buren st	Stowers	J.D.	Maine	White	2 mos	11 yrs	15 yrs	No
2	10	2	273	Hastings st	Stoye	Fred	Germany	White	2 yrs	7 yrs	7 yrs	yes
2	7	13	51	Ruble st	Strabanow	Ferdinand	Germany	White	20 yrs	20 yrs	20 yrs	Yes
1	30	15	4800	Loomis st	Strabein	Conrad	Germany	White	10 yrs	25 yrs	25 yrs	yes
2	10	10	534	Leavitt st	Strabel	Frank	Illinois	White	1 mo	10 yrs	10 yrs	No
2	7	3	24	Barber st	Strabel	Jno	Germany	White	16 yrs	16 yrs	16 yrs	Yes
3	16	16	245	Center av	Strable	Mike	Austria	White	5 yrs	18 yrs	18 yrs	Yes
1	30	13	6015	Ada st	Strachan	A.L.	Illinois	White	4 mos	27 yrs	27 yrs	No
1	30	5	6005	School st	Strachan	Jas	Scotland	White	8 yrs	8 yrs	8 yrs	yes
2	5	11	111	19th st	Strachata	Frank	Bohemia	White	2 yrs	8 yrs	8 yrs	yes
2	19	13	205	Taylor st	Strachota	Maty	Foreign	White	2 yrs	16 yrs	16 yrs	yes
3	16	10	71	Division st	Strachutski	Martin	Poland	White	1 mo	8 yrs	8 yrs	yes
1	3	5	3025	Cottage Grove av	Strach	Carl	England	White	4 mos	4 mos	22 yrs	yes
3	14	8	574	N. Robey st	Strack	F.	Germany	White	1 yr	11 yrs	11 yrs	Yes
1	34	4	6423	Sheridan av	Strack	M.E.	Indiana	White	1 yr	7 yrs	7 yrs	No
1	34	17	116th and	Portland av	Strackbein	W.J.	New York	White	2 yrs	3 yrs	3 yrs	No
4	22	11	269	Larrabee st	Stracke	H.	Germany	White	30 yrs	30 yrs	30 yrs	yes
4	22	11	276	Larrabee st	Stracke	Otto	Illinois	White	24 yrs	24 yrs	24 yrs	No
1	4	12	3554	Cottage Grove ave	Stradelman	Peter	Minn	White	1 mo	2 yrs	2 yrs	No
1	32	4	462	Bowman av	Straden	Jacob E.	Illinois	White	6 yrs	26 yrs	32 yrs	No
1	2	14	2425	Michigan av	Strader	Jacob	Ohio	White	23 yrs	23 yrs	23 yrs	No
1	2	14	2425	Michigan av	Strader	Louis	Illinois	White	21 yrs	21 yrs	21 yrs	No
		7	163	Center av	Straesle	B.	Germany	White	11 yrs	21 yrs	21 yrs	Yes

Illustration 9.3: This excerpt from Chicago voter registration records indicates that F. Strack was born in Germany and registered to vote October 16, 1888. He has resided in Illinois for 11 years, in Cook County for 11 years, and in Precinct 8 of Ward 14 for one year. He was naturalized in 1876 in the Circuit Court of Allegheny County, Pennsylvania.

From these statistics you learn he lived in Pennsylvania, possibly in Pittsburgh, before coming to Illinois in 1877. He likely came directly to Chicago, because the length of time in Cook County is the same as for the state. He moved to his current address within the last year, because that is the length of time he has lived in this precinct.

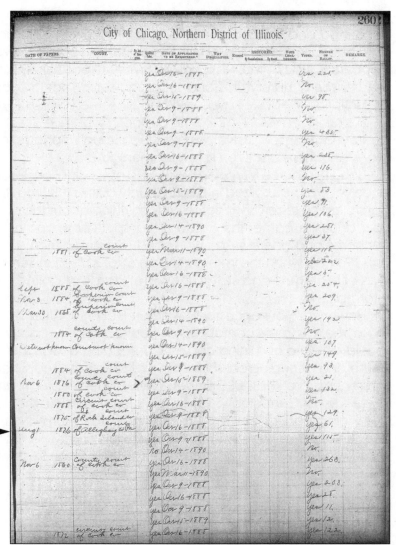

To learn more about when he came to the United States, you would research how many years of residency was required in the 1870s before applying for citizenship and then refocus your efforts around that date. Source: *Record and Index of Persons Registered and Poll Lists of Voters*, City of Chicago Board of Election Commissioners 1888–1890, Volume 7 SC–WE, Roll 30–1787, Newberry Library.

Registered and Poll Lists of Voters. It covers 1888 to 1890 and 1892 and can be accessed at the Illinois Regional Archives Depository (IRAD), the National Archives—Great Lakes, and the Newberry Library. It is also searchable on Ancestry.com (subscription Web site, available free at some libraries). The time period covered makes it a good substitute for the destroyed 1890 census. Names are listed in rough alphabetical order, and there are even a few women.

Using this source is a good news–bad news situation. If your ancestor was naturalized in Cook County during this time, the naturalization records will not tell you anything about the date your ancestor came, the mode of transportation, and his or her homeland address. You won't find that kind of rich detail until 1904–06, when the Immigration and Naturalization Service was established and set up new standards of collecting information.

However, if your ancestor was naturalized in another state, those records may contain what you're seeking, and you should look into obtaining copies. Contact the county court-house or a genealogical society in that area, and see where the records are kept. USGenWeb (www.usgenweb.org) and Cyndi's List of Genealogy Sites on the Internet (www.cyndislist. com) are good places to start looking for this information. If your ancestor completed the naturalization process in Cook County, a copy of the out-of-state record should be filed with the Cook County documents.

❑ Strategy No. 4: Church Records

Some denominations keep records showing where their members come from and where they go to. These records can give valuable clues about the time of arrival in the United States and the place of residence in the previous country. Look for "Communicants" or "Lists of Families" in the records of Episcopalian and Lutheran churches. Catholic churches don't keep these records in the same way; for instance, there are lists of communicants, but nothing beyond names and dates when First Communion was received.

Finding religious records is a search in itself. It has been greatly helped by the dedicated work of Scott Holl, former staffer at the Newberry Library. His *Guide to Chicago Church and Synagogue Records* covers most religious bodies and lists locations of archives, denominational Web sites, materials held by the Newberry Library, and film numbers of records that the Latter-day Saints have microfilmed. It is available at the Local and Family History reference desk at the Newberry Library and is posted on the genealogy section of the Newberry Web site, www.newberry.org.

To find religious records in Cook County towns, first determine if the church or synagogue is still in existence. A history of the town can be helpful. Check with the local library or historical society. Many histories are held by the Newberry Library and the Chicago Historical Society. If the place of worship exists, call or write the office administrator to learn their research policy. If possible, do your research in person rather than rely on a staffer who has a million other things to do besides answer genealogical requests. Mail requests should always be accompanied by a donation and an appreciation of the staffer's time.

If the place of worship no longer exists, the town history may tell you if it merged with another, and that place should have the records. If it closed, the records are generally sent to denominational archives; Holl's guide can help with that.

❏ Strategy No. 5: Naturalization Records

These records are the best place to look for your ancestor's arrival date if your ancestor was naturalized in 1904 to 1906 or after. Starting in that time period, the Declaration of Intention (to become a citizen) gives you the name of the ship, the arrival date in the United States, the place of arrival, and the place of departure. The declaration is often accompanied by the Certificate of Arrival from official government records. When you have this, you can go

COMMUNICANTS.

No.	NAME	DATE ENTERED	HOW AND WHENCE RECEIVED
80	Willis D. Chapman Jr.	Aug 12 1907	St. Luke's Evanston
81	Gertrude Maynard Chapman (Mrs)	" "	" "
82	Daniel Bowen Wheaton	July 1 1897	Christ Woodlawn
83	Earl Bent	Jan 6, 1808	St. Peter's Chicago
84	H. Dyer Bent	Jan 1, 1908	St. Peter's Chicago
85	Alys McCloud (Mrs)	Apr 12 1908	Confirmation
86	Ione Woodward Easter (Mrs)	" " "	"
87	Anna (Hansen) Holmes	" " "	"
88	Elsa Stichweh	" " "	"
89	Marjorie Fitzpatrick	" " "	"
90	Donald Anderson	" " "	"
91	Leroy Nilles	" "	"
92	Emil W. Coel	" " "	"
93	Louis Anderson	" " "	"
94	Earnest Jason Ford	" 15th "	"
95	Fred F. Gradler	" 12th "	"
96	Emma Dorothy Gradler (Mrs)	" " "	Recd from R.C. Church
97	Dora Miller (Miss)	May 9 1908	England
98	Martha Edwards (Miss)	May 17 1908	"
99	Ansell Victor Coffman (Dr)	May 17 1908	St. Mark's Evanston
100	Theodora Robin Bowers (Mrs)	July 1 1908	Our Saviour Chicago
101	Susan Marie Moore (Mrs)	July 1 1908	St. Simon's Sheridan Park
102	William Hand	July 9 1908	St. Mark's Evanston
103	Annie Hand (Mrs)	July 9 1908	St. Mark's Evanston
104	Annie C. Burch (Mrs)	Jan 1 1907	St George's London, Ont.
105	Edith Louise Ford (Mrs)	Apr 1 1908	Epiphany, Chicago
106	Sarah W. Anderson (Mrs)	June 10 1909	Confirmation
107	Jessie L. Anderson (Miss)	" " "	"
108	Kathrine S. Anderson (Miss)	" " "	"
	Rampsey	Oct 14 1908	St Simon's Chicago
110	Elise (Mrs)	" " "	" "
112	Harley Seymour Hibbard	Sep 22, 1908	Holy Trinity Winnipeg
113	Frances Emily Hibbard (Mrs)	Sep 22 1908	" "
114	Edward Warren Kidder	Sept 24 1908	St. Mark's Evanston
115	Irene Stevens Kidder (Mrs)	Sept 24 1908	" "
	Annie Shepard (Mrs)	Sept 29 1908	Atonement Edgewater
	May Atwood Cairol (Mrs)	Oct 6 1883	Original member
	Elizabeth Neumann (Mrs)	Sept 24 1908	St Paul Canton, O.
		Dec 7 1908	St Barnabas Chicago

Illustration 9.4: Annie Burch, no. 104, joined this congregation from St. George's [Church] in London, Ontario. Harley and Frances Hibbard, nos. 112 and 113, joined from Holy Trinity [Church], Winnipeg. Knowing the previous church and its location points you to those church records as well as city directories and Canadian censuses to gain more insight into when these folks immigrated. Source: St. Matthew's Episcopal Church, Evanston, Illinois, Microfilm 823, Item 4, Newberry Library. Used with permission of Rev. Jane Henderson, Rector, St. Matthew's.

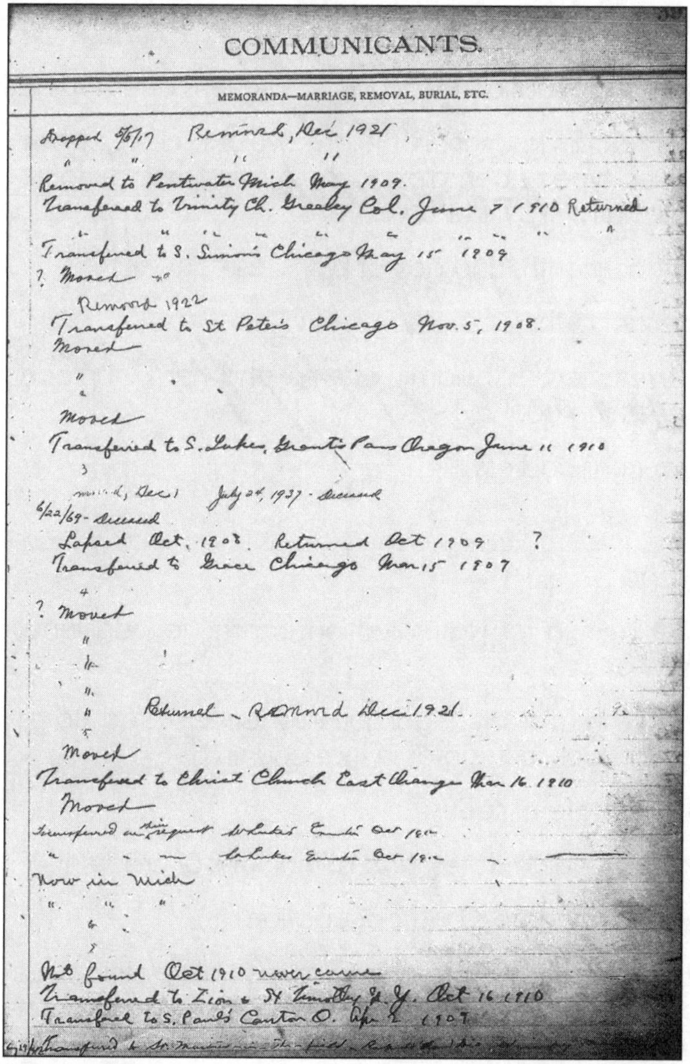
COMMUNICANTS.

MEMORANDA—MARRIAGE, REMOVAL, BURIAL, ETC.

Dropped 5/5/17 Removed, Dec 1921

Removed to Pentwater Mich May 1909.
Transferred to Trinity Ch. Greeley Col. June 7 1910 Returned

Transferred to S. Simon's Chicago May 15 1909
? Moved
Removed 1922
Transferred to St Peter's Chicago Nov. 5, 1908.
Moved

Moved
Transferred to S. Lukes, Grants Pass Oregon June 11 1910

moved, Dec 1 July 24, 1937 - deceased
6/22/69 - deceased
Lapsed Oct. 1908. Returned Oct 1909 ?
Transferred to Grace Chicago Mar 15 1907

? Moved

Returned - Removed Dec 1921.

Moved
Transferred to Christ Church East Orange Mar 16 1910
Moved
Transferred on their request St Lukes Evanston Oct 1910
St Lukes Evanston Oct 1910
Now in Mich

Not found Oct 1910 never came
Transferred to Zion & St Timothy N.Y. Oct 16 1910
Transferred to S. Paul's Canton O. Apr 2 1907

Illustration 9.4

directly to the films of passenger lists and get the records—saving you a tremendous amount of work.

Bonus information found in declarations after 1904–06:

• physical description (height, weight, color of hair and eyes, type of complexion, any distinguishing marks; later declarations have a photo)

• year, month, and day of birth

• exact birthplace

• if married, first name of wife and her birthplace (often just the country)

• current address

• occupation

• age

The Petition for Naturalization can have additional information:

• date immigrant began journey to the United States (helps you look for records in that country)

• birth date of spouse

• names, birth dates, and birthplaces of children

• current address and occupation

• information on any denials of petition of citizenship (the date and court name lead you to court records)

• names and addresses of character witnesses and length of time they have known the immigrant (helps you place your ancestor in a particular locale)

Things You Should Know
About the Naturalization Process

From 1802 to 1906, these were the requirements to become naturalized:

1. The petitioner had to live in the United States for five years and in the state or territory where he or she filed the naturalization petition for one year. (After September 22, 1922, the requirement was to be in the United States for one year total.)

2. During that time, the petitioner had to be of good moral character.

3. The petitioner filed a Declaration of Intention to become a citizen (often referred to as *first papers*).

4. The petitioner had to wait three years (later revised to two years) and not get in trouble with the law.

5. The petitioner was to file a Petition for Admission to Citizenship (often referred to as *final papers*).

6. The petitioner had it approved in court.

7. The petitioner renounced allegiance to the ruler of his or her former country and to any title of nobility and took an oath to uphold the U.S. Constitution.

Generally you will not find naturalization records for your female ancestors prior to 1922. An 1855 law said that women who married U.S. citizens received citizenship through their spouses. Some wives applied on their own, as did some single women and widows, but few before the twentieth century, because of their inability to vote once becoming a citizen and because of the cost of court fees.

The usual proof of citizenship for women up to 1922 was the marriage certificate and the husband's U.S. birth record or naturalization record. Prior to 1906, it's hit or miss whether the wife is listed on the husband's naturalization records. The INS issued a Certificate of Derivative Citizenship for women

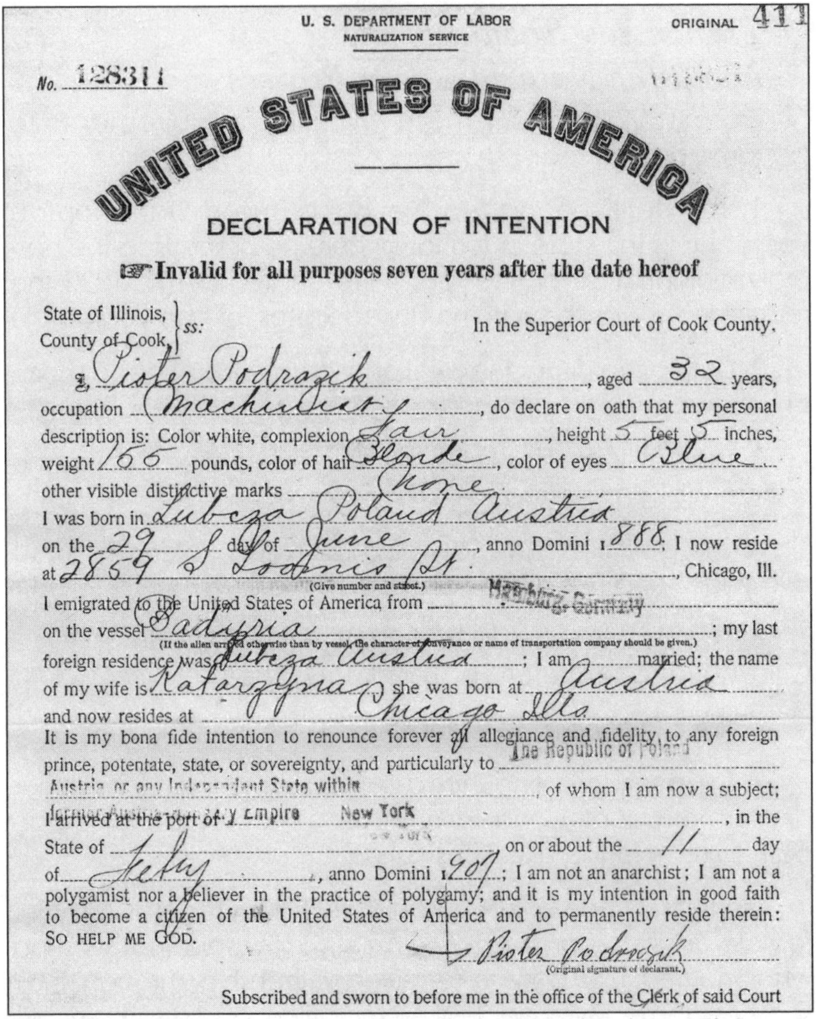

U. S. DEPARTMENT OF LABOR
NATURALIZATION SERVICE

ORIGINAL 411

No. 128311

UNITED STATES OF AMERICA

DECLARATION OF INTENTION

Invalid for all purposes seven years after the date hereof

State of Illinois, County of Cook, } ss: In the Superior Court of Cook County.

I, Pioter Podrazik, aged 32 years, occupation Machinist, do declare on oath that my personal description is: Color white, complexion fair, height 5 feet 5 inches, weight 165 pounds, color of hair Blonde, color of eyes Blue other visible distinctive marks None

I was born in Lubcza Poland Austria on the 29 day of June anno Domini 1888; I now reside at 2859 S Loomis St. (Give number and street.), Chicago, Ill.

I emigrated to the United States of America from Hamburg, Germany on the vessel Batavia (If the alien arrived otherwise than by vessel, the character of conveyance or name of transportation company should be given.); my last foreign residence was Lubcza Austria; I am married; the name of my wife is Katarzyna she was born at Austria and now resides at Chicago Ills

It is my bona fide intention to renounce forever all allegiance and fidelity to any foreign prince, potentate, state, or sovereignty, and particularly to The Republic of Poland Austria or any Independent State within former Austro-Hungary Empire, of whom I am now a subject; I arrived at the port of New York, in the State of New York, on or about the 11 day of Feby, anno Domini 1907; I am not an anarchist; I am not a polygamist nor a believer in the practice of polygamy; and it is my intention in good faith to become a citizen of the United States of America and to permanently reside therein: So help me God.

Pioter Podrazik
(Original signature of declarant.)

Subscribed and sworn to before me in the office of the Clerk of said Court

Illustration 9.5: The road to U.S. citizenship for Polish immigrant Pioter (Peter) Podrazik began with filing a Declaration of Intention on February 14, 1921. This is the so-called first papers. Courtesy of Walter J. Podrazik.

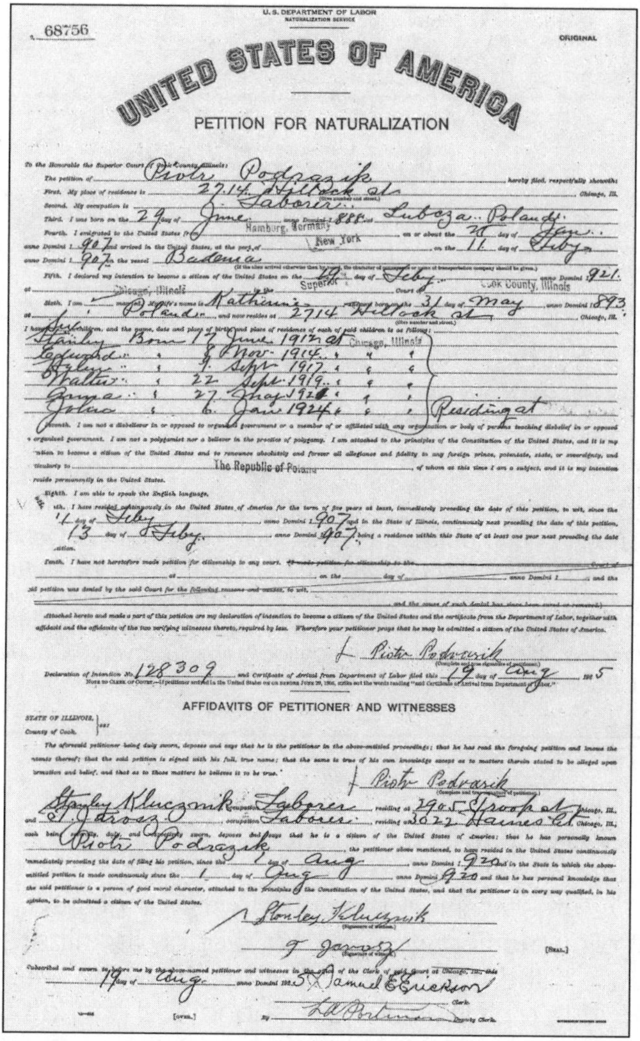

U.S. DEPARTMENT OF LABOR
NATURALIZATION SERVICE

No. 68756 ORIGINAL

UNITED STATES OF AMERICA

PETITION FOR NATURALIZATION

To the Honorable the Superior Court of Cook County, Illinois:

The petition of Piotr Podrazik hereby filed, respectfully showeth:

First. My place of residence is 2714 Hillock st. Chicago, Ill.

Second. My occupation is Laborer.

Third. I was born on the 29 day of June anno Domini 1888 at Lubcza, Poland.

Fourth. I emigrated to the United States from Hamburg, Germany on or about the 28 day of Jan anno Domini 1907 and arrived in the United States, at the port of New York on the 11 day of Feby anno Domini 1907 on the vessel Badenia.

Fifth. I declared my intention to become a citizen of the United States on the 19 day of Feby anno Domini 1921 at Chicago, Illinois in the Superior Court of Cook County, Illinois.

Sixth. I am married. My wife's name is Katherine; she was born on the 31 day of May, anno Domini 1893 at Poland, and now resides at 2714 Hillock st. Chicago, Ill.

I have six children, and the name, date and place of birth, and place of residence of each of said children is as follows:

Stanley Born 17 June 1912 at Chicago, Illinois
Edward " 8 Nov 1914 " " "
Helen " 9 Sept 1917 " " "
Walter " 22 Sept 1919 " " "
Anna " 27 May 1921 " " "
Jolia " 6 Jan 1924 " " " Residing at

Seventh. I am not a disbeliever in or opposed to organized government or a member of or affiliated with any organization or body of persons teaching disbelief in or opposed to organized government. I am not a polygamist nor a believer in the practice of polygamy. I am attached to the principles of the Constitution of the United States, and it is my intention to become a citizen of the United States and to renounce absolutely and forever all allegiance and fidelity to any foreign prince, potentate, state, or sovereignty, and particularly to The Republic of Poland of whom at this time I am a subject, and it is my intention to reside permanently in the United States.

Eighth. I am able to speak the English language.

Ninth. I have resided continuously in the United States of America for the term of five years at least, immediately preceding the date of this petition, to wit, since the 11 day of Feby, anno Domini 1907 and in the State of Illinois, continuously next preceding the date of this petition, since the 13 day of Feby, anno Domini 1907, being a residence within this State of at least one year next preceding the date of this petition.

Tenth. I have not heretofore made petition for citizenship to any court. ~~(I made petition for citizenship to the ______ Court of ______ at ______ on the ______ day of ______, anno Domini 1___, and the said petition was denied by the said Court for the following reasons and causes, to wit, ______ and the cause of such denial has since been cured or removed.)~~

Attached hereto and made a part of this petition are my declaration of intention to become a citizen of the United States and the certificate from the Department of Labor, together with affidavit and the affidavits of the two verifying witnesses thereto, required by law. Wherefore your petitioner prays that he may be admitted a citizen of the United States of America.

Piotr Podrazik
(Complete and true signature of petitioner.)

Declaration of Intention No. 128309 and Certificate of Arrival from Department of Labor filed this 19 day of Aug 1925

NOTE TO CLERK OF COURT.—If petitioner arrived in the United States on or before June 29, 1906, strike out the words reading "and Certificate of Arrival from Department of Labor."

AFFIDAVITS OF PETITIONER AND WITNESSES

STATE OF ILLINOIS, County of Cook, } ss:

The aforesaid petitioner being duly sworn, deposes and says that he is the petitioner in the above-entitled proceedings; that he has read the foregoing petition and knows the contents thereof; that the said petition is signed with his full, true name; that the same is true of his own knowledge except as to matters therein stated to be alleged upon information and belief, and that as to those matters he believes it to be true.

Piotr Podrazik
(Complete and true signature of petitioner.)

Stanley Kluczynik, occupation Laborer, residing at 2905 Throop st, Chicago, Ill., and T. Jarosz, occupation Laborer, residing at 3022 Haines Ct, Chicago, Ill., each being severally, duly, and respectively sworn, deposes and says that he is a citizen of the United States of America; that he has personally known Piotr Podrazik, the petitioner above mentioned, to have resided in the United States continuously immediately preceding the date of filing his petition, since the 1 day of Aug, anno Domini 1920 and in the State in which the above-entitled petition is made continuously since the 1 day of Aug anno Domini 1920 and that he has personal knowledge that the said petitioner is a person of good moral character, attached to the principles of the Constitution of the United States, and that the petitioner is in every way qualified, in his opinion, to be admitted a citizen of the United States.

Stanley Kluczynik
(Signature of witness.)

T. Jarosz
(Signature of witness.)

[SEAL.]

Subscribed and sworn to before me by the above-named petitioner and witnesses in the office of the Clerk of said Court at Chicago, Ill., this 19 day of Aug anno Domini 1925

Samuel E. Erickson, Clerk.
By L. A. Portman, Deputy Clerk.

[OVER.]

Illustration 9.6: Four years later, in 1925, Peter returned to court to file his Petition for Naturalization. The document included the birth date of his wife and the birth dates and birthplaces of their children. Peter stated that he arrived in the United States (specifically, the port of New York) on February 11, 1907. He must have traveled straight to Illinois, having resided there since February 13, 1907. A gap between arrival and residence should point you to the passenger list to see where the initial destination was. Character witnesses and their descendants can be sources of photos and information about your ancestor. Courtesy of Walter J. Podrazik.

CERTIFICATE OF ARRIVAL—FOR NATURALIZATION PURPOSES
tificate is for the use of the person applying for it only, and is issued for naturalization purposes in compliance with
Act of June 29, 1906, sec. 4, subd. 2, par. 4, requiring a certificate from the Department of Labor stating the date,
e, and manner of arrival in the United States.)

U. S. DEPARTMENT OF LABOR

BUREAU OF NATURALIZATION

CERTIFICATE OF ARRIVAL DIVISION
ELLIS ISLAND, NEW YORK   MAY 2 3 1925

ᴬ is to certify that the following-named alien was legally admitted into the United States on the date
anner described below, at Ellis Island, New York.

Name of alien: Podrazik, Piotr

Date of arrival: February 11, 1907

Manner of arrival: Badenia   7529

ᴱCTION OF THE SECRETARY OF LABOR:

[signature]
Commissioner of Naturalization   By _____
                                                                  Chief of Division.
2-8-24   GOVERNMENT PRINTING OFFICE   14—2072

Illustration 9.7: Accompanying Peter's petition is an official Certificate of Arrival from the Bureau of Naturalization (part of the INS, Immigration and Naturalization Service), confirming the date, port, and name of the ship. The typed name ("Badenia") is much easier to read than the one on the Declaration of Intention, which looks like "Badyria." Courtesy of Walter J. Podrazik.

married prior to 1922 starting in 1929 for those whose husbands had naturalized and then in 1940 for those whose husbands were U.S. born.

In 1922 the Married Women's Act was passed, stating that all alien married women had to apply for citizenship on their own. If the husband had naturalized, the wife could jump to filing a petition. If the husband had not naturalized, she had to file her declaration first.

Children born abroad became citizens when the father did. Prior to 1906, children were rarely listed on the father's naturalization records. Lack of legal proof led to some kids going to court after age 21. You will find these records under Minors' Petitions, meaning they entered the U.S. while minors.

There are many nuances to naturalization, and there's

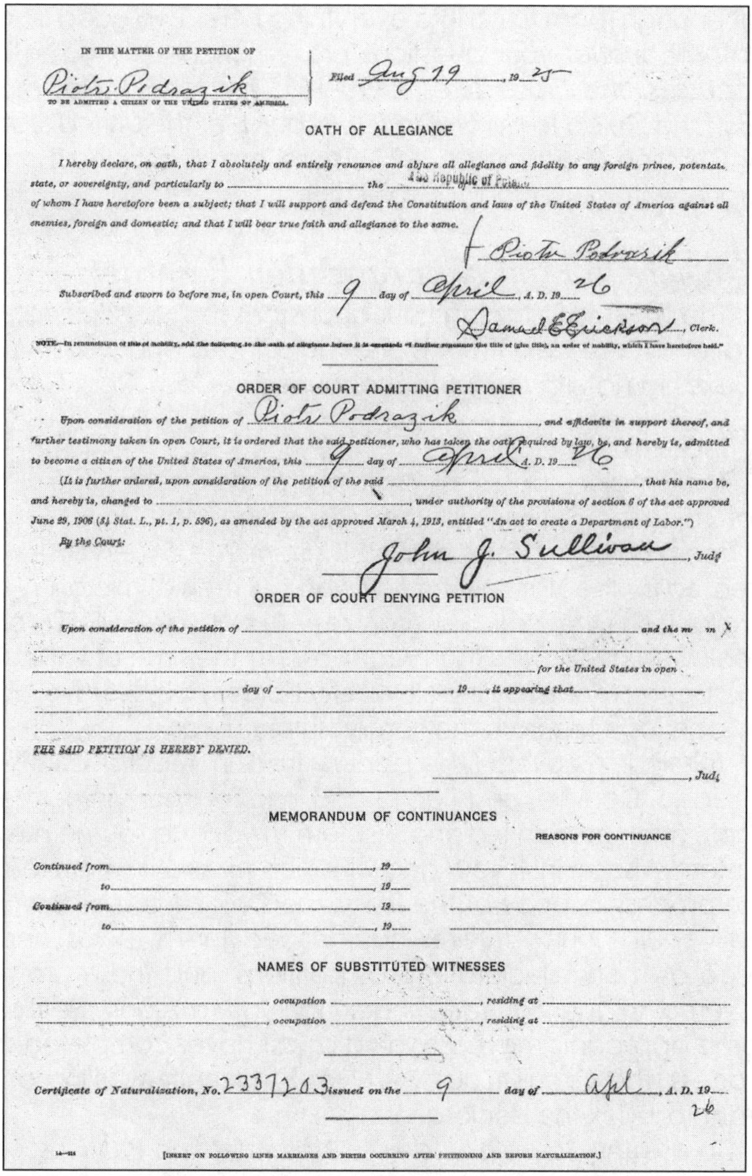

IN THE MATTER OF THE PETITION OF

Piotr Podrazik

TO BE ADMITTED A CITIZEN OF THE UNITED STATES OF AMERICA.

Filed Aug 19 1925

OATH OF ALLEGIANCE

I hereby declare, on oath, that I absolutely and entirely renounce and abjure all allegiance and fidelity to any foreign prince, potentate, state, or sovereignty, and particularly to .... the The Republic of Poland of whom I have heretofore been a subject; that I will support and defend the Constitution and laws of the United States of America against all enemies, foreign and domestic; and that I will bear true faith and allegiance to the same.

Piotr Podrazik

Subscribed and sworn to before me, in open Court, this 9 day of April, A. D. 1926

Samuel E Erickson, Clerk.

NOTE.—In renunciation of title of nobility, add the following to the oath of allegiance before it is executed: "I further renounce the title of (give title), an order of nobility, which I have heretofore held."

ORDER OF COURT ADMITTING PETITIONER

Upon consideration of the petition of Piotr Podrazik, and affidavits in support thereof, and further testimony taken in open Court, it is ordered that the said petitioner, who has taken the oath required by law, be, and hereby is, admitted to become a citizen of the United States of America, this 9 day of April, A. D. 1926

(It is further ordered, upon consideration of the petition of the said ...., that his name be, and hereby is, changed to ...., under authority of the provisions of section 6 of the act approved June 29, 1906 (34 Stat. L., pt. 1, p. 596), as amended by the act approved March 4, 1913, entitled "An act to create a Department of Labor.")

By the Court:

John J. Sullivan, Judge

ORDER OF COURT DENYING PETITION

Upon consideration of the petition of .... and the m .... for the United States in open .... day of ...., 19...., it appearing that ....

THE SAID PETITION IS HEREBY DENIED.

........, Judge

MEMORANDUM OF CONTINUANCES

REASONS FOR CONTINUANCE

Continued from ...., 19....
to ...., 19....
Continued from ...., 19....
to ...., 19....

NAMES OF SUBSTITUTED WITNESSES

........, occupation ...., residing at ....
........, occupation ...., residing at ....

Certificate of Naturalization, No. 2337203 issued on the 9 day of Apl, A. D. 1926

[INSERT ON FOLLOWING LINES MARRIAGES AND BIRTHS OCCURRING AFTER PETITIONING AND BEFORE NATURALIZATION.]

Illustration 9.8: On April 9, 1926, Peter renounced the claims of the land of his birth and swore allegiance to the United States of America. Notice the space provided above Judge Sullivan's signature to legally change the immigrant's name. Courtesy of Walter J. Podrazik.

not enough room to go into everything here. Two good books that will answer your questions are *American Naturalization Processes and Procedures, 1790–1985* by John J. Newman, 1985, and *Guide to Naturalization Records of the United States* by Christina K. Schaefer, 1997. These are available at most libraries with genealogical collections.

Where to Find Naturalization Records

The first step in finding your ancestor's record is to find the citation in an index. There is one major index and two smaller indexes to naturalizations that occurred in Cook County.

Indexes

The major index is called the *Soundex Index to Naturalization Petitions for the U.S. District and Circuit Courts, Northern District of Illinois and INS District #9 —1840–1950*. It was created by the National Archives on 179 reels of microfilm. It is available at the National Archives—Great Lakes, IRAD, and Cook County Circuit Court Archives. (At the time of writing, it had been ordered by the Newberry Library.) It is also available on loan for a fee from the Family History Library.

This index covers *final papers* filed in federal courts in Chicago, Danville, and Peoria and in local courts in northern Illinois, northwestern Indiana, eastern Iowa, and southern and eastern Wisconsin. If your ancestor completed the naturalization process, a copy of the first papers will be there also. But the Circuit Court Archives has noticed that it holds about twice as many declarations as petitions, and these are not covered in the *Soundex Index to Naturalization Petitions*. Some applicants moved or died or just never completed the process. The Circuit Court Archives is currently working on a grant to index the declarations.

To use the *Soundex Index to Naturalization Petitions*, you need to know how to code your ancestor's surname (last name) to the Soundex format. See "Soundex and Miracode Indexes" in Chapter 10. It's also important to know that Cook County naturalizations prior to 1871 don't show up in this index, because those records were destroyed in the Chicago Fire of

October 1871.

The Circuit Court Archives will search the *Soundex Index to Naturalization Petitions* for a fee. A separate fee is charged for a copy of the file. Forms can be downloaded from the Web site, www.cookcountyclerkofcourt.org.

There are a couple of smaller indexes. One is the Calumet City Court Naturalization Index. It indexes nine volumes of Calumet City, Cook County naturalizations c. 1906–1952, primarily Poles and Italians who completed final papers after filing first papers elsewhere. The index is at the South Suburban Genealogical and Historical Society, which also holds the documents from 1929 to 1954. Contact:

South Suburban Genealogical and Historical Society
3000 W. 170th Place
Hazel Crest, IL 60429-1174
708/335-3340
www.rootsweb.com/~ssghs
ssghs@usa.net

There is a small fee for nonmembers to use the SSGHS library. Mail research is offered for a fee; see "Research Policy" on the Web site.

Another index covers close to 4,000 individuals who completed final papers in Chicago Heights, Cook County, from about 1907 to 1954. The index is at the South Suburban Genealogical and Historical Society, while the documents are at the Chicago Heights Public Library. Contact:

Chicago Heights Public Library
25 W. 15th Street
Chicago Heights, IL 60411
708/754-0323
www2.sls.lib.il.us/CHS

The Family History Library in Salt Lake City has some separate indexes that went into the *Soundex Index to Naturalization Petitions*. It may be worth looking at these if you can't find your ancestor in the main index. See the Family History Library catalog at www.familysearch.org and do a place search for "Illinois, Cook—Naturalization and Citizenship—Indexes."

Records

Once you learn the court in which your ancestor filed for naturalization, and the date he or she became a citizen, you can locate the records. Your options depend on whether the papers were filed in county courts or federal court.

• The Cook County Circuit Court Archives holds the records that were filed in county courts from 1871 to 1929. After 1929 all naturalizations were filed in federal courts. They do not have records that were filed in Cook County towns other than Chicago, such as Calumet City and Blue Island. As mentioned earlier, Calumet City records are held by the South Suburban Genealogical and Historical Society.

• The National Archives—Great Lakes has the following records that were filed in federal courts in Chicago: Declarations of Intention 1872 to 1982, petitions 1872 to February 1975, and indexes 1872 to 1961. Be aware that there are gaps and incomplete files in these holdings. If you go in person, you'll need to make an appointment with an archivist for the Textual Research Room. If you're researching from a distance, Great Lakes will mail a copy of the naturalization file for a fee if you provide the information on the index entry.

• IRAD holds some 1871–1929 records for county courts (Circuit Court, County Court, Criminal Court, Superior Court), which include minors and military filings. IRAD has a record of naturalization petitions filed by women from 1923 to 1924. Staff will search for free (limit of two names per request) and provide photocopies for a fee.

• The Family History Center in Wilmette holds some Cook County naturalizations. Records filed in County Court, Circuit Court, or Superior Court from 1871 to 1929 are available on loan for a fee at other Family History Centers and the Newberry Library.

• The Immigration and Naturalization Service (INS) collected duplicate records of all naturalizations after September 26, 1906. In 2003, this federal agency became the U.S. Citizenship and Immigration Services (USCIS), a bureau of the U.S. Department of Homeland Security. Use Form G–639 and provide as much information as possible. Fees may apply depending on the amount of search time and photocopying. To obtain the form and instructions, call the Forms Request Line (800/870-3676), stop by the Forms Kiosk in the lobby of the Chicago District Office (address below), or download from http://uscis.gov/graphics/formsfee/forms/g-639.htm.

For records dating from 1906 to 1956, send the form to:

USCIS Headquarters
425 "Eye" Street, NW, 2nd Floor
ULLICO Building
Washington, DC 20536

For records after 1956, send the form to the district office in charge of the state where the immigrant lived. The Chicago District Office has charge of Illinois, Indiana, and Wisconsin. Contact:

USCIS Chicago District Office
10 W. Jackson Boulevard
Chicago, IL 60604
312/360-1346

❏ Strategy No. 6: Passenger Lists

Passenger lists are proof positive of when your ancestor came to America. It's a great feeling to see that name in black and white. But getting to that name can be a long and difficult process, for these reasons:

• There are many places you must look for the information.

• There is no master index—you'll have to search port by port.

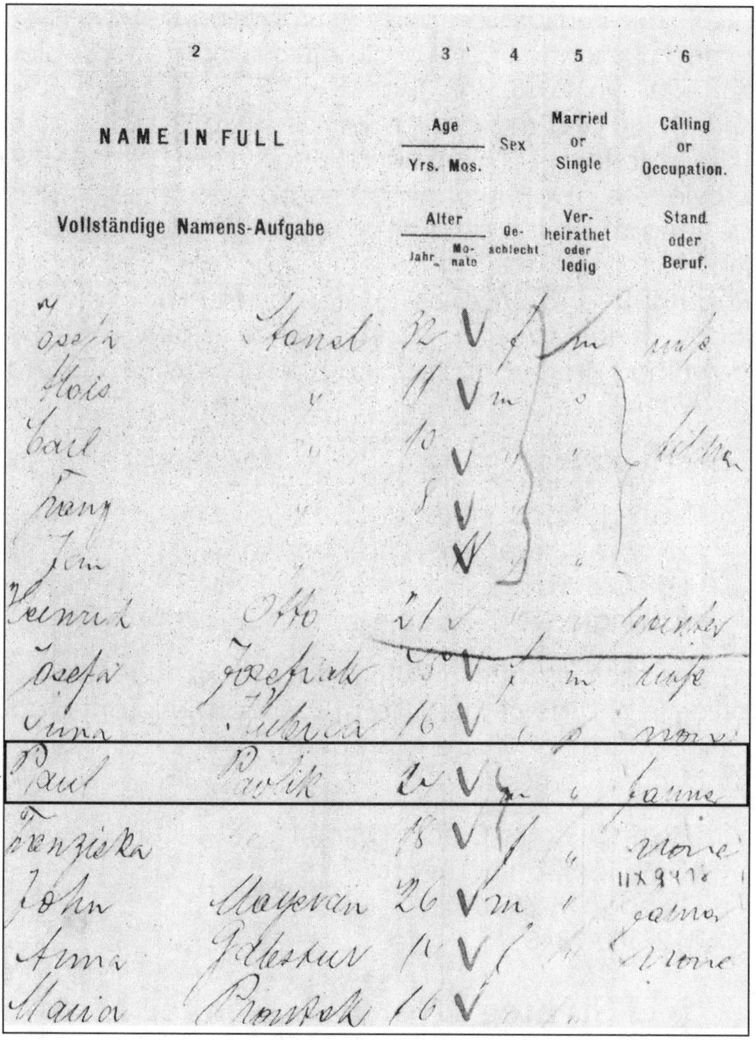

Illustration 9.9: Excerpt from passenger list of the S. S. Furst Bismarck, arrived in New York City on April 26, 1902. Source: "Passenger and crew lists of vessels arriving at New York," Family History Library film #1404020.

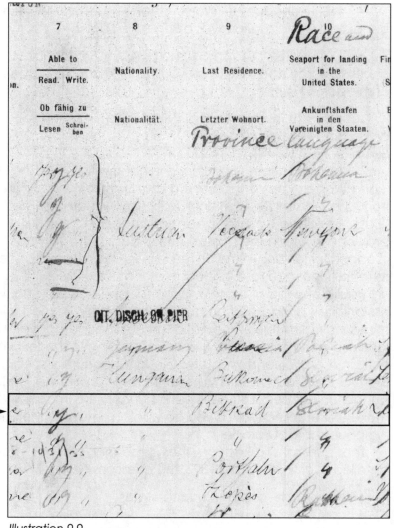

Illustration 9.9

- You'll encounter worse than usual handwriting, because the information was being taken down in a hurry.

- Your ancestor may have shortened or Americanized his or her surname after arrival, so you won't know the name he or she started with.

Let's look at the example of Paul Pavlik (Illustration 9.9). He arrived in New York City in 1902 aboard the ship S.S. *Furst Bismarck* from Hamburg, Germany. A record like this is where you'll earn your stripes in deciphering handwriting. (Tip: The Ellis Island Web site has a text version of basic information pulled from the passenger list entry.) Notice how category no. 9, "Last Residence," has been changed to record the province in which the passenger resided. Category no. 10, "Seaport for landing in the United States," has been changed to record the race and language of the passenger.

Paul is 24 years old, single, a farmer, and able to read. His nationality is Hungarian (the person creating the list used ditto marks indicating the same nationality as the line above). He last lived in the province of Bikrzad, according to the text version on the Ellis Island Web site. The language Paul speaks is Slovak. *That fact makes him ethnically Slovak.* He is not Hungarian just because he lived in Hungary. It's important to make those distinctions as you go back in time with the shifting boundaries of Europe.

The questions asked on the passenger lists got more detailed over time. Before 1893, the questions generally were:

- name, age, sex, and marital status
- country of origin
- occupation
- date and port of departure
- date and port of arrival in the United States

After 1907, the following questions were added:

- physical description

- detailed birthplace (the town, the county or province,

and the country)

- last residence in home country (added in 1893)
- name and address of nearest relative in home country
- name and address of relative or friend in the United States
- final destination in the United States: state, city, or town
- dates and places of any previous trips to the United States
- person who paid for the current passage (gives clue to other relatives)
- remarks on health (passengers with infectious diseases were barred from entering the United States)
- whether the passenger had sufficient funds to get to the final destination

Because of Chicago's location in the center of the country, immigrants did not arrive directly until the advent of air transportation. Instead, they either landed at East Coast or West Coast ports and journeyed inland via trains, wagons, or stagecoaches; arrived at southern ports and went up the Mississippi River; or traveled overland and by water through Canada and the Great Lakes states.

At certain periods, different ethnic groups favored different ports. Many Germans, for instance, came through New Orleans in the nineteenth century on their way to St. Louis and Chicago. Irish and English often went to Canada before crossing into the United States. Poor eastern European immigrants might take the cheapest fare to an out-of-the-way port. For a successful search, you'll need to figure out the most likely ports for your ancestor. John Colletta's 2002 book _They Came in Ships_ should be your first stop. Colletta talks about the routes different groups in Europe used over time. Often their point of embarkation determined their U.S. port of arrival.

Not every immigrant came through Ellis Island. Because of

its connection to the Statue of Liberty, New York City might be the first place you think of. There were many other possibilities:

East Coast Ports
- Baltimore, MD
- Boston, MA
  - Philadelpha, PA
- Portland, ME
- Providence, RI

West Coast Ports
- Astoria, OR
- Los Angeles, CA
- San Francisco, CA
- Seattle, WA

Southern Coast Ports
- Galveston, TX
- Mobile, AL

Mexican Border Crossings
- El Paso, TX
- Nogales, AZ

Canadian Border Crossings
- St. Albans, VT
- Skagway, AK

Check out the National Archives article "Immigration Records" (posted at www.archives.gov/research_room/genealogy/ immigrant_arrivals/passenger_records.html) and go to Part 5, "Available 1800–1959 Immigration Records," for a complete list of ports.

Ethnic Indexes

Start your search with this type of index if you don't know your ancestor's arrival date. For a positive ID, it helps to know as much as possible, such as your ancestor's age upon arrival and names of family members your ancestor was traveling with. The Newberry Library names many ethnic indexes in its guide "Passenger Lists," available in the genealogy section of its Web site or as a handout in the Local and Family History area on the second floor. Examples are *Armenian Immigrants: Boston 1891–1901, New York 1880–1897; Italians to America, 1880–1901;* and *The Swedish Emigrant.* You can generally find these items at libraries with strong genealogy collections. Search library catalogs with "[name of ethnic group] genealogy" (for example, "French genealogy") as a subject to find items specific to the group you're tracking.

Remember, indexes are only as good as the indexers. Just because you can't find your ancestor doesn't mean his or her record doesn't exist. As John Colletta says, your ancestor didn't swim here. If you look long enough and hard enough, you should be able to find documentation.

Port Indexes

To use these successfully, first narrow down the time period and the list of possible ports. Keep careful records of what you've looked at—you'll encounter many name variations that you'll have to weigh against the other things you know about your ancestor to determine if you have a match.

The National Archives created many Soundex port indexes (see Chapter 10 for instructions), and a number of them are available at the Great Lakes facility and other regional branches. Many of the indexes may be obtained on loan for a fee from the Family History Library. Ancestry.com recently began a section of passenger list databases, accessible at an additional cost above its basic subscription. In the Chicago area, the Wilmette Family History Center and the National Archives—Great Lakes offer free in-facility use of Ancestry.com's passenger resources.

Selected Index Holdings

This is an alphabetical list of indexes to major ports, arranged by date span from earliest to latest, and stating where you will find the indexes. It is a selected list and does not cover every research facility in the Midwest.

Baltimore

1820–52	Ancestry.com (subscription)
	Wisconsin Historical Society (Madison, WI)
1820–97	Harold Washington Library Center
	Allen County Public Library (Fort Wayne, IN)
1851–72	Ancestry.com (subscription)

Baltimore cont.
1897–1952   National Archives—Great Lakes

Boston
1821–50   Ancestry.com (subscription)

1848–91   Harold Washington Library Center
             Allen County Public Library
             Wisconsin Historical Society

1902–20   National Archives—Great Lakes
             Wisconsin Historical Society

Detroit
1906–54   National Archives—Great Lakes
             Allen County Public Library

Galveston
1896–1951   National Archives—Great Lakes
             Wisconsin Historical Society

New Orleans
1820–50   Ancestry.com (subscription)

1853–1952   National Archives—Great Lakes

1853–1952   Allen County Public Library
             Wisconsin Historical Society

New York
1820–46   National Archives—Great Lakes
             Allen County Public Library
             Wisconsin Historical Society

1820–50   Ancestry.com (subscription)

1851–91   Ancestry.com (subscription)

1892–1924   Statue of Liberty–Ellis Island Foundation
             Web site (www.ellisisland.org; free)

1897–1902   National Archives—Great Lakes
             Allen County Public Library
             Wisconsin Historical Society

1902–43   Newberry Library
             Allen County Public Library
             Wisconsin Historical Society

Philadelphia

1800–50	Ancestry.com (subscription)
1800–1906	Harold Washington Library Center Allen County Public Library
1800–1948	Wisconsin Historical Society
1883–1948	Allen County Public Library

St. Albans

1895–1952	National Archives—Great Lakes Allen County Public Library
1924–52	Allen County Public Library

Obtaining Copies of Passenger Lists

Once you find your ancestor in an index, you'll want to look at the ship's *manifest* (list of passengers) to learn all the information recorded about your forebear. You can also often find another family members traveling on the same ship. You have several options for viewing and obtaining copies of manifests.

• The National Archives has the most extensive collection of passenger lists. Check with the branch closest to you and see if they have the microfilm you want. If not, in most cases you can purchase the reel (interlibrary loan is not an option for passenger records).

For a fee, the National Archives in Washington will make a copy of your ancestor's record. You must provide the name of the port, the name of the ship, and the date of arrival. Use NATF Form 81, Ship Passenger Arrival Records, available at regional facilities or by e-mail at www.archives.gov/global_pages/inquire_form.html.

• The Family History Library holds copies of many of the National Archives microfilms. You can get them on loan for a fee at the Newberry Library or a Family History Center near you. Check the Family History Library catalog under "[name of port]-Emigration and Immigration." Sometimes you'll have to order more than one film because the arrival dates are split across two reels.

• The Ellis Island Web site has images of New York City arrivals dating from 1892 to 1924. You can view images for free online, but if you want copies, you must order them for a fee. You can't just give the site sponsor a credit card and then print the passenger list from your computer, at least not at the date of this book's publication.

• Ancestry.com has digitized images of several ports' passenger lists. You will either need to pay a subscription fee or print the list at research facilities with public access.

• There are research facilities that house microfilm holdings of lists (see next section).

Selected List Holdings
To find passenger list holdings on microfilm, scan this section for the name of the port and the date span you want. The facilities following the date spans are places in the greater Chicago and Midwest area. Again, this is a selected roster and does not cover every research facility.

Baltimore

1820–91	Arlington Heights Memorial Library
	Wisconsin Historical Society (Madison, WI)
1820–1909	Allen County Public Library (Fort Wayne, IN)

Boston

1820–91	Arlington Heights Memorial Library
	Wisconsin Historical Society
1820–1943	Allen County Public Library

Detroit

| 1946–57 | National Archives—Great Lakes |

Galveston

| 1896–1948 | National Archives—Great Lakes |
| 1896–1951 | Allen County Public Library |

New Orleans

| 1800–1902 | Wisconsin Historical Society |
| 1820–75 | Arlington Heights Memorial Library |

New Orleans cont.
1820–1902   Newberry Library
             Allen County Public Library
New York
1820–97   Arlington Heights Memorial Library
             Wisconsin Historical Society

1820–1940   Allen County Public Library

1846–97   National Archives—Great Lakes

Philadelphia
1800–82   Arlington Heights Memorial Library
             Wisconsin Historical Society

1800–1945   Allen County Public Library

St. Albans
1924–49   Allen County Public Library

Special Note Concerning Hamburg Emigration Lists

If you can't find your ancestor in U.S. records, you may want to look on the other side of the ocean. Hamburg, Germany, became one of the premier ports in Europe about 1900. Until World War I, 50 percent of Russian Jews came via Hamburg. It was the port of choice as well for subjects of the Austria–Hungary Empire, for Romanians, and for many Scandinavians.

The emigration lists kept by the Hamburg steamship companies from 1850 to 1934 have survived. They are available on microfilm from the Family History Library for a fee (in the Chicago area, the Wilmette Family History Center has the 1850–1934 index on permanent loan). An index to the years 1891 to 1906 has been posted online at the Link to Your Roots Web site (www.linktoyourroots.hamburg.de). Plans are to post 1907 to 1908 shortly and continue with the twentieth century, the years of peak emigration. After 1934 is reached, data for the mid-nineteenth century will be added. Searching is free, but there is a fee in euros to view complete information. Similar to the Ellis Island Web site, you may also purchase reproductions of the emigration lists and related memorabilia.

When Did My Ancestor Come to America?

Points to Remember

❑ *The U.S. census is a starting point for information about immigration and naturalization:*

• Be wary, however, of your ancestor's immigration or naturalization answers—always check against other evidence (such as naturalization records) before jumping into passenger lists.

❑ *If your ancestor was naturalized in 1904 to 1906 or after, naturalization records are the best place to find his or her arrival date; check indexes first and then obtain the records:*

• A Declaration of Intention provides this information:
—arrival date and place in the U.S.
—name of ship or railroad
—place of departure
—physical description
—year, month, and day of birth
—exact birthplace
—current address
—occupation
—age
—if married, name and birthplace of wife

When Did My Ancestor Come to America?

• A Petition for Naturalization provides this information:

—date immigrant began journey to the U. S.

—current address and occupation

—birth date of spouse

—names, birth dates, and birthplaces of children

—data on any denials of previous petitions

—names and addresses of character witnesses and the length of time the immigrant has been known by them

❏ *Not every immigrant came through Ellis Island; other points of entry include:*

• East Coast ports

• West Coast ports

• Southern ports

• Mexican border crossings

• Canadian border crossings

❏ *Strategies for searching passenger lists include the following:*

• Look in ethnic indexes.

• Look in port indexes (after narrowing down the time period and possible ports).

• Try Hamburg emigration lists.

Part II

Practical
Advice

10   Nuts and Bolts of the U.S. Census

Census research is fundamental to finding your ancestors. That's why it figures in so many chapters of this book. To save space, I've consolidated the nitty-gritty of using the census into this chapter. Master the concepts here and you are well on your way to filling out your family tree.

Tips for Finding Your Ancestor's Entry

There are many indexes by name—start looking for your ancestor in these to save wear and tear on your eyeballs. Keep the following points in mind as you look:

• The census taker might have misspelled your ancestor's name. Try looking under variations, for example, Swensen for Swenson and Coleman for Kollman. An ethnic name may have been written down the way the census taker heard it pronounced.

• Because of a census taker's bad handwriting, the indexers may get the name wrong.

• The name may have been missed in the index if the microfilm was too dark or scratched to be read.

CD and computer indexes let you search by variations in names and also by other factors. You may be able to set them to give you all Schwartzes born in Germany living in Hillside, for instance.

If you can't find your ancestor by name, go in the back door and search by address. This method involves obtaining a street address for the year of the census or close to it, using maps of the *enumeration district* (the district assigned to each enumerator, meaning census taker) to locate the proper area, and then searching until you find the address and see who's living there.

The Newberry Library offers a fee-based search service for the U.S. censuses it holds. One search is for indexes, and another is for the census entry when you have a citation from an index. Because of license restrictions, the Newberry cannot use electronic databases in its search service, though you are welcome to use the databases in person. Request forms are on the Newberry Web site (www.newberry.org in the genealogy section under "Services"). Or you can call or write for them. Contact:

Newberry Library
Local and Family History Section
60 W. Walton Street
Chicago, IL 60610
312/255-3512

Census Indexes

The listing that follows appears in reverse chronological order, starting with the latest available census, in keeping with the genealogical principle of starting with the most recent events and working backward. Note: Indexes on the two main subscription Web sites, Ancestry.com and Heritage QuestOnline, are constantly being upgraded. Check back frequently to see if coverage has been expanded for the year of interest, for instance including every name enumerated, not just heads of household.

– 1930 –

By Name:
• Every-name index on Ancestry.com (subscription Web site), at the Newberry Library, Arlington Heights Memorial Library, Elmhurst Public Library, and other libraries.

By Address:
• Enumeration district maps of Chicago (no suburbs), at the Newberry Library and online at www.alookatcook.com/1930/index.htm.

• Enumeration district maps of Chicago and Cook County, at the National Archives—Great Lakes.

• Cross-index of Chicago streets and enumeration districts on microfilm, at the National Archives—Great Lakes and the Newberry Library.

• Database of enumeration district descriptions online at the National Archives Web site, http://1930census.archives. gov/beginSearch.asp. Search by place-names or institution names (for example, schools, hospitals, orphanages).

• Written descriptions of Illinois enumeration district boundaries on microfilm, at the National Archives—Great Lakes, the Newberry Library, and the Harold Washington Library Center. Online descriptions of Cook County townships at www.alookatcook.com/1930/index.htm.

– 1920 –

By Name:
• Head of household index on Ancestry.com and HeritageQuest Online (subscription Web sites). Others in household listed only if surname differs. At the Newberry Library, the Arlington Heights Memorial Library, the Elmhurst Public Library, and others.

• Soundex system index on microfilm, at the Newberry Library, the National Archives—Great Lakes, and the Harold Washington Library Center and on loan for a fee from the Family History Library in Salt Lake City, Utah, through nationwide Family History Centers.

By Address:
• Enumeration district maps of Chicago (no suburbs), at the Newberry Library and online at www.alookatcook.com/ 1920/index.htm.

• Written descriptions of Illinois enumeration district boundaries on microfilm, at the National Archives—Great Lakes, the Newberry Library, and the Harold Washington Library Center. Online descriptions of Cook County townships at www.alookatcook.com/1920/index.htm.

– 1910 –

By Name:

• Every-name index on HeritageQuest Online (subscription Web site), at the Newberry Library, the Arlington Heights Memorial Library, the Elmhurst Public Library, and other libraries.

• Head of household index on Ancestry.com (subscription Web site). Others in household listed only if surname differs. At the Newberry Library, the Arlington Heights Memorial Library, the Elmhurst Public Library, and other libraries.

• Soundex system index (also known as the Miracode index) on microfilm, at the Newberry Library, the National Archives—Great Lakes, the Harold Washington Library Center, and other libraries. Available on loan for a fee from the Family History Library in Salt Lake City through nationwide Family History Centers.

By Address:

• Enumeration district maps of Chicago (no suburbs), at the Newberry Library and online at www.alookatcook. com/1910/index.htm.

• Cross-index of Chicago streets and enumeration districts on microfiche, at the National Archives—Great Lakes and the Newberry Library.

• Written descriptions of Illinois enumeration district boundaries on microfilm, at the National Archives—Great Lakes and the Harold Washington Library Center. Online descriptions of Cook County townships at www.alookatcook. com/1910/index.htm.

– 1900 –

By Name:

• Every-name index on Ancestry.com (subscription Web site), at the Newberry Library, the Arlington Heights Memorial Library, the Elmhurst Public Library, and other libraries.

• Head of household index on HeritageQuest Online (subscription Web site). Others in household listed only if surname differs. At the Newberry Library, the Arlington Heights Memorial Library, the Elmhurst Public Library, and other libraries.

• Soundex system index on microfilm, at the Newberry Library, the National Archives—Great Lakes, the Harold Washington Library Center, and other libraries. Available on loan for a fee from the Family History Library in Salt Lake City through nationwide Family History Centers.

By Address:
• Enumeration district maps of Chicago (no suburbs), at the Newberry Library. Arranged by ward; ward maps also available. Online enumeration district and ward maps at www.alookatcook.com/1900/index.htm.

• Written descriptions of Illinois enumeration district boundaries on microfilm, at the National Archives—Great Lakes and the Harold Washington Library Center. At time of publication, the Look at Cook Web site did not have any descriptions for 1900 Cook County townships.

– 1890 –
• Virtually destroyed in a 1921 fire at the Bureau of the Census in Washington, D.C. One microfilm reel of fragments was compiled, including a few Illinois counties but not Cook.

– 1880 –
By Name:
• Every-name index on the Web site of the Church of Jesus Christ of Latter-day Saints, www.familysearch.org (free), and Ancestry.com (subscription), at the Newberry Library, the Arlington Heights Memorial Library, the Elmhurst Public Library, and other libraries.

• Every-name index on 55 CDs from the Church of Jesus Christ of Latter-day Saints, at the Newberry Library and other libraries. May be purchased from the church.

• Soundex system index (only covers households with children age ten and under in 1880) on microfilm, at the Newberry Library, the National Archives—Great Lakes, and the Harold Washington Library Center. Available on loan for a fee from the Family History Library in Salt Lake City through nationwide Family History Centers.

By Address:
• Enumeration district maps of Chicago and Cook County, at the Newberry Library. Chicago arranged by ward; ward maps also available. Online maps of Chicago and Cicero township at www.alookatcook.com/1880/index.htm.

• Written descriptions of Illinois enumeration district boundaries on microfilm, at the National Archives—Great Lakes and the Newberry Library.

• Cross-index to Cook County townships and localities by reel and page numbers, at www.alookatcook.com/1880/index.htm.

– 1870 –
By Name:
• Every-name index on Ancestry.com (subscription Web site), at the Newberry Library, the Arlington Heights Memorial Library, the Elmhurst Public Library, and other libraries.

• Head of household index on HeritageQuest Online (subscription Web site). Others in household listed only if surname differs. At the Newberry Library, the Arlington Heights Memorial Library, the Elmhurst Public Library, and other libraries.

• HeritageQuest index for Illinois on CD, at many libraries. May be purchased from the company.

• Book, *Chicago, Illinois 1870 Census Index*, Bradley W. Steuart, ed., Bountiful, Utah: Precision Indexing, 1990. At the National Archives—Great Lakes and the Newberry Library. Also includes Cook County communities.

• Surname index by ward, at the Illinois State Archives.

• Name index for townships of Bremen, Calumet, Orland, and Palos, in the 1982–84 issues of *Where the Trails Cross*, publication of the South Suburban Genealogical and Historical Society. At the Newberry Library, the Chicago Public Library, the Oak Lawn Public Library, and other libraries.

By Address:

• Enumeration district map of Chicago, at the Newberry Library (includes dates census takers came through each area) and online at www.alookatcook.com/1870/index.htm.

• Written descriptions of Illinois enumeration district boundaries on microfilm, at the National Archives—Great Lakes and the Newberry Library.

• 1870 landownership map of Cook County on microfiche, at the Newberry Library, the Richard J. Daley Library at the University of Illinois at Chicago, the Illinois State Library, and other libraries. Useful to learn where ancestor's farm was located.

– *1860* –

By Name:

• Every-name index on Ancestry.com (subscription Web site). At the Newberry Library, the Arlington Heights Memorial Library, the Elmhurst Public Library, and other libraries.

• Head of household index on HeritageQuest Online (subscription Web site). Others in household listed only if surname differs. At the Newberry Library, the Arlington Heights Memorial Library, the Elmhurst Public Library, and other libraries.

• Book, *Illinois 1860 Census Index, North*, Ronald Vern Jackson, Bountiful, Utah: Accelerated Indexing Systems, 1987. At the Newberry Library, the Arlington Heights Memorial Library, the Winnetka Public Library, and many other libraries.

• *Name Index to Early Illinois Records* on microfilm, at the Illinois State Archives, the Newberry Library, and the Chicago Historical Society.

• Name index for townships of Lemont, Orland, Palos, Thornton, and Worth in the 1973–79 issues of *Where the Trails Cross*, publication of the South Suburban Genealogical and Historical Society. At the Newberry Library, the Chicago Public

Library, the Oak Lawn Public Library, and other libraries.

By Address:
• Written descriptions of enumeration district boundaries on microfilm, at the National Archives—Great Lakes and the Newberry Library.

• 1861 landownership map of Cook County on microfiche, at the Newberry Library, the Richard J. Daley Library at the University of Illinois at Chicago, the Illinois State Library, and other libraries. Useful to learn where ancestor's farm was located.

– 1850 –

By Name:
• Every-name index on Ancestry.com (subscription Web site), at the Newberry Library, the Arlington Heights Memorial Library, the Elmhurst Public Library, and other libraries.

• Every-name index, at the Illinois State Archives.

• Book, *Illinois 1850 Census Index*, Ronald Vern Jackson and Gary Ronald Teeples, Bountiful, Utah: Accelerated Indexing Systems, 1976. At the Newberry Library and the National Archives—Great Lakes. Heads of households only.

• Book, *Surname Index to the 1850 Federal Census of Chicago, Cook County, Illinois*, Gertrude W. Lundberg, Bernice C. Richard, Chicago: Genealogical Services and Publications, 1976. At the Newberry Library, the Arlington Heights Memorial Library, the Wisconsin Historical Society, and many others.

• Book, *Cook County Illinois: 1850 Federal Census, Not Including the City of Chicago*, Gertrude W. Lundberg, Chicago: Chicago Genealogical Society, 1987. At the Newberry Library, the Arlington Heights Memorial Library, the Oak Lawn Public Library, the Wheaton Public Library, and many other libraries.

• Name index for townships of Bloom, Bremen, Lemont, Palos, Thornton, and Worth in the 1970–74 issues of *Where the Trails Cross*, publication of the South Suburban Genealogical and Historical Society. At the Newberry Library, the Chicago Public Library, the Oak Lawn Public Library, and other libraries.

By Address:
• Written descriptions of enumeration district boundaries on microfilm, at the National Archives—Great Lakes and the Newberry Library.

• 1851 landownership map of Cook County on micro-fiche, at the Newberry Library, the Richard J. Daley Library at the University of Illinois at Chicago, the Illinois State Library, and other libraries. Useful to learn where ancestor's farm was located.

– *1840* –

By Name:
• Head of household index on Ancestry.com (subscription Web site). Others in household listed only if surname differs. At the Newberry Library, the Arlington Heights Memorial Library, the Elmhurst Public Library, and other libraries.

• Book, *Illinois 1840 Census Index*, Ronald Vern Jackson and Gary Ronald Teeples, Bountiful, Utah: Accelerated Indexing Systems, 1977. At the Naperville Public Library, the Oak Lawn Public Library, the Schaumburg Public Library, the Allen County Public Library, and many other libraries.

• Book, *Illinois 1840 Census Index* (Volume 1, Counties Adams–DuPage), Maxine W. Wormer, Thomson, Illinois: Heritage House, 1973. At the Newberry Library, the Arlington Heights Memorial Library, the Wheaton Public Library, and many others. Heads of households only.

• Name index, at the Illinois State Archives.

• Cook County indexed in the 1970 issues of *Chicago Genealogist* (Volume 2, Numbers 1–4), published by the Chicago Genealogical Society. At the Newberry Library, the

Chicago Public Library, the Arlington Heights Memorial Library, and many other libraries.

By Address:
• Written descriptions of enumeration district boundaries on microfilm, at the National Archives—Great Lakes and the Newberry Library.

Soundex and Miracode Indexes

The U.S. Census Bureau developed indexes to the census when Social Security was established in the 1930s. Many people who were eligible for Social Security benefits had been born at home and had no birth certificates. The government accepted a listing in a census as proof of age. To make these entries more accessible, an index was created that enabled surnames to be found the way they sounded, not the way they were spelled. This index was called the Soundex. It involves deleting certain letters and substituting numbers to make a three-digit code preceded by the first letter of the surname. For instance, my name, DuMelle, is coded D540.

The Soundex system was also used for indexing passenger lists and naturalization records. It is used today in driver's license numbers, by Illinois and some other states. Knowing how to use the Soundex will help you a great deal in your research.

The Miracode index is another name for the Soundex system used in the 1910 census. The Miracode index works the same way as the Soundex. The main difference is that you get a volume, an enumeration district, and a family number citation instead of an enumeration district, a sheet, and a line citation on the index cards. The Miracode was used only for the 1910 census. The cards were printed instead of handwritten, so they can be easier to read.

Using Soundex and Miracode Indexes

Follow these steps to work with Soundex and Miracode indexes:

1. Code the surname (last name). See Illustrations 10.1 and 10.2.

2. Select the microfilm reel that contains that code, either by looking through the drawers or consulting a catalog. Within each code, the index cards are arranged alphabetically by first name. If your ancestor's first name was Hans, go to the "H" section of your code to begin your search. Tip: Many men were enumerated by their initials, so if you don't find him under "Hans," for example, then look under "H." He may also have Americanized his name to Hank or Henry.

3. The index cards contain an abstract of the census entry. They will, however, give you enough information (age, birthplace, address, and names of others in the household) to determine if this is the correct Hans Braun. The census entry will have more information about the family, such as their occupations and the birthplaces of their parents. Don't stop with the index; always look at the census entry.

4. When you find your ancestor's entry, make a photocopy or write down the information. Copy the enumeration district (ED) number, sheet number, and line number for the 1880, 1900, and 1920 census. Copy the ED and family number for the 1910 census. (There is no Soundex or Miracode index for the 1890 or 1930 census for Illinois. The Census Bureau only indexed as far back as 1880, because that was what was needed for Social Security purposes in the 1930s. The 1880 Soundex covers only families with children age ten and under. You will need to use another index if your ancestor was not a small child or did not have children at that point in time.)

5. Using your ED information, find the reel that contains that ED. It is easiest to look at the National Archives catalogs that are put out for patron use at research facilities. They are also available online at www.archives.gov/publications/ genealogy_microfilm_catalogs.html.

The Soundex Coding System

The Soundex is a coded surname (last name) index based on the way a surname sounds rather than by the way it is spelled. Surnames that sound the same, but are spelled differently, like BROWN and BROWNE, are filed under the same code. The Soundex coding system was developed so that you can find a surname even though it may have been recorded under various spellings.

To search for a particular surname, you must first work out its code. Every Soundex code consists of a letter and three numbers. The letter is always the first letter of the surname. The numbers are assigned to the remaining letters of the surname according to the Soundex guide.

Using the boxes in the middle panel, follow these steps:

STEP 1 On line 1, write the surname you are coding, placing one letter in each box.

STEP 2 On line 2, write the first letter of the surname in the first box.

STEP 3 On line 1, disregarding the first letter, slash through the letters A, E, I, O, U, W, Y, and H.

STEP 4 On line 2, write the numbers found on the Soundex Coding Guide for the first three remaining unslashed letters. Add zeros to any empty boxes. Disregard any additional letters.

NAMES WITH DOUBLE LETTERS

If the surname has any double letters, they should be treated as one letter. For example, the two "t"s in Ritter are coded with one "3" (R360).

NAMES WITH LETTERS SIDE-BY-SIDE THAT HAVE THE SAME NUMBER

A surname may have different letters side-by-side that have the same code number. For example, PF in Pfister (1 is the number for both P and F); CKS in Jackson (2 is the number for C, K, and S.) These letters should be treated as one letter.

NAMES WITH PREFIXES

Mc and Mac are not considered prefixes.
If a surname has a prefix, such as Van, Con, De, Di, La, or Le, code both with and without the prefix because it might be listed under either code.

"H" AND "W" AS CONSONANT SEPARATORS

"H" or "W" are completely disregarded except as initial letters. In any other part of the surname, the letters "H" and "W" are treated as if they are not there. If "H" or "W" separate two consonants that have the same Soundex code, the consonant to the right of the "H" or "W" should not be coded. For example: Ashcraft is coded A-261 (A, 2 for S, C ignored, 6 for the R, 1 for the F). Burroughs is coded B-620 (B, 6 is for R, 2 for G, S is ignored, 0 because there are no more letters to code).

It is very important to remember that not all Bureau of the Census employees Soundexed a name strictly according to the rules. For example, Ashcraft may sometimes be found under A226.

Illustrations 10.1, 10.2: Official government instructions for using the Soundex system of indexes. These indexes were used for the 1880, 1900, 1910, and 1920 censuses. No Soundex was done for Illinois in the 1930 census. Source: National Archives and Records Administration, "Census Soundex" brochure, 2002.

Soundex Coding Guide

Number	Represents Letter	
1	B, F, P, V	
2	C, G, J, K, Q, S, X, Z	Disregard the letters A, E, I, O, U, H, W, *and* Y.
3	D, T	
4	L	
5	M, N	
6	R	

Line 1
Line 2

Line 1
Line 2

Line 1
Line 2

With your ancestor's name correctly coded, you are ready to use the microfilmed Soundex card index, which is organized by state, thereunder by Soundex code number, and **thereunder alphabetically by first name or initial.**

FAMILY CARD

Soundex Code →

1880

A130			OHIO			
Abbott, Alvira A.			VOL. 18	E.D. 233		
(HEAD OF FAMILY)			SHEET 10	LINE 42		
W	F	56	Vermont			
(COLOR)	(SEX)	(AGE)	(BIRTHPLACE)			
Defiance						
(COUNTY)						
Defiance		Perry	(M.C.D.)* —			
(CITY)		(STREET)	(HOUSE NO.)			

(OTHER MEMBERS OF FAMILY)

NAME	RELATIONSHIP	AGE	BIRTHPLACE
Abbott, Henry E.	S	33	Mass.
" Willie A.	S	27	New Hamp.
Cushing, Julia A.	D	35	New Hamp.
Cushing, Richard E.	GS	7	New York

* "M.C.D." *stands for* "minor civil division."

Illustration 10.2

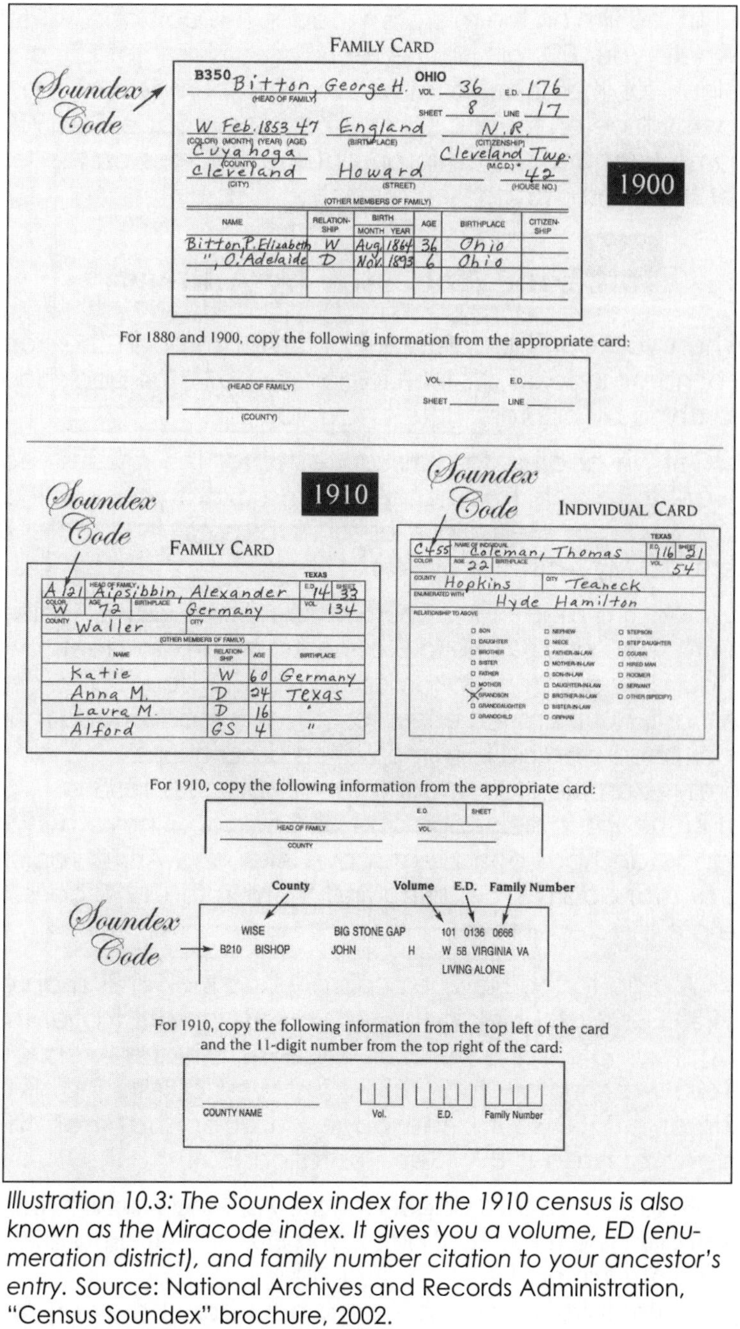

Illustration 10.3: The Soundex index for the 1910 census is also known as the Miracode index. It gives you a volume, ED (enumeration district), and family number citation to your ancestor's entry. Source: National Archives and Records Administration, "Census Soundex" brochure, 2002.

6. Put the film on the microfilm reader. The box label will tell you where your ED falls on the reel. Forward to that ED, and then look for the sheet number and line number. All these numbers will be on the top right of the census page. For 1910, the family number is listed in one of the columns on the left side of the census page (see Illustration 1.4).

Find Your Ancestor by Address

When you can't locate your ancestor through the front door of name indexes, it's time to go around to the back door of searching by address. Here's how you do it:

1. Get an address for your ancestor for the census year you want to search. If you can't get the exact year, get it as close as you can. (See "Sources for Addresses" in Chapter 6, "Where Did My Ancestor Live?")

2. Look at a map of the enumeration districts (EDs). Another option for 1930 and 1910 is to use the cross-index to streets and EDs. You can also read a description of ED boundaries and figure it out, but it's much easier to look at a ready-made map that has been created from the written descriptions.

In my example, I am looking for the address 1655 W. 17th Street in the Pilsen neighborhood of Chicago. I have a 1930 mortgage and bail bond that shows Alex and Anna Kopicki living at that address. I want to find them in the 1930 census. These are the steps I take:

A. I go to the Newberry Library and look in its map of 1930 EDs. First, I look in the index map in front to get the approximate page number. Because Ashland Avenue is 1600 west, I know that 1655 is just west of Ashland. 17th Street is 1700 south. The page number that has the general area is 89. (See Illustration 10.4.)

B. Turning to that page, I locate Ashland Avenue, then 17th, and next the 1600 block. The ED for that area is 796. (See Illustration 10.5.)

Note: If your address is on a boundary between two

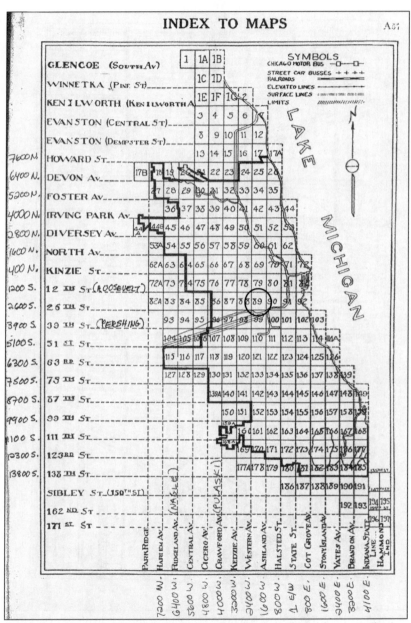

Illustration 10.4: Start here to find the enumeration district for a particular Chicago address. Source: 1930 Chicago census finding aid, Newberry Library.

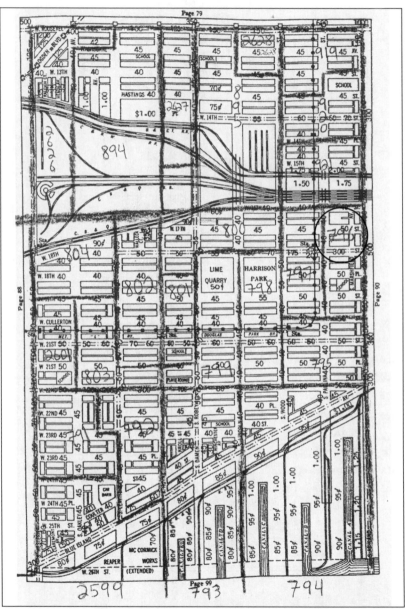

Illustration 10.5: The heavy lines are ED boundaries, drawn over a land valuation map (ignore dollar and cent figures). Source: 1930 Chicago census finding aid, page 89, Newberry Library.

22   *Illinois*

Coles   EDs 15-1 to 15-8

412. Coles   EDs 15-9 to 15-31

Clinton   EDs 14-1 to 14-29

413. Cook   EDs 16-1977 to 16-1979, 16-2910 (void), 16-1980 to 16-1983, 16-2911, 16-1984 to 16-1989, 16-2912, 16-1990 to 16-1996

414. Cook   EDs 16-1997 to 16-2005, 16-2913 (void), 16-2026, 16-2332, 16-2027, 16-2014 to 16-2025

415. Cook   EDs 16-2006 to 16-2013, 16-2029, 16-2334, 16-2030 to 16-2031, 16-2028, 16-2032 to 16-2033, 16-2067, 16-2065 to 16-2066, 16-2068, 16-2034 to 16-2047, 16-2058, 16-2359, 16-2059, 16-2360, 16-2063 to 16-2064

416. Cook   EDs 16-2048 (NP), 16-2049 to 16-2055, 16-2060, 16-2056 to 16-2057, 16-2061 to 16-2062, 16-1, 16-2377 to 16-2378, 16-2, 16-2379, 16-3 to 16-5, 16-2380, 16-6 to 16-8, 16-2381, 16-9 to 16-10, 16-2382, 16-11, 16-2383, 16-12 to 16-15

417. Cook, Chicago City   EDs 16-16 to 16-19, 16-2384, 16-20, 16-2385, 16-21 to 16-23, 16-2386, 16-24 to 16-25, 16-2387, 16-26, 16-2388, 16-27 (NP), 16-2389 to 16-2390, 16-28, 16-2391, 16-29, 16-2392 to 16-2393, 16-30 to 16-34, 16-2394, 16-35 to 16-36, 16-2395, 16-37, 16-2396, 16-38, 16-2397, 16-39 to 16-41, 16-2398, 16-42 to 16-45, 16-2399, 16-46, 16-2400, 16-47 to 16-48, 16-2401, 16-49 to 16-50, 16-2402, 16-51, 16-2403

418. Cook, Chicago City   EDs 16-52, 16-2404 to 16-2405, 16-53 to 16-54, 16-2406, 16-55 to 16-56, 16-2407, 16-57 to 16-69, 16-2408, 16-70, 16-2409, 16-71 to 16-75, 16-2410, 16-76, 16-2411, 16-77 to 16-78, 16-2412, 16-79, 16-2413, 16-80, 16-2414, 16-81 to 16-83

419. Cook, Chicago City   EDs 16-84 to 16-87, 16-2415, 16-88 to 16-90, 16-2416 (NP), 16-91 to 16-94, 16-2417, 16-95 to 16-96, 16-2418, 16-97 to 16-100, 16-2419, 16-101, 16-2420, 16-102, 16-2421, 16-103 to 16-104, 16-2422, 16-105, 16-2423 (NP), 16-2424, 16-106, 16-2425, 16-107 to 16-112, 16-2426

420. Cook, Chicago City   EDs 16-113 to 16-126, 16-2427, 16-127 to 16-128, 16-2428, 16-129 to 16-131, 16-2429, 16-132 to 16-137, 16-2430, 16-138 to 16-141, 16-2431, 16-142 to 16-143

421. Cook, Chicago City   EDs 16-144 to 16-145, 16-2432, 16-146 to 16-150, 16-2433, 16-151 to 16-180

422. Cook, Chicago City   EDs 16-181 to 16-207

423. Cook, Chicago City   EDs 16-208 to 16-236

424. Cook, Chicago City   EDs 16-237 to 16-268

425. Cook, Chicago City   EDs 16-269 to 16-296

426. Cook, Chicago City   EDs 16-297 to 16-316

427. Cook, Chicago City   EDs 16-317 to 16-322, 16-323 (NP), 16-2434, 16-324 to 16-331, 16-2435, 16-332 to 16-338, 16-339 (NP), 16-340

428. Cook, Chicago City   EDs 16-341 to 16-344, 16-2436, 16-345 to 16-362, 16-364

429. Cook, Chicago City   EDs 16-363, 16-365 to 16-367, 16-368 (NP), 16-2437 to 16-2438, 16-369 to 16-372, 16-2439, 16-373, 16-2440 to 16-2444, 16-374, 16-2445 to 16-2446, 16-375, 16-2447 to 16-2449, 16-376 to 16-379

430. Cook, Chicago City   EDs 16-380 to 16-381, 16-2450, 16-382 to 16-398, 16-399 (NP), 16-2451, 16-400

431. Cook, Chicago City   EDs 16-401 to 16-413, 16-2452 to 16-2453, 16-2454 (NP), 16-414, 16-2455

432. Cook, Chicago City   EDs 16-415 to 16-417, 16-2456 to 16-2457, 16-418, 16-2458 to 16-2459, 16-419, 16-2460 to 16-2461, 16-420, 16-2462, 16-421 to 16-423, 16-2463, 16-424, 16-2464, 16-425, 16-2465, 16-426, 16-2466, 16-428, 16-2467, 16-429

433. Cook, Chicago City   EDs 16-427, 16-430, 16-2468, 16-431, 16-2469, 16-432 to 16-433, 16-2470, 16-434 to 16-435, 16-2471 to 16-2472, 16-436, 16-2473, 16-437, 16-2474, 16-438 to 16-439, 16-2475 to 16-2476, 16-440, 16-2477 to 16-2481, 16-441,

16-2482, 16-2483 (NP), 16-442, 16-2484, 16-443, 16-2485, 16-444, 16-2486, 16-445, 16-2487 (NP), 16-2488, 16-446

434. Cook, Chicago City   EDs 16-447 to 16-450, 16-2489, 16-451, 16-2490, 16-452, 16-2491, 16-453 to 16-454, 16-2492, 16-455, 16-2493, 16-456 to 16-457, 16-2494, 16-458 to 16-459, 16-2495 to 16-2496, 16-460, 16-2497, 16-461, 16-2498, 16-462, 16-2499, 16-463 to 16-464, 16-2500, 16-465 to 16-466, 16-2501, 16-467

435. Cook, Chicago City   EDs 16-468 to 16-470, 16-2502, 16-471, 16-2503 to 16-2504, 16-472, 16-2505 to 16-2506, 16-473 (NP), 16-2507 to 16-2508, 16-2509 (NP), 16-474 to 16-481, 16-2510 (NP), 16-2511, 16-482, 16-2512, 16-483, 16-2513

436. Cook, Chicago City   EDs 16-2514 to 16-2515, 16-484, 16-2516 to 16-2517 (NP), 16-485, 16-2518, 16-2519 (NP), 16-2520, 16-486, 16-2521, 16-487 to 16-490, 16-2522, 16-491 to 16-492, 16-2523, 16-493, 16-2524, 16-494, 16-2525, 16-495 to 16-496, 16-2526, 16-497, 16-2527, 16-498, 16-2528, 16-499, 16-2529, 16-500, 16-2530

437. Cook, Chicago City   EDs 16-501 to 16-502, 16-2531, 16-503 (NP), 16-2532 to 16-2533 (NP), 16-504 (NP), 16-2534, 16-505, 16-2535, 16-506 to 16-508, 16-2536, 16-509 to 16-525

438. Cook, Chicago City   EDs 16-526 to 16-527, 16-2537, 16-528, 16-2538, 16-529 to 16-530, 16-2539, 16-531 to 16-535, 16-2540, 16-536 to 16-546, 16-2540, 16-547, 16-2541

439. Cook, Chicago City   EDs 16-548, 16-2542, 16-549, 16-2543, 16-550, 16-2544, 16-551 to 16-552, 16-2545, 16-553 to 16-554, 16-2546, 16-555 to 16-556, 16-2547, 16-557 to 16-559, 16-2548, 16-560 to 16-565

440. Cook, Chicago City   EDs 16-566 to 16-568, 16-2549, 16-569, 16-570 (NP), 16-2550, 16-571, 16-2551 to 16-2552, 16-572, 16-2558, 16-573, 16-2554, 16-574, 16-2555, 16-575, 16-2556 to 16-2558, 16-576, 16-2559 to 16-2561, 16-577 to 16-579

441. Cook, Chicago City   EDs 16-2562, 16-580 to 16-587, 16-2590, 16-588 to 16-589, 16-591 to 16-592, 16-2563, 16-593 to 16-2600

442. Cook, Chicago City   EDs 16-601 to 16-620, 16-2564, 16-621 to 16-622, 16-2565, 16-623 to 16-625

443. Cook, Chicago City   EDs 16-626 to 16-631, 16-2908, 16-632 to 16-649, 16-2566

444. Cook, Chicago City   EDs 16-650 to 16-671

445. Cook, Chicago City   EDs 16-672 to 16-673, 16-2567, 16-674 to 16-675, 16-2568, 16-676 to 16-682, 16-2569, 16-683, 16-2570, 16-684, 16-2571, 16-685 to 16-689, 16-691

446. Cook, Chicago City   EDs 16-690, 16-692 to 16-698, 16-2572 (NP), 16-699 to 16-712

447. Cook, Chicago City   EDs 16-713 to 16-735, 16-736 (NP)

448. Cook, Chicago City   EDs 16-737, 16-2573, 16-738 to 16-740, 16-2574, 16-741 to 16-750, 16-2575, 16-751, 16-2576, 16-752 to 16-753, 16-2577

449. Cook, Chicago City   EDs 16-754 to 16-756, 16-2578, 16-757, 16-2579 to 16-2581, 16-758 to 16-760, 16-2582, 16-761 to 16-765, 16-2583, 16-766 to 16-771

450. Cook, Chicago City   EDs 16-772 to 16-774, 16-2584, 16-775, 16-2585, 16-776, 16-2586, 16-777, 16-2587 to 16-2588, 16-778, 16-2589, 16-779, 16-2590, 16-780 to 16-781, 16-2591, 16-782, 16-2592, 16-783 to 16-785, 16-2594 (NP), 16-786, 16-2595, 16-787 to 16-788, 16-2596, 16-789, 16-2597 to 16-2598 (NP), 16-790, 16-2599, 16-791

451. Cook, Chicago City   EDs 16-792 to 16-804, 16-2600 (NP), 16-805, 16-2601, 16-806, 16-2602, 16-804, 16-2603 to 16-2604,

Illustration 10.6: The number in the left column is the reel number. The prefix "16" was assigned to all Cook County EDs in the 1930 census. Source: National Archives and Records Administration, *1930 Federal Population Census* catalog, page 22, 2002.

EDs, you can check the written ED descriptions to see how it was divided, or simply check both EDs on the census. In general, when the boundary is a street running north and south, one ED takes the east side of the street (odd numbers) and the other takes the west side of the street (even numbers). When the boundary is a street running east and west, one ED takes the south side of the street (odd numbers) and the other takes the north side of the street (even numbers).

C. I take the ED number and go to the 1930 census catalog. I look at the reel descriptions for Cook County, Chicago City until I find ED 796. It is on Reel 451. (See Illustration 10.6.)

D. I take Reel 451 from the drawer and go to my assigned microfilm reader. First, I find the start of ED 796. Then, I look at the left margin of the page where the street name is listed. I look for 17th Street and then the house number, 1655. I may have to go through the whole ED before I find 1655 W. 17th Street—it depends on how the census taker walked the route. Homes that were missed on the initial canvass may be listed at the end of the ED.

E. I locate 1655 W. 17th Street and learn that Alex and Anna Kopicki are not living there! The house is occupied by two renters: the Bruno Orzechowski family and Bernard Herzynowski. (See Illustration 10.7.) The Kopickis evidently moved between the time of my documents and the census, which was taken in April. I will need to do more research to learn where they went.

Follow the same steps A through E for other census years. The exception is 1900, where you have to know the ward of the address before using the map. Ward maps are available at the Newberry Library and also online at www. alookatcook.com.

Find a Chicago Address Online

The Look at Cook Web site (see p. 194) provides very helpful ED maps and boundary descriptions for 1870 to 1930 (suburbs are descriptions only for 1910 to 1930). Using the site can be a great alternative to in-person research. To see why, open your Internet browser and follow my steps below:

1. Using the same example of 1655 W. 17th Street, I go to www.alookatcook.com and select 1930. Then I click on "1930 Chicago City Ward Map."

2. I find the general area and click on the ward number, 21. It takes me to a map of EDs in Ward 21. The map has street names as they existed then (for example, Lincoln Street, which is now Wood Street).

3. I know 1655 W. 17th Street is west of Ashland (1600 west) and east of Paulina (1700 west). So the ED is 796.

4. I return to the 1930 index page and click on "NARA Roll Numbers by Ward." I scroll to Ward 21. ED 796 is on Reel T626–451 (which has EDs 792–805 as the first ones listed). The prefix T626 identifies the 1930 census in NARA's system; you only need the last three digits for pulling the reel.

Find a Suburban Address Online

Currently there are not as many online resources for localities outside Chicago, and they generally pertain to 1930, 1920, and 1910. Follow along on your computer to learn how to use one of these resources for 1930.

1. I want to find 411 N. Elmwood Avenue in Oak Park. I go to the 1930 Census Microfilm Locator on the National Archives Web site, http://1930census.archives.gov/beginSearch.asp.

2. I select "Illinois" from the list of states on the left side of the page. I click "Continue" and go to a page where I can search by county, city, or place. I choose to search by county and select "Cook."

3. I go to "Refine Your City/County Results." I type "Oak Park" in the box and click on "Search Geographic Places."

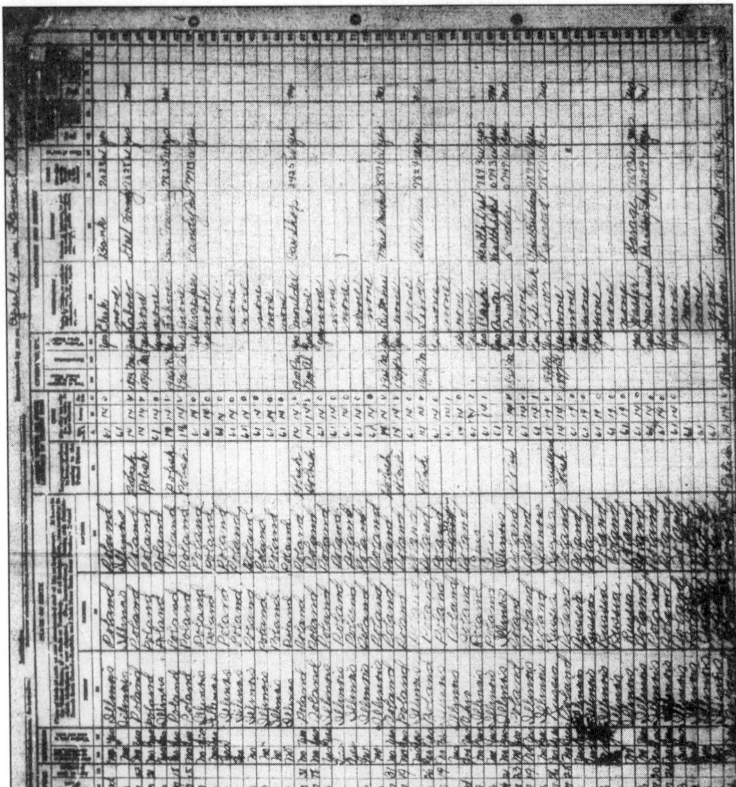

Illustration 10.7: The street name is written vertically in the left margin, next to the census line numbers. The house number is given in the first column after the street name. Source: 1930 U.S. Census, Reel 451, ED 796, Sheet 5B, Lines 86–93.

4. There are four microfilm rolls with 46 EDs for Oak Park. Only the boundaries of each ED are listed, not interior streets. I go to my current *Chicagoland Atlas* and see that ED 16–2259 is bounded by Chicago Avenue, Cuyler Avenue, South Boulevard, and East Avenue. It includes the 400 block of north Elmwood Avenue. It is on T626, Reel 504. The designation "T626" identifies the 1930 census in NARA's system. The prefix "16" was assigned by the Census Bureau to Cook County EDs.

5. Now I can go to a facility and pull Reel 504. First, I find the start of ED 2259. (The box label will tell me where this ED is in relation to others on the reel.) Then, I look at the left margin of the page where the street name is listed. I look for Elmwood Avenue and then the house number, 411. I may have to go through the whole ED before I find 411 N. Elmwood Avenue— it depends on how the census taker walked the route. Homes that were missed on the initial canvass may be listed at the end of the ED.

Where to Find the Census

Remember, you want to see the full census. Many of the indexes give you information, but they are abstracts and don't transcribe all the questions, for reasons of space.

You have several options for finding the census:

• View digitized images online at Ancestry.com or HeritageQuest Online (subscription Web sites), available at the Newberry Library, the Arlington Heights Memorial Library, the Elmhurst Public Library, and other libraries. These Web sites have all census years. While convenient, some digital scans can be poor quality, and you usually don't have the option of printing onto 11 x 17 inch paper as you do with microfilm printers.

• View microfilm available at many research facilities (see list that follows).

• Borrow microfilm to view for a fee at a Latter-day Saints Family History Center. See www.familysearch.org and click on

"Library" and then "Family History Centers" to find a location near you. Use the online catalog (www.familysearch.org/Eng/Library/FHLC/frameset_fhlc.asp) to find the film number. The Web site POINTers in Person (www.rootsweb.com/~itappcnc) also lists film numbers for the Illinois census.

• Rent microfilm through the National Archives or a participating library for a fee. For information, call NARA at 301/604–3699 or see www.archives.gov/publications/microfilm_catalogs/how_to_rent_microfilm.html.

Census Holdings at Major Research Facilities

Following is a list of the main Chicago and Midwest research facilities with microfilm holdings by year. Use this list in conjunction with the census index list, pp. 177–185, to determine the best place for you to spend your time. For instance, the Chicago Historical Society houses many years of the census but few indexes, so if your primary research goal is the census, you're better off at another place that has everything together.

• **1930:** Harold Washington Library Center, National Archives—Great Lakes, Newberry Library, Allen County Public Library (Fort Wayne, Indiana), Wisconsin Historical Society (Madison, Wisconsin).

• **1920:** Harold Washington Library Center, National Archives—Great Lakes, Newberry Library, Richard J. Daley Library at University of Illinois at Chicago, Allen County Public Library, Wisconsin Historical Society.

• **1910:** Arlington Heights Memorial Library, Harold Washington Library Center, National Archives—Great Lakes, Newberry Library, Richard J. Daley Library at University of Illinois at Chicago, Allen County Public Library, Wisconsin Historical Society.

• **1900:** Arlington Heights Memorial Library, Chicago Historical Society, Harold Washington Library Center, National Archives—Great Lakes, Newberry Library,

Richard J. Daley Library at University of Illinois at Chicago, Allen County Public Library, Wisconsin Historical Society.

• **1890:** Virtually destroyed in a 1921 fire at the Census Bureau in Washington, D.C. One microfilm reel of fragments was compiled, including a few Illinois counties but not Cook. National Archives—Great Lakes, Newberry Library, Allen County Public Library.

• **1880:** Chicago Historical Society, Harold Washington Library Center, National Archives—Great Lakes, Newberry Library, Richard J. Daley Library at University of Illinois at Chicago, Allen County Public Library, Wisconsin Historical Society.

• **1870:** Chicago Historical Society, Harold Washington Library Center, National Archives—Great Lakes, Newberry Library, Richard J. Daley Library at University of Illinois at Chicago, Allen County Public Library, Wisconsin Historical Society.

• **1860:** Chicago Historical Society, Harold Washington Library Center, National Archives—Great Lakes, Newberry Library, Richard J. Daley Library at University of Illinois at Chicago, Allen County Public Library, Wisconsin Historical Society.

• **1850:** Chicago Historical Society, Harold Washington Library Center, National Archives—Great Lakes, Newberry Library, Richard J. Daley Library at University of Illinois at Chicago, Allen County Public Library, Wisconsin Historical Society.

• **1840:** Chicago Historical Society, Harold Washington Library Center, National Archives—Great Lakes, Newberry Library, Richard J. Daley Library at University of Illinois at Chicago, Allen County Public Library, Wisconsin Historical Society.

Nuts and Bolts of the U.S. Census

Points to Remember

❑ *Some things to keep in mind for specific censuses:*

• **1930:** There is no Soundex index for Illinois.

• **1910:** The Miracode index gives you a slightly different set of numbers (volume number, ED number, and family number) to locate the census entry.

• **1900:** You'll need to know the ward in Chicago when searching by address.

• **1890:** Returns for Cook County no longer exist.

• **1880:** The Soundex index only covers households with children age ten and under.

• **1840:** Only head of household is named in the census.

❑ *"Front door" methods of finding your ancestor's entry:*

• Start with name indexes.

• Look at variations and possible misspellings of your ancestor's surname.

• Your ancestor may have Americanized his or her first name (for example, Henry or Hank for Hans or Mary for Marijona).

Nuts and Bolts of the U.S. Census

• Use other facts (such as birthplace, age, occupation, children's names, or spouse's name) to make a positive ID when the name is off.

❑ *"Back door" methods of finding your ancestor's entry:*

• Get an address as close to the census year as possible (from city directory, document, letter, and so on).

• Find a map, written description, or cross-index of the EDs.

• Locate the ED the street address falls within.

• Search through the ED until you find the address.

• Persons missed on the initial canvass may show up at the end of the ED.

11 Nuts and Bolts of Newspaper Searching

Historic newspapers can fill in details of your ancestor's lives and flesh out the times they lived in. Whether you read old papers for background or specifics, there are things you need to know to be successful.

Before You Start

Nowhere is the frustrating fact of big-city genealogical research more apparent than the category of newspapers. Chicago has long been known as a newspaperman's town for good reason. For most of the city's history there were *at least* four major dailies. That's not counting ethnic, neighborhood, and suburban papers.

Scores of titles are preserved in research facilities in the Chicago area. The bad news is that few of them are indexed. To find death notices when you have a death date is not so bad. But looking for an article about an event with only a range of years to go by—well, you'd better start to practice with a white cane now, because you'll go blind.

The first thing to do when trying to locate an item about your ancestor is to find out what newspapers existed at the time. Use the lists that follow as a starting point. Then check the Illinois Newspaper Project (www.library.uiuc.edu/inp) for other titles. The three places that have the most extensive collections of historic newspapers are the Chicago Historical Society, the Harold Washington Library Center, and the Abraham Lincoln Presidential Library (formerly the Illinois State Historical Library).

You need to check *all* possible papers to do a thorough search. Time and again I hear people say, "My ancestor didn't have an obituary," because they looked in one paper and couldn't find anything. Often families placed notices only in the paper that they and their friends and neighbors read. It could be a foreign-language newspaper, if they were immigrants. It could be their local paper rather than the city paper, if they lived in a suburb. It could be the morning edition, or the evening edition, or the weekly edition. You have to be open to all the possibilities.

See what indexes are available before firing up the microfilm reader. Save yourself the work if you can. Indexes, and obituary and other search services, are listed later in this chapter. If you have to scroll through reels of microfilm, at least you'll be entertained by the old ads and illustrations you'll encounter along the way. Happy hunting!

Selected Chicago Newspapers and Where to Find Them

These lists are indications of key holdings at the facilities with the most easily accessed historical titles in the area. The lists do not include every paper ever published in Chicago, so be sure to ask the librarians for other recommended titles in their collection that might be appropriate for your research (reflecting the time period, locations, or ethnic group of your subject).

Note: Check with the library for exact beginning and ending dates of publication and/or holdings. Also be careful to specify which era you are seeking, since several newspapers had similar names in different eras. Key to abbreviations:

CHS = Chicago Historical Society
HWLC = Harold Washington Library Center
NL = Newberry Library
UIC = University of Illinois at Chicago's Richard J. Daley Library
* = with gaps

Major English-Language Papers

This list is keyed primarily to the holdings of the Harold Washington Library Center, with citations at three other facilities offered as well. Be sure to verify with staff the actual holdings from a specific period. Do not assume that all the issues are there from a given period of years. There are often gaps anywhere in the run (indicated by an asterisk).

The holdings are arranged in chronological order, rather than alphabetical order by title, because that approach is most useful to genealogists searching through an era. The dates given in the "Years Held" column are the dates of holdings and do not always correspond with the beginning and ending dates of publication.

YEARS HELD	TITLE	FACILITY
1833–45*	Chicago Democrat	HWLC, CHS
1835–42*	Chicago American	HWLC CHS (1835–37*) NL (1839–42*)
1842–43*	Chicago Express	HWLC, NL CHS (1843*)
1844–1929	Chicago Daily Journal/ Evening Journal	HWLC CHS (1844–49*, 1855–61*, 1904–16*, 1921–29*) NL (1844–90*)
1849–present	Chicago Tribune	HWLC, UIC CHS (1860–72*, 1963–present) NL (1849–58*, 1860–84*, 1914–20*, 1928–64)
1852–57	Daily Democratic Press	HWLC, CHS
1855–82	Chicago Times	HWLC CHS (1855–65*, 1876–77*) NL (1855–60*, 1864–82*, 1884*)
1872–1914	Inter-Ocean	HWLC CHS (1872–94*, 1902–14) NL (daily edition 1880–86*, 1889–98*, 1902–14*)
1875–1978	Chicago Daily News (continued next page)	HWLC, UIC, CHS NL (1877*, 1878–1935; also

YEARS HELD	TITLE	FACILITY
1875–1978	Chicago Daily News (continued)	morning edition, various titles, 1881–82*, 1892–1901*)
1881–1914	Chicago Record-Herald	HWLC
1881–1918	Chicago Herald	HWLC CHS (1885–89*, 1893–95*, 1914–18*)
1882–1901	Chicago Times-Herald	HWLC CHS (1895–1901*)
1883–93	Chicago Daily Globe	HWLC
1885–95*	Chicago Mail/Evening Mail	HWLC, CHS
1890–1932*	Chicago Evening Post	HWLC, CHS NL (1871*, 1894*)
1898–1907	Chicago Chronicle	HWLC CHS (1895–1907*)
1901–39*	Chicago American	HWLC CHS (1912–14*)
1918–39	Chicago Herald-Examiner	HWLC CHS (1918–21*)
1929–48	Chicago Daily Times	HWLC UIC (1929–47)
1939–53	Chicago Herald-American	HWLC CHS (1939–49*)
1941–48	Chicago Sun	HWLC, CHS, UIC NL (1941*)
1948–present	Chicago Sun-Times	HWLC, CHS, UIC
1953–62	Chicago American	HWLC UIC (1950–62) CHS (1959*)
1962–69	Chicago's American (continued next page)	HWLC UIC (1962–68)

YEARS HELD	TITLE	FACILITY
1962–69	Chicago's American (continued)	CHS (1963*, 1968*)
1969–74	Chicago Today	HWLC, UIC CHS (1969*)

Ethnic Newspapers

African-American

1909–present	Chicago Defender: HWLC (city and weekend editions), UIC (Saturday edition 1909–65, daily edition 1966–present)	
1943–47	Chicago Bee: UIC	

German

1862–76*	Chicago Sonntags-Zeitung: NL
1889–1918	Abendpost/Sonntag Post: HWLC
1896–98*	Abend-Presse: NL

Italian

1886–89*	Italia: CHS
1901–18*	

Jewish

1879–87*	Occident: CHS
1896*	

Polish

1890–1971	Dziennik Chicagoski: Library of the Polish Museum of America

Scandinavian

1882 (1 issue)	Svenska Arbetaren (Swedish): CHS
1883–84*	
1891–93*	Norden (Norwegian): CHS

Neighborhood Newspapers

1882 (1 issue)	*Hyde Park Herald:* CHS
1884–89*	
1918–34	
1936–85	
1987–present	
1903–04*	*Daily Calumet:* CHS
1906–15*	
1917*	
1919–37*	
1905–10	*Englewood Times:* CHS
1912–22	
1905–06	*Ravenswood Citizen:* HWLC
1910–13	
1920	
1924–26	*Southtown Economist:* HWLC
1931–58	
1960–63	
1975–87	
1930–43	*Uptown News & The Northside Citizen:* HWLC
1932–51*	*Auburn Parker:* CHS
1932–59*	*Woodlawn Booster:* CHS
1935–66*	*Garfieldian:* CHS
1974–76*	*Lawndale News:* CHS
1987–88*	
1990–91*	

Indexes to Chicago Newspapers

Looking at the list that follows, you can see how the early years and the more recent years have been indexed, but there remains a huge gap between the 1850s and 1970s.

The *Chicago Tribune Historical Archive* helps fill that gaping hole. It is a selective full-text database, consisting of three sections:

• 2.5 million obituaries and death notices from 1860 to 1984

• Nearly 3 million clippings from the *Tribune's morgue* (in-house reference file), from the 1920s to 1984.

• More than 16,000 front pages from the early 1900s to 1984.

The *Historical Archive* is available from NewsBank (www.newsbank.com), a subscription Web site that you can use at the Chicago Historical Society and many public libraries. You can search by name and era, and your hits come up as full-text articles or transcriptions you can print out.

ProQuest Information and Learning Company is building a complete full-text digital version of the *Chicago Tribune*. Issues from 1890 to 1946 are now part of the electronic subscription *ProQuest Historical Newspapers* (available at the Newberry Library, Arlington Heights Memorial Library, Skokie Public Library, and other libraries). The company plans to complete the issues from 1849 to 1889 and 1947 to 1984 by 2006. ProQuest's *Tribune* includes all the ads, illustrations, and photos in each issue (unlike NewsBank's product), all fully searchable by keyword or article type. You can display full page images and browse them as you would a printed newspaper.

With these two innovations from ProQuest and NewsBank, you can look up ancestors without having to get the death date! Once you get the date from the death notice, you can easily proceed to other newspapers. You can also see what the headlines were on the date your ancestor was born or married.

General Indexes

1833–46	Various newspapers in the book *Vital Records from Chicago Newspapers 1833–46*, published by Chicago Genealogical Society, 1971: NL, CHS, HWLC, and others
May 1835–October 1842	*Chicago American:* CHS
1840–55 and 1857–61	*Chicago Democrat:* CHS
1844–45 and 1847–52	*Chicago Daily Journal:* CHS
1855	*Chicago Democratic Press:* CHS
1860–1984	*Chicago Tribune: Chicago Tribune Historical Archive* online (www.newsbank.com) at CHS, Des Plaines Public Library, Evanston Public Library, and many others
1904–12	*Chicago Record-Herald:* CHS
1972–present	*Chicago Tribune:* Bell & Howell's printed index at many libraries
1976–present	*Chicago Sun-Times:* Bell & Howell's printed index at many libraries
1985–present: full text	*Chicago Tribune:* www.chicagotribune.com/ archives and ProQuest *Chicago Tribune* database online with Chicago Public Library card at http://piscator2.chipublib.org/ ChicagoAuth.asp
	Chicago Sun-Times: ProQuest Illinois Newsstand database online with Chicago Public Library card at http://piscator2.chipublib.org/ ChicagoAuth.asp

Obituary Indexes

1988–97	*Chicago Tribune:* Ancestry.com (subscription Web site) at many libraries
1988–95	*Chicago Sun-Times:* Ancestry.com (subscription Web site) at many libraries

Selected Suburban
Cook County Newspapers

Almost every community has had at least one newspaper cover the comings and goings of its citizens. To conserve space, only a few are listed here. Use the Illinois Newspaper Project to locate titles covering Cook County towns, and then check with libraries and historical societies in those locations. The Harold Washington Library Center holds many suburban titles in the Lerner Newspapers group on microfilm dating from the 1920s to the 1990s. See the "Lerner Newspapers" chronology online at www. chipublib.org/008subject/005genref/gislrnr.html.

* = with gaps

Evanston
1872–1914	*Evanston Index:* Evanston Public Library
1925–present	*Evanston Review:* Evanston Public Library

Oak Park
1887–present	Various titles: Oak Park Public Library (indexed 1887–present)

Skokie
1943–present*	Various titles: Skokie Public Library (obituary index 1963–present online at www.skokie.lib.il.us/ Abstracts/SPLSearchObits.asp)

Winnetka
1917–present	*Winnetka Talk:* Winnetka Public Library (obituary index 1917–present)

Obituary and Other Search Services

The Abraham Lincoln Presidential Library will search for articles on an occurrence if you provide the full name(s), exact date (day, month, and year), and city and county of the occurrence. There is a small fee for Illinois residents and a larger fee for non-Illinois residents. Further information on the library's search policy can be found online or if you call.

Send your paid request with a SASE to:

Abraham Lincoln Presidential Library
112 N. Sixth Street
Springfield, IL 62701-1310
217/524-7216
www.state.il.us/hpa/lib

The library also makes its microfilm newspaper collection of 4,900 Illinois titles available on interlibrary loan to patrons in the continental United States. Contact your local public library to arrange loans; there may be a small fee.

The Newberry Library offers fee-based death notice or obituary searches of its *Chicago Daily News* and *Chicago Tribune* holdings (which are not complete runs). Details and forms are at the genealogy section of the Newberry Web site, www.newberry.org, or call the Local and Family History reference desk (312/255-3512) and ask for forms to be sent. You can also place a phone order with a credit card.

Most historical and genealogical societies will look for obituaries or articles for a fee. They usually have lower prices for members. You can find societies through the Internet (see Chapter 15, "Top Web Sites for Chicago-Area Research") or by picking up literature at places like the Newberry and the National Archives—Great Lakes.

Two fee-based sources for ethnic obituaries are the Polish Genealogical Society of America and the Balzekas Museum of Lithuanian Culture. Their contact information is in Chapter 16, "Ethnic Resources." John Corrigan offers a fee-based search for Irish obituaries. His index includes 16,000+ names, and more continue to be added. He has nearly completed an index of the Irish weekly *The Chicago Citizen* for its entire run (1882–1928). There are two gaps in publication, one for the early 1880s and one for some of the World War I years. Send him a SASE or an e-mail. Contact:

John Corrigan
P.O. Box 428151
Evergreen Park, IL 60805
jc4321@sbcglobal.net

Nuts and Bolts
of Newspaper Searching

Points to Remember

❑ *Helpful hints for searching newspapers:*

• Search on your ancestor's name in NewsBank's *Chicago Tribune Historical Archive* or ProQuest's searchable *Chicago Tribune*.

• If you have a hit, look in other papers on and near that date for further coverage.

• Use the Illinois Newspaper Project (www. library.uiuc.edu/inp) to locate suburban titles.

• Think of the circles to which your ancestor belonged, and search for publications serving those circles, for instance:
  —community or neighborhood newspaper
  —trade, professional, or employee journal
  —fraternal publication
  —veterans' publication

• Use indexes and search services whenever possible. Inquire at historical societies and libraries.

• Ask librarians about publications covering a time period, location, or group of interest.

12   Nuts and Bolts of Birth and Death Records

This chapter goes into detail about obtaining two crucial kinds of vital records created by Cook County—those pertaining to births and deaths. You'll learn about the available indexes and the years each covers. Then you'll find information on the government agencies and research facilities that hold the records and what their policies are. For discussions on non-governmental records, such as baptismal and burial registers kept by churches, see Chapter 2 ("When (and Where) Was My Ancestor Born?") and Chapter 8 ("When Did My Ancestor Die and Where Is My Ancestor Buried?").

Birth Records

One key date to keep in mind when searching for government records is 1916. That is the year the state of Illinois made vital records registration mandatory. Prior to 1916, with the prevalence of home births, registration was often lax. Even after 1916, there were lapses.

Another date to remember is 1871, the year of the Chicago Fire. When the Cook County Courthouse burned, all county vital records prior to that time went up in flames.

The circumstances of 1871 and 1916 mean there may not be a birth record for your ancestor created at the time of the birth. The next section explains methods of finding later records and alternative records.

Indexes to Birth Records

Start your search in an index. It's much easier to find someone in an index than scrolling through reels and reels of microfilm. It saves money, too, if you're ordering a certificate from the Cook County Bureau of Vital Statistics and can provide the certificate or register number. Check general indexes first, then ones for delayed filing and corrected filings.

General Indexes
The *Cook County Birth Index 1871–1916* is on microfiche and is available at the Newberry Library, the Illinois Regional Archives Depository in Chicago, and the Family History Center in Wilmette. The Newberry Library will search this index for a small fee.

There are a couple quirks with this index. An ID number beginning with the letters A to E refers to a birth register. An ampersand ("&") in the INT (middle initial) column means the baby was not named at the time of registration and is indexed by a combination of the father's first initial and the mother's first name. It's also a signal that you should look for a corrected birth certificate.

For years after 1916, try the listings of elementary school graduates in the Chicago Public Schools. The *Board of Education Proceedings* gives birth dates starting in the 1933–34 school year and continuing through the 1971–72 school year. The dates begin about where the *Cook County Birth Index 1871–1916* leaves off and continue to about 1958. In each *Proceedings* book, there are two sections of graduates: one in June, toward the back of the book, and one in January or February, toward the front. Names are alphabetized within an alphabetical listing of schools, so you'll have to scan the columns. The Harold Washington Library Center holds the 1933–34 to 1971–72 volumes. The Richard J. Daley Library at the University of Illinois at Chicago has 1960–61 to 1971–72. For an example of graduates' birth dates, see Chapter 2, "When (and Where) Was My Ancestor Born?".

If your ancestor is listed in the *Social Security Death Index*, the exact birth date is often given. See the section "Indexes to Death Records" later in this chapter.

Indexes to Delayed Filings

Many people discovered they had no birth certificate on file when they needed to get a copy for work or school or for pension benefits. Home births tended to be overlooked prior to 1916, and even into the 1920s and 1930s, midwives and physicians could fail to file certificates. Therefore a delayed birth certificate had to be created, with the facts attested to by a parent, the physician, or someone else who had knowledge of the birth.

A few of the delayed birth certificates are indexed in the *Cook County Birth Index 1871–1916*. The majority are on seven reels of microfilm that make up *Chicago Delayed Birth Indexes, 1871–1948*. Entries look like this:

| Silverman, David | 3/15/1891 | #78351 | 6/12/1941 |
| (name) | (birthdate) | (cert. no.) | (file date) |

Names are not in strict alphabetical order—I found Silvermans interspersed with Silvers and Silversteins. In the Chicago area, the Family History Center in Wilmette holds this index. The films are also available on loan through Family History Centers and the Newberry Library for a fee. Check the Family History Library catalog for film numbers (online at www.familysearch.org, or on microfiche or CD at Family History Centers). For an example of a delayed filing, see Chapter 3 ("Who Were the Parents of My Ancestor?").

Indexes to Corrected Filings

Mistakes in spelling, omitted information, or no first name are all reasons for filing a corrected (also called amended) birth certificate. Corrected names are usually but not always indexed in the *Cook County Birth Index 1871–1916*, and other types of corrections rarely show up in that index. Try looking in *Chicago, Illinois Birth Corrections and Indexes, 1871–1915*, on microfilm at the Family History Library. There are five reels of indexes. What makes them tricky is that the original name, not the corrected name, is usually what is indexed. There are six additional reels of corrections, which lack indexes. A later series of corrections, covering 1916 to 1918, has no indexes either. For film numbers, check the Family History Library catalog at www.familysearch. org and do a place search for "Illinois, Cook, Chicago—Vital Records Indexes." The catalog is also on microfiche and CDs at Family History Centers. The films are available on loan through Family History Centers and the Newberry Library for a fee. For an example of a corrected filing, see Chapter 3.

Sources for Birth Certificates

I've listed government agencies and research facilities according to the chronological order of their holdings. That way it's easy to see who to contact for a particular year.

Cook County Bureau of Vital Statistics
Years: 1871–Present

Genealogy copies of birth certificates are limited to those that are 75 years or older, per the Illinois Vital Records Act. To obtain a copy of a more recent certificate, you have to prove you are a close relation.

Unlike smaller counties, you are not able to conduct a search yourself—instead, the staff does it for you. It is rare that you can get a genealogy request the same day. Most have to be retrieved from the warehouse, and that can take several weeks. In-person payment is cash only.

One fee is charged if the certificate number is provided, while a higher fee applies if the certificate number is not given. There is a fee for each additional copy ordered. Request forms are available at the bureau, its Web site, suburban locations, and the Newberry Library Local and Family History reference desk. Some Chicago-area currency exchanges also offer vital record services for an additional fee.

You can order online or by phone with a credit card through VitalChek, which provides these services to the bureau. It is the most expensive way to obtain certificates—and the fastest. The documents are pulled by Vital Statistics employees. Additional fees apply for shipping and handling.

Genealogical orders are sent by regular mail; no expedited delivery is available. Contact:

Cook County Clerk
Bureau of Vital Statistics
Attn.: Genealogy
P.O. Box 642570
Chicago, IL 60664-2570
312/603-7790
fax: 312/603-4899
www.cookctyclerk.com/sub/vital_records.asp
312/603-7799 (accepts credit card orders)
www.vitalchek.com (for online orders)

Main office location:
Cook County Building
118 N. Clark Street
(Randolph Street entrance, lower concourse level)
Chicago, IL 60602

Suburban locations:
Bridgeview Courthouse
10220 S. 76th Avenue, Room 238
Bridgeview, IL 60455
708/974-6150

Markham Courthouse
16501 S. Kedzie, Room 238
Markham, IL 60428
708/210-4150

Suburban locations (cont.):
Maywood Courthouse
1311 Maybrook Square, Room 109
Maywood, IL 60153
708/865-6010

Rolling Meadows Courthouse
2121 Euclid Avenue, Room 238
Rolling Meadows, IL 60008
847/818-2850

Skokie Courthouse
5600 W. Old Orchard Road, Room 149
Skokie, IL 60077
847/470-7233

Illinois Regional Archives Depository (IRAD) at Northeastern Illinois University

Years: 1871–1915

The records at this facility are birth registers, which contain the same information as birth certificates: mother's maiden name, father's occupation, and so on.

You may print copies yourself for a photocopying fee. You can also use IRAD's reference service by mail; there is a limit of two requests at a time. Searches are free, and there is a nominal charge for copies. Contact:

Illinois Regional Archives Depository
Ronald Williams Library
Northeastern Illinois University
5500 N. St. Louis Avenue
Chicago, IL 60625-4699
773/442-4506
www.sos.state.il.us/departments/archives/irad/iradhome.html

Family History Library
Birth Certificates and Birth Registers:
Years: 1871–1922 (Chicago)
1878–94 and 1916–22 (suburban Cook County)

Hospital Birth Records:
Years: 1896–1933 (Chicago)

Birth Corrections:
Years: 1871–1918 (Chicago)

Delayed Births:
Years: 1871–1918 (Chicago)

If your ancestor's record falls within the years that the Church of Jesus Christ of Latter-day Saints have microfilmed, their resources are the best way to go. The cost is less than you'll pay through the Cook County Bureau of Vital Statistics or the Illinois Department of Public Health, and you can conduct searches yourself rather than wonder if a clerk did a good job.

A Word About Hospital Birth Records

I didn't discuss this category under indexes because none exist. You'll have to search by year. The Church of Jesus Christ of Latter-day Saints has microfilmed case records and birth records from 1896 to 1933 for a number of facilities that served the immigrant population of Chicago. You may have good luck if your ancestor's family lived near the Maxwell Street Dispensary, the Stockyards Clinic, the Newberry Clinic, the Chicago Lying-in Hospital, or the Chicago Maternity Center. Frequently the hospital record was the only record made of the birth. There are three reels of birth records and 11 reels of "applications to hospital," which include some birth records. The originals are at the archives of Northwestern Memorial Hospital.

You can borrow the microfilm for hospital birth records and the other categories listed earlier from the Family History Library at Family History Centers affiliated with the church and at certain libraries, such as the Newberry Library. You'll pay a small loan fee and be able to view the film at the facility for about a month. Two renewals of 60 days each are possible. Photocopying charges vary with the facility. For film numbers, consult the Family History Library catalog at www.familysearch. org and do a place search for "Illinois, Cook, Chicago—Vital Records" or "Illinois, Cook—Vital Records." The catalog is also available on microfiche and CD at Family History Centers. There are ten Family History Centers in the Greater Chicago area; you can find locations of these and others on the church's genealogy Web site. The Wilmette, Illinois, location has many Cook County vital records on permanent loan. You can search and print without having to wait for material to be sent from Salt Lake City. See fuller description in Chapter 14, "What to Expect at Chicago-Area Research Facilities." Contact:

Family History Library
35 North West Temple Street
Salt Lake City, UT 84150-3400
801/240-2331
www.familysearch.org

Family History Center
2727 Lake Avenue
Wilmette, IL 60091 (no mail inquiries because of limited staff)
847/251-9818

Illinois Department of Public Health
Years: 1916–Present

Genealogical copies are limited to those that are 75 years or older, per the Illinois Vital Records Act. But if you can prove that the person is deceased, you can obtain his or her birth record (only for records after 1916). You need to fill out a special application form to do this. Request it at the address below, or send an e-mail to vitalrecords@idph.state.il.us. Copies of your application and the record you request are sent to the Illinois Department of Public Aid to ensure you are not attempting to file for welfare benefits.

Birth certificates for living people younger than 75 years old (born 1931 or later at the time of this book's publication in 2005) are open only to the person on the certificate, his or her parents, or his or her legal guardian.

There is a higher fee for a copy of the original birth certificate and a lower fee for a computer abstract. Don't get the abstract—you want to see the original with all the information on it, including the parents' names. The only things you get on the abstract are name, birth date, birthplace, and state file number. Fees apply for each additional copy. Order forms are available by mail or at the IDPH Web site. Contact:

Illinois Department of Public Health
Division of Vital Records
605 W. Jefferson Street
Springfield, IL 62702-5097
217/782-6553 (automated information)
fax: 217/523-2648 (accepts credit card orders)
www.idph.state.il.us/vitalrecords/index.htm
online ordering: through VitalChek at www.vitalchek.com

Death Records

It's been my experience that death registration was better kept than birth registration prior to 1916, when the state of Illinois started enforcing vital records registration. Still, you may have ancestors who don't show up in an index of death certificates. Sometimes they can be in the *Cook County Coroner's Inquest Record Index, 1872–1911* at the Illinois Regional Archives Depository. Other indexes to try are discussed in the section below.

Indexes to Death Records

To locate your ancestor's death certificate, first look at an index to get the death date. The three major ones are *Cook County Death Index 1871–1916, Illinois Death Index 1916–1950*, and the *Social Security Death Index* (covers deaths 1937 to the present).

The *Cook County Death Index 1871–1916* is available on microfiche at the Newberry Library and the Illinois Regional Archives Depository in Chicago. It can also be obtained on loan for a fee from Family History Centers affiliated with the Church of Jesus Christ of Latter-day Saints. The Newberry Library will search this index for a small fee. The index is also partially online as part of the *Pre-1916 Illinois Death Index* compiled by the Illinois State Archives (www.sos.state.il.us/departments/archives/death.html). It should be completely online by early 2005.

The *Illinois Death Index 1916–1950* was compiled by the Illinois State Archives. The most complete version is on its Web site, www.sos.state.il.us/departments/archives/idphdeathindex.html. The goal is to list all deaths 50 years old, so they are not quite current yet. A microfiche version with deaths up to 1947 is available at the Newberry Library and IRAD.

The *Social Security Death Index* is available at several Web sites (RootsWeb.com and Ancestry.com are my favorites) and is also on CD at Family History Centers. Though this index covers much of the U.S. population, people who did not pay into the Social Security system will not be listed. These include housewives, self-employed individuals, and, until recently, government workers. The CD version allows for browsing (helpful in catching typos) and reports overseas deaths, two things the Web versions do not have, according to Kathleen Hinckley in her 1999 book *Locating Lost Family Members & Friends*.

Another index is *Sam Fink's Index*, compiled from Chicago newspaper death notices covering 1833 to 1889 (the bulk of the notices are from 1856 to 1874) and Cook County death records from 1878 to 1884. Coverage is therefore spotty. It is available on microfilm at the Newberry Library and on loan for a fee through Family History Centers.

The Church of Jesus Christ of Latter-day Saints has microfilmed a WPA index done in the 1930s, *Chicago Deaths 1871–1933*. It is often called the out-of-town index because it includes some residents of Chicago who died while away

NAME	ADDRESS		DATE OF DEATH MO. - DAY - YEAR			REGISTER NUMBER	
KAASBOELL ADOLPH 16 FAY		K	12	2	83	270	17
KAASHEINSKY CLARA 226 CLEAVER		F	7	19	78	344	40
KAAT ANNIE M 348 W CHICAGO		L	7	16	84	180	26
KAATZ ANNA 601 CENTRE		C	12	10	74	296	33
KAATZ ANNA 1054 N KEDZIE			5	15	29	15194	22
KAATZ AUGUST 52 FRY		P1	3	21	99	235	41
KAATZ DOROTHEA 3236 EMERALD		J	11	6	62	211	8
KAATZ EDWARD 258 WASHINGTON BLVD			2	7	27	3983	20
KAATZ FANNIE 34 GILPIN PL		H1	3	2	95	238	40
KAATZ FLORENCE 4254 N SAWYER			12	18	27	34040	20
KAATZ HOWARD 1951 S SAWYER			2	23	28	4858	15
KAATZ JOHN 84 EMERALD		B	10	29	72	86	3
KAATZ JOHN 1422 CORNELIA			9	12	12	31801	5
KAATZ MARCELLA 4254 N SAWYER			2	13	18	4247	11
KAATZ MARCUS 66 E 56			6	16	20	19906	13
KAATZ MAX 570 S HALSTED		4	6	29	06	241	1
KAATZ REGINA DUNNING ILL		O-T	1	27	24	266	16
KAATZ RUDOLPH SPOKANE WASH		OT	11	21	30	3843	22
KAATZ SARAH 66 E 56			2	9	24	3709	17
KAATZ WILHELMINE 4830 LAFLIN		D1	3	11	93	235	31
KAATZMEN SAM AUGUSTANA HOSP			9	24	08	22763	1
KAAUTZ FRITZ 4440 WENTWORTH		TL	7	27	82	18	16
KAAVIATKOWSKI ANNA DUNNING ILL		OT	6	11	19	1398	11
KABANCZYK MARY 4342 S WESTERN			2	28	33	5905	26
KABA FEMALE 242 TELL CT		SB	3	29	12	584	4
KABACHAK ALICE 757 W CONGRESS			1	31	17	3660	10
KABACINSKA MARYANNA 8736 MARQUETTE			2	7	16	4269	9
KABACINSKI ANNABELLE 2042 W SUPERIOR			7	23	22	20290	15
KABACINSKI IGNATZ 2042 W SUPERIOR			5	31	14	16479	7
KABACINSKI INFANT 2518 SOUTHPORT			3	24	29	9644	22
KABACINSKI MARY 2847 KILBOURN			12	9	28	35656	21
KABACINSKI MICHAEL 128 CORNELL		M	2	23	85	51	4

Illustration 12.1: Excerpt from Chicago Deaths 1871–1933. Rudolph Kaatz died in Spokane, Washington (top arrow). You would contact the courthouse in Spokane County, Washington, for Rudolph's death certificate. Death certificates are filed at the place the death occurred. The abbreviation "OT" = out of town.

The abbreviation "SB" = stillbirth. An example is Kaba, female, stillborn March 29, 1912 (middle arrow). Compare the listing for Kabacinski, infant, died March 24, 1929 (bottom arrow). Even if the child lives only for a few minutes, Illinois law considers it a live birth.

Other abbreviations used in the index are "HP" = Hyde Park, "LV" = Lake View, and "TL" = Town of Lake (the town, more properly township, of Lake stretched from State Street to approximately 7200 west and from 39th Street to 87th Street), signifying deaths that took place when these communities were independent of Chicago. Source: Family History Library film #1295948, deaths K–Lap.

on vacation or business and were shipped back to the city for burial. It also includes some stillbirths. This is a good one to check if you know your ancestor lived in the vicinity and is not showing up in the Cook County or Illinois indexes.

Another tip: I have had good success locating Chicago and Cook County residents in the *California Death Index 1940–1997*. California is a popular retirement destination. The index is available on RootsWeb.com at http://vitals.rootsweb.com/ca/death/search.cgi.

Sources for Death Certificates

As with the section "Sources for Birth Certificates," the places that follow appear according to the chronological order of their holdings. You can go down the list and spot the ones that have the year you need.

Cook County Bureau of Vital Statistics
Years: 1871–Present

More recent death certificates, those issued 20 years or less before the date of your request, are considered confidential under the Illinois Vital Records Act. You must prove you are a family member or are the executor of the estate to access them.

Tip: One way to obtain a death certificate number is to contact the cemetery and get the burial permit number, which is usually numbered the same as the certificate. This only works if you have knowledge of where your ancestor is buried.

The procedure for obtaining death certificates is the same as for birth certificates. You cannot conduct a search yourself; the staff must do it for you. Rarely can you get a genealogy request the same day. Most have to be retrieved from the warehouse. Be prepared for a wait of several weeks. In-person payment is cash only.

One fee is charged if the certificate number is provided, while a higher fee applies if the certificate number is not given. There is a fee for each additional copy ordered. Request forms are available at the bureau, its Web site, suburban locations, and the Newberry Library Local and Family History reference desk. Some Chicago-area currency exchanges also offer vital record services for an additional fee.

You can order online or by phone with a credit card through VitalChek, which provides these services to the bureau. It is the most expensive way to obtain certificates—and the fastest. The documents are pulled by Vital Statistics employees. Additional fees apply for shipping and handling. Genealogical orders are sent by regular mail; no expedited delivery is available. Contact:

Cook County Clerk
Bureau of Vital Statistics
Attn.: Genealogy
P.O. Box 642570
Chicago, IL 60664-2570
312/603-7790
fax: 312/603-4899
www.cookctyclerk.com/sub/vital_records.asp
312/603-7799 (accepts credit card orders)
www.vitalchek.com (for online orders)

Main office location:
Cook County Building
118 N. Clark Street
(Randolph Street entrance, lower concourse level)
Chicago, IL 60602

Suburban locations:
Bridgeview Courthouse
10220 S. 76th Avenue, Room 238
Bridgeview, IL 60455
708/974-6150

Markham Courthouse
16501 S. Kedzie, Room 238
Markham, IL 60428
708/210-4150

Suburban locations (cont.):
Maywood Courthouse
1311 Maybrook Square, Room 109
Maywood, IL 60153
708/865-6010

Rolling Meadows Courthouse
2121 Euclid Avenue, Room 238
Rolling Meadows, IL 60008
847/818-2850

Skokie Courthouse
5600 W. Old Orchard Road, Room 149
Skokie, IL 60077
847/470-7233

Illinois Regional Archives Depository (IRAD) at Northeastern Illinois University
Years: 1878–1909 (Cook County suburbs only—no Chicago records)
You may print copies yourself for a photocopying fee. You can also use IRAD's reference service by mail; there is a limit of two requests at a time. Searches are free, and there is a nominal charge for copies. Contact:

Illinois Regional Archives Depository
Ronald Williams Library
Northeastern Illinois University
5500 N. St. Louis Avenue
Chicago, IL 60625-4699
773/442-4506
www.sos.state.il.us/departments/archives/irad/iradhome.html

Family History Library
Years: 1878–1947 (Chicago)
1878–1909 and 1916–22 (Cook County suburbs)
The famed genealogical library in Salt Lake City, Utah, makes its microfilm holdings available on loan to Family History

Centers affiliated with the Church of Jesus Christ of Latter-day Saints and to certain libraries, such as the Newberry Library. You'll pay a small loan fee and be able to view the film for about a month. Two renewals of 60 days each are possible. Photocopying charges vary with the facility. For film numbers, consult the Family History Library catalog at www.familysearch. org and do a place search for "Illinois, Cook, Chicago—Vital Records" or "Illinois, Cook—Vital Records." The catalog is also available on microfiche and CD at Family History Centers. There are ten Family History Centers in the Greater Chicago area; you can find locations of these and others on the church's genealogy Web site. The Wilmette, Illinois, location holds a good selection of Cook County vital records. You can walk in and use them without waiting for material to be sent from Salt Lake City. See fuller description in Chapter 14 ("What to Expect at Chicago-Area Research Facilities"). Contact:

> Family History Library
> 35 North West Temple Street
> Salt Lake City, UT 84150-3400
> 801/240-2331
> www.familysearch.org
>
> Family History Center
> 2727 Lake Avenue
> Wilmette, IL 60091
> (no mail inquiries because of limited staff)
> 847/251-9818.

Illinois State Archives
Years: 1916–47
     These years are only available in person from the Illinois State Archives. Because of excessive demand and limited staff, mail request service was discontinued as of November 15, 2002. Genealogist Mary Lou Johnsrud lives near the archives and will obtain death certificates for a small fee by mail. Her request forms are available at the Newberry Library Local and

Family History reference desk, or contact:

Mary Lou Johnsrud
127 N. State Street
Springfield, IL 62702
genehelper@juno.com

Archives contact information:
Illinois State Archives
Reference Unit
Margaret Cross Norton Building
Capitol Complex
Springfield, IL 62756
217/782-3556
fax: 217/524-3930
www.sos.state.il.us/departments/archives/services.html

Illinois Department of Public Health
Years: 1916–Present
Access to death records for third parties is limited to deaths that occurred 20 years prior to the current year. If you do not know the date of death, the department can search indexes for a fee. If the record is found and is more than 20 years old, you'll get one copy without an additional charge.

There is a higher fee for a certified copy of a death certificate. Lower fees are charged for genealogical copies of death certificates more than 20 years old. Fees apply for each additional copy. Order forms are available by mail or at the IDPH Web site. Contact:

Illinois Department of Public Health
Division of Vital Records
605 W. Jefferson Street
Springfield, IL 62702-5097
217/782-6553 (automated information)
fax: 217/523-2648 (accepts credit card orders)
www.idph.state.il.us/vitalrecords/index.htm
online ordering: through VitalChek at
www.vitalchek.com

Nuts and Bolts of Birth and Death Records

Points to Remember

❏ *Confidentiality rules for third-party requests:*

• Birth records: 75 years or older from current date

• Death records: 20 years or older from current date

❏ *Who has what for birth records (all of Cook County unless otherwise noted):*

• Cook County Bureau of Vital Statistics
1871–present

• Ilinois Regional Archives Depository at Northeastern Illinois University
1871–1915

• Family History Library
1871–1922 (Chicago)
1878–94 and 1916–22
(suburban Cook County)
1896–1933
(Chicago hospital birth records)
1871–1918 (Chicago birth corrections)
1871–1918 (Chicago delayed births)

• Illinois Department of Public Health
1916–present

(Continued next page)

Nuts and Bolts of Birth and Death Records

❑ *Who has what for death records (all of Cook County unless otherwise noted):*

- Cook County Bureau of Vital Statistics
  1871–present

- Illinois Regional Archives Depository at Northeastern Illinois University
  1878–1909 (Cook County suburbs only)

- Family History Library
  1878–1947 (Chicago)
  1878–1909 and 1916–22
  (Cook County suburbs)

- Illinois State Archives
  1916–47

- Illinois Department of Public Health
  1916–present

13   How to Use Machines and Catalogs

In your quest for ancestors, you'll be using some of the same skills you used back in school. Two basic skills are knowing how to use microfilm and microfiche machines, and how to use library catalogs.

Microfilm and Microfiche Machines

Not everything is on the Internet. Many genealogical materials are on microfilm or microfiche (*microform* is the library term that refers to both types).

Microfilm comes in narrow or wide reels housed in boxes (narrow is 16mm, wide is 35mm). You'll be using it most often for newspapers, censuses, telephone directories, city directories, church records, and passenger lists.

Microfiche are flat cards about the size of large index cards, housed in open envelopes. You'll encounter them for indexes, directories, catalogs, family histories, and other books. Their thinness means they take up less space than reels of microfilm holding an equivalent amount of information.

You'll use special machines to read and make copies of microfilm and microfiche. Each facility has different machines. I'm going to discuss the most common. If you're not sure how to use a particular machine, the staff will be happy to show you—they know the quirks of the equipment. Note: Maintenance is often the first item slashed in budget cuts. Consider making a donation to a "friends of the library" group if you are frequently frustrated by out-of-order signs.

Each place you go has different policies on machine use. You may need to sign up or make a reservation. Paying for copies may be via coins or copy cards or at a central desk. Don't be shy about calling in advance or telling staff that this is your first visit and finding out what you need to know. Be courteous to fellow researchers and vacate your spot when your time slot is finished or when a staffer asks you to do so.

Microfilm Reader (Overhead Viewer)

This type of microfilm reader (see Illustration 13.1) projects the image from overhead onto a white reading surface. The angle may be bothersome if you wear bifocals; switching to a straight-ahead viewer can help. Some machines have button controls to advance and rewind the film; others use hand cranks (but I've never seen them for left-handed users).

How to Load Film in an Overhead Viewer Microfilm Reader

1. Turn the power switch on so the light comes on and you can see what you're doing.

2. Position your reel so the end of the film is coming from the bottom of the reel. Fit the diamond-shaped hole onto the spindle and push it firmly until it seats—you'll hear a click. If the film isn't on firmly, it'll slide off the spindle and you'll have a big mess rolling it up again. (Sometimes reels with round holes won't fit onto diamond-shaped spindles. Ask the staff for a machine that accepts round-hole reels.)

3. Take the end of the film and thread it over the roller, under the glass, over the second roller, and into the take-up reel (see Illustration 13.2). The film must be between the two pieces of glass to focus correctly. You can either use the button to open the glass (it should close when you advance the film) or lift it with a finger. It doesn't matter which way the film comes into the take-up reel, because when you fast-forward to get the film started, the machine will wind it correctly.

4. Fast-forward through the *leader* (blank length of film) until you are at the beginning of the material. Use the carrier handle if necessary to rotate the film so you're

Illustration 13.1: Microfilm reader (overhead viewer type). Photo by Grace DuMelle.

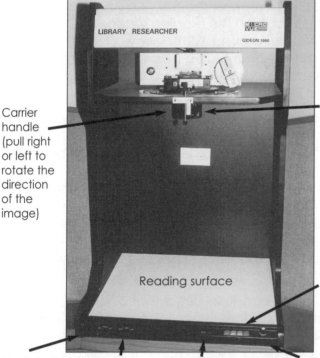

Zoom and focus rings (twist right or left on the zoom to make the image bigger or smaller; twist right or left on the focus to make the image sharper)

Carrier handle (pull right or left to rotate the direction of the image)

Reading surface

Buttons for fast-reverse (red), reverse, forward, fast-forward (red)

On and off buttons

Light setting (high or low)

Scan control (centers the image)

Speed control (optional; regulates speed of forward and reverse buttons)

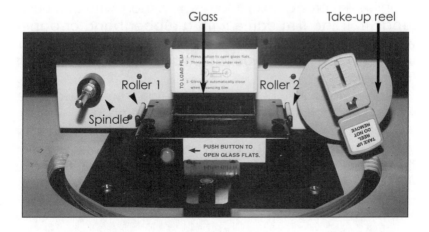

Glass

Take-up reel

Roller 1

Roller 2

Spindle

TO LOAD FILM

PUSH BUTTON TO OPEN GLASS FLATS.

TAKE UP REEL DO NOT REMOVE

not reading it sideways and getting a crick in your neck. Next, use the zoom ring to make the image larger or smaller, and use the focus ring to make it sharper. The scan button helps you center the image on the reading surface. It's especially useful when you're working with narrow (16mm) film. The speed knob (an optional feature) controls how fast the forward and reverse buttons work. There are low and high settings for the amount of light.

5. Things to watch for: If you're taking notes on the reading surface, it's easy to accidentally press the buttons and lose your place. It's also easy to forget there's a shelf above you and hit your head as you stand up.

Pay attention to hand cramps from pressing buttons or using hand cranks. I've gotten a couple cases of tendonitis in my eagerness to search as many films as possible. Take breaks to shake your hands out and do wrist exercises. Alternate film work with book work. Your ancestors will still be there when you get back.

6. Follow the Golden Rule. Just like at Blockbuster, rewind the film when you are done, by holding the rewind button. If the whole film winds up on the take-up reel, don't just drop it back in the box; instead, take a moment to get another reel and put it back to the beginning, or at least bring this to a staffer's attention. Few things are as frustrating as starting a session of film work and having the first reel start at the end.

If the film breaks, take it to a staff person, who can easily repair it. If the film came with a rubber band or paper wrapper around it, replace them before you box the film; they help keep the film wound tight and less likely to come off the reel.

Turn off the light when you are retrieving more film, and be sure to switch off the machine when you're done.

Note: The wide slot on the take-up reel makes it easier for you to thread the film. This convenience comes at a price for the research facility: $15 or more apiece. Please don't remove the reels if they are labeled "Do not remove." They will break, and then you and others will spend extra time threading film

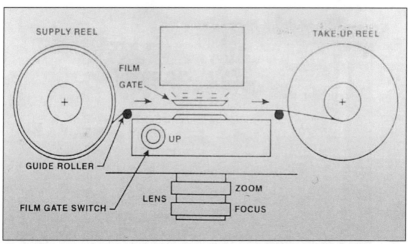

SUPPLY REEL   TAKE-UP REEL

FILM
GATE

UP

GUIDE ROLLER

FILM GATE SWITCH   LENS   ZOOM

FOCUS

Illustration 13.2: Follow the diagram to correctly thread an overhead viewer type of microfilm reader. Photos by Grace DuMelle.

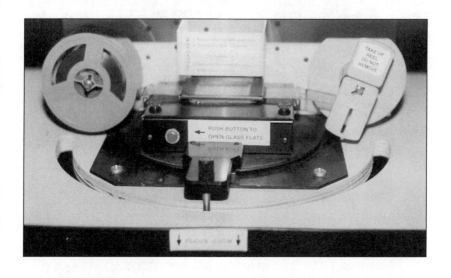

onto standard reels. Some places allow you to remove both reels for printing; others require you to rewind. Find out what the policy is before you do it.

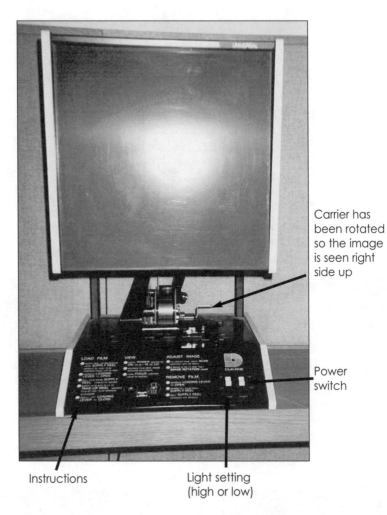

Carrier has been rotated so the image is seen right side up

Power switch

Instructions

Light setting (high or low)

Illustration 13.3: Microfilm reader (straight-ahead viewer type). Photo by Grace DuMelle.

Microfilm Reader (Straight-Ahead Viewer)

With this kind of microfilm reader (see Illustration 13.3), you are supplying the power to move forward and backward. It can be fatiguing to go through many films. There is also no zoom capability. Despite these factors, it is often easier to read faded or poorly reproduced films on this viewer.

How to Load Film in a Straight-Ahead Microfilm Viewer

1. Turn the power switch on so your work area is illuminated.

2. Position your reel so the end of the film comes from the top of the reel (see Illustration 13.4). Match the hole in the reel to the spindle and push firmly until it seats.

3. No worry about rollers here. Flip the lever attached to the glass halves to "Open" and thread the free end of the film (the *leader*) between the halves and into the take-up reel (doubling the end of the leader helps it to stay in). You'll want to place the film on the take-up reel overhand, so it advances clockwise from the start (it will take you extra time to get it to wind in the right direction if you don't).

4. Flip the lever to "Close" and crank past the leader to the beginning of the material. Swing the carrier left or right if necessary to orient the film. Use the scan lever to center the page. The focus knob in the middle makes the image sharper.

5. When you want to rewind, set the lever to "Open" and you'll be done faster. Remember to turn off the light when retrieving films and when you are finished. Given that this microfilm reader is hand-powered, you're less likely to advance the whole film onto the take-up reel, but if you do, please put it back to the beginning. Replace any rubber bands or wrappers. Follow the facility's preference in either refiling the film or leaving it for the staff to do.

Scan lever
(centers the image)

Lever to open and close
glass halves

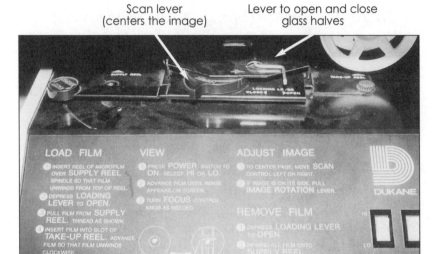

Hand crank to move film forward or backward   Focus knob

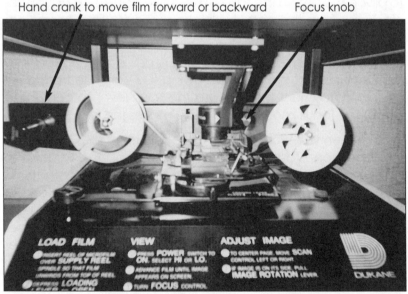

Illustration 13.4: The straight-ahead viewer type of microfilm reader features easy-to-follow instructions on the base of the machine. Photos by Grace DuMelle.

Microfiche Reader

Of all the machines discussed in this chapter, the microfiche reader is the easiest to use. You can review many fiche quickly once you know how. Note that some fiche may require a reader with high-power magnification. Ask staff to direct you to such a machine if the text is unusually small on screen.

How to Load Fiche in a Microfiche Reader

1. Turn the power switch on (generally located on the front of the reader).

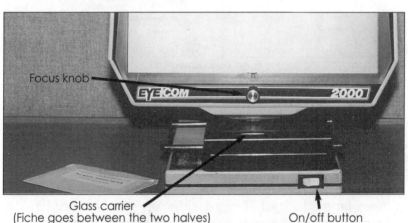

Focus knob

Glass carrier
(Fiche goes between the two halves)

On/off button

Illustration 13.5: Microfiche reader. Photos by Grace DuMelle.

Illustration 13.6: Read the fiche by pushing the handle up and down or side to side. Photo by Grace DuMelle.

---

2. Pull the handle toward you so the two halves of the glass carrier open (see Illustration 13.5). Place the fiche in the carrier (generally face up) and push the handle away from you to see it on screen. You may have to play with the fiche a few times to get it right side up—each machine is different. (I always have to flop the fiche around, so don't feel bad.)

3. Adjust the focus by means of a knob in the center of the machine.

4. To get where you want to go on the fiche, move the handle up and down or side to side (see Illustration 13.6). You'll get the hang of it quickly. Some microfiche readers have a yellow index line on-screen to help you mark your place in lists. A knob or lever controls the position of the line.

5. Switch off the machine when you are retrieving new fiche and when you are finished.

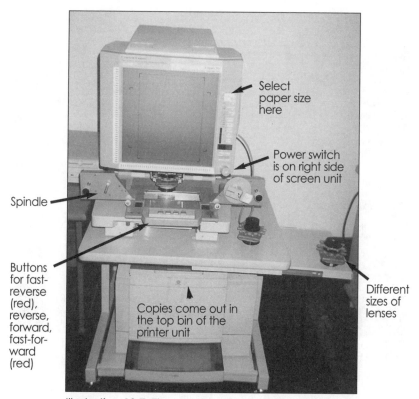

Select paper size here

Power switch is on right side of screen unit

Spindle

Buttons for fast-reverse (red), reverse, forward, fast-for-ward (red)

Copies come out in the top bin of the printer unit

Different sizes of lenses

Illustration 13.7: The combination reader–printer allows you to both read and make copies from microfilm and microfiche. Photo by Grace DuMelle.

Combination Microfilm/Microfiche Reader-Printer

Many facilities use machines on which you can both read and print. Illustration 13.7 shows a common brand, which prints 8.5 x 11 inch and 11 x 17 inch copies and has several sizes of zoom lenses. It uses buttons to advance and rewind the film, like the overhead viewer shown earlier. It also offers advanced options, such as masking (deleting unwanted areas from the image) and printing either positive or negative (making a negative image—white type on black back-

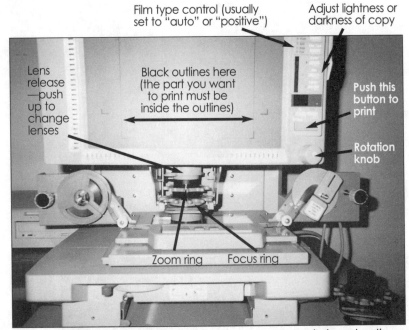

Illustration 13.8: Combination machines have many controls and options. It's best to ask a staff person before you make copies you're not happy with. Photo by Grace DuMelle.

ground—can help bring out faint handwriting). Illustrations 13.7 and 13.8 show the glass carrier, which accepts microfiche as well as microfilm.

How to Load Film in a Reader–Printer

1. Turn the power switch on (located on the right side of screen unit). Pull the carrier handle toward you so the glass halves open.

2. A loading diagram above the spindle tells you the film comes from the top of the reel. Seat it on the spindle (both round-hole and diamond-hole reels will fit) and thread the free end under the roller, under the glass, under the second roller, and into the take-up reel. Push the carrier handle away from you to close the glass halves. Use the rotation knob to adjust orientation.

3. The top ring of the lens is the zoom, and the bottom ring is the focus. A fixed lens (no zoom) is handy for getting an entire census page on one sheet of paper. To change a lens, push up the lens release, pull out the current lens, then insert the new lens into the channels and push until it clicks into place. The lens release will lower by itself.

4. To make a copy:

• Find the page you want.

• Center it between the black outlines on the screen—whatever's outside the outlines will not print.

• Make sure the film type is set the way you want it, positive or negative (the default is usually "auto," which senses the type and prints accordingly).

• Choose your paper size, either 8.5 x 11 inches or 11 x 17 inches (some machines will print legal size, 8.5 x 14 inches).

• Set the number of copies you want.

• Press the "Start" button to print. The copy comes out in the bin underneath the work surface.

Note: Facilities must pay for toner and paper as well as maintenance on the machines. Copy charges are set with these costs in mind. Ask staff to show you how to make the best copies. If the film or fiche is dark to begin with, there may be little anyone can do.

How to Load Fiche in a Reader–Printer

1. Turn the power switch on (located on the right side of the screen unit).

2. Pull the carrier handle toward you so the glass halves open. Insert the microfiche and push the handle away from you to see it on-screen. Play around with it until it's right side up. Adjust the focus and zoom to your liking.

3. Move the carrier handle up and down or side to side

to find what you want to print.

4. To make a print, follow the steps outlined in the microfilm section above.

Library Catalogs

As you research your family history, you're going to start with *primary sources*. These are materials created by or in the possession of your ancestors; examples include letters, journals, address books, diplomas, Social Security cards, membership cards, paycheck stubs, and similar items.

Once you glean all you can from these kinds of things, you'll need to turn to *secondary sources*. These are materials created about your ancestors or that give a "big picture" look at your ancestors' place in the scheme of things. Examples are biographies, published family histories, college yearbooks, church anniversary books, books about ethnic communities in Chicago, and histories of Cook County towns.

The way to find secondary sources is through library catalogs. For years these were in the form of card catalogs: 3 x 5 inch cards in wooden drawers held in place with metal rods. Most places by now have done away with the cards in favor of computer catalogs, because these can be put online and researchers can look for materials from their homes, offices, and classrooms.

The basics of searching remain the same even if the format has been updated electronically. You search by author, by title, or by subject.

Searching by Author

Searching by author is useful when you know the person's name and want to see what else he or she has written, or if the library has a particular book by that author. Say you've used John Colletta's *They Came in Ships* and you're curious if he has anything more that can help you.

If you're using a computer catalog, you type "Colletta, John" in the search box and choose "Author" as the type of search. Then hit the "Search" or "Go" button. The first title by Colletta that comes up is *Finding Italian Roots: The Complete Guide for Americans*. Titles are listed in alphabetical order, so the next book is *They Came in Ships*.

If you're using a card catalog, go to the drawer that would contain "Coll—." Flip through the cards until you find the one headed "Colletta, John" and then see what books of his this library has.

If you don't find anything, it may mean you don't have the correct spelling of the name, or it may mean that this particular library does not have any books by this author. A reference librarian will be glad to help you.

Searching by Title

Searching by title is pretty straightforward. The main thing to know is that common words at the start of a title, such as "The," "A," and "An," are ignored in cataloging. For example, if you were looking for the book *The Dutch in South Cook County Since 1847*, it would be alphabetized under "D," not "T."

In a computer catalog, type "Dutch in South Cook County" in the search box; you don't need to put the whole title in. Choose "Title" as the type of search and click "Search" or "Go."

In a card catalog, go to the drawer that would contain "Dutch in —" and flip through the title cards looking for the one you want. Again, not finding it may mean either you are mistaken about the title or the facility you're in does not have a copy.

Searching by Subject

Searching by subject is going to be the most useful category for you. This is where you'll go fishing and find the greatest things for your research. This is where you find out if there is a book on Assyrians in Chicago, or records of Oak Woods Cemetery, or a map of Germany in 1742.

Most libraries use Library of Congress subject headings. These are standard headings issued by our national library in Washington, D.C. There are a few that will be very useful to you:

• To find all types of genealogy materials for a particular location, look under "[Name of town] [Name of state] Genealogy."

Example: "Evanston Illinois Genealogy"

• To find newspaper holdings, look under "Newspapers [Name of state] [Name of city]."

Example: "Newspapers Illinois Cicero"

• For materials on ethnic groups, look under "[Name of group] Genealogy" or "[Name of group—Americans] [Name of state] Genealogy."

Examples: "Greeks Genealogy" (leads you to materials about Greeks in Greece and other locations); "Greek-Americans Illinois Genealogy" (limits the location to Illinois)

In a computer catalog, type the subject heading in the search box and choose "Subject" as the type of search. Click "Search" or "Go." The nice thing about computer catalogs is that you can pull up a record and then click on the linked subject headings in it, thereby expanding your search.

In a card catalog, go to the drawer that contains the section of the alphabet for your heading: "Evan—" for "Evanston Illinois Genealogy," for example. It's important to know that subject headings come *after* all the author cards. The subject cards are filed in alphabetical order, so "Evanston Illinois Genealogy" will be after "Evanston Illinois Biography" and before "Evanston Illinois History."

When You Find Items You Want to Look At

You can print a list of what you find in a computer catalog, e-mail it to yourself, or download it to a floppy disk. With a card catalog, you have to take notes. The main thing is to get the title and *call number* (the number the library assigns it) so you can find it on the shelves or in the drawers. Many facilities are *closed-stack* (the book shelves are off-limits to readers); in these places, you'll fill out *call slips* (listing the items you want to look at) and have the staff retrieve the items for you. Closed-stack libraries don't let you check out materials to take home. You often can obtain them on interlibrary loan through your public library or the library of a university or college you are an alumnus of. There may be a small fee. The Family History Library in Salt Lake City does not lend books, but most microform items can be loaned for a fee to Family History Centers nationwide.

Using library catalogs takes a little bit of time, but it pays off. You may find a publication that gives you a new strategy for a fact that's eluded you. You may discover a published family history that saves you years of work. You won't know what's out there unless you look!

How to Use Machines and Catalogs

Points to Remember

❑ *Microfilm comes in 16mm or 35mm reels of film.*

❑ *Microfiche are flat cards about the size of index cards.*

❑ *Using microfilm readers:*

• Make sure the reel you want to use is seated on the spindle.

• Remember to thread it between the two pieces of glass.

• Prevent tendonitis by taking breaks and alternating film work with book work.

• Report backward film and breaks to a staffer.

• Ask about the facility's policy on removing take-up reels before you do it.

• Rewind film when done and replace rubber bands or paper wrappers.

• Shut off the light.

❑ *Using microfiche readers:*

• Place the fiche between the two halves of glass.

• Orient the fiche to be right side up.

• Move the handle up and down or side to side to get where you want to go.

How to Use Machines and Catalogs

❏ *Making prints on a reader-printer:*

• Adjust the zoom or the type of lens if necessary.

• Center the image inside the black outlines on the screen.

• Adjust the focus.

• Choose the film type (positive or negative).

• Choose the paper size.

• Select the number of copies.

• Press the "Start" or "Print" button.

❏ *Using library catalogs:*

• Library catalogs are the best way to find secondary sources (materials created about your ancestors or that provide a "big picture" look).

• Searching by subject is the most useful kind of search for genealogy. Standard headings include:
—"[Name of town] [Name of state] Genealogy" (for materials about a location)
—"Newspapers [Name of state] [Name of city] (for newspaper holdings)
—"[Name of group] Genealogy" or "[Name of group—Americans] [Name of state] Genealogy" (for materials on ethnic groups)

14 What to Expect at Chicago-Area Research Facilities

When you start doing research in person, a few simple tips will make your visits productive and pleasant:

• Your first visit to a facility is going to be largely devoted to learning about that facility: where the materials are kept, how you access them, how you work the microfilm machines, and so on. You might have a long list of research you want to do, but you'll probably only cross one or two things off your list on this initial visit. If you know that going in, you won't be frustrated. It helps to call in advance or check the Web site about things like handicapped access and orientations for first-time users.

• Budget cuts the last few years have seriously affected staffing at nearly all the facilities you'll be using. You'll likely encounter fewer and less experienced staff. Please be understanding; these places are trying to do the best they can. If you pitch a fit, you're not going to get much help. Be polite and be patient. And if you're in a position to donate or become a member or lobby your government representative, your support will be greatly appreciated.

• Respect the rules. They are there to ensure a fair and long-lasting use of materials for everybody. Use a pencil if requested. Turn off your cell phone. Sign in for computers or microfilm machines if required, and vacate them promptly when asked or when your time is up.

• Bring the notes you need to do your work. If you don't bring Aunt Violet's death date, for example, you'll waste time looking up that piece of information at the facility, rather than going right to the new research you had planned to do on her. Take copies of documents, not the originals, and put an address label on your notebook in case you leave it somewhere.

Chicago Historical Society (CHS)

Location:
Chicago Historical Society
Clark Street at North Avenue
Chicago, IL 60610

The Research Center is located on the third floor. CHS is easily accessible by public transportation; a public parking lot is available at LaSalle and Stockton streets with discounted parking rates for CHS visitors (have your ticket validated at the lobby desk).

Hours:
Normally open Tuesday, Thursday, Friday, and Saturday from 10 A.M. to 4:30 P.M.; Wednesday from 1 P.M. to 4:30 P.M. Closed on Sunday and Monday. Please check Web site for any temporary closings.

Fees:
There is no charge to use the Research Center. There is a per copy charge for computer printouts, microfilm copies, and book copies. Image copies are slightly higher. Fees for image rights are available at the Rights and Reproduction counter.

Rules of Use:
Obtain a research pass from the attendant at the lobby desk before taking the stairs or elevator to the third floor. Coats, briefcases, backpacks, umbrellas, cameras, notebooks, large purses, and similar items must be stored in the free coat check area on the main floor. You may take a laptop computer. Bring a photo ID on your first visit to obtain a reader's card, good for one year. You must sign in at each visit. Materials do not circulate and are not interlibrary loaned. To obtain most books, microfilm, and collection materials, you will need to fill out a call slip to have them brought to your

Illustration 14.1: The Chicago Historical Society is conveniently located near the Newberry Library, only about a 20-minute walk or 10-minute bus ride away. Courtesy of the Chicago Historical Society.

Illustration 14.2: Renovated a few years ago, the Research Center at the Chicago Historical Society is a marvel of space and light. The society's previous cramped quarters were crowned with a booming grandfather clock, which startled patrons with its chiming. Courtesy of the Chicago Historical Society/John Alderson.

seat. There is an extensive collection of "ready print" photographs that you can look through (gloves are available for your use); for others you will need to fill out a call slip. Food and drink are not allowed; you can use pencils only. The staff in the Rights and Reproduction area does all the photocopying.

Holdings Summary:
The Chicago Historical Society has a complete collection of Chicago city directories and Chicago telephone directories; criss-cross directories (directories organized by address) for certain years; and volumes of the *Chicago Blue Book*, listing the prominent citizens of the city from 1890 to 1916. Individuals may also be referenced in the card catalog, the biography clipping files, and biographical dictionaries. CHS also has extensive holdings of Chicago newspapers on microfilm. Selected Chicago high school and professional school yearbooks, church publications, and some historical information on Chicago businesses are available. The Research Center also has resources for tracing the histories of homes (City of Chicago building permits, real estate and architectural periodicals, fire insurance maps) that are also helpful when studying families and individuals. Additionally, materials on Chicago neighborhoods and the ethnic populations of Chicago are available.

Services:
A card catalog lists all published and manuscript collections. This is supplemented by an online catalog that lists more recent acquisitions. Databases from the *Chicago Tribune* are available to use on-site; these include the *Chicago Tribune Historical Archive*, which contains clippings from the 1920s to 1984 and death notices and obituaries from 1860 to 1984, and the *Chicago Tribune Online*, which includes complete text of stories from 1985 to the present. Selected years of the Chicago city directories are online and may be used in the Research Center. These can be searched by name, address, or occupation. Research specialists are always available when the center is open and are very

helpful in getting you started with research on your topic of interest. Research specialists are, however, limited in their availability to answer questions over the phone, so it is best to visit the center in person.

Contact:
For general information about the Research Center and its holdings, visit the Web site at www.chicagohistory.org (click on "Research + Collections"), or call 312/642-4600 and ask for the Research Center.

Chicago Public Library

Location:
Harold Washington Library Center (HWLC)
400 S. State Street
Chicago, IL 60605

HWLC is the central library of the Chicago Public Library system. It is accessible by public transportation; public parking facilities are available nearby.

Select branch locations:
Sulzer Regional Library
4455 N. Lincoln Avenue
Chicago, IL 60625

Woodson Regional Library
9525 S. Halsted Street
Chicago, IL 60628

Hours:
Hours for HWLC are Monday through Thursday from 9 A.M. to 7 P.M.; Friday and Saturday from 9 A.M. to 5 P.M.; Sunday from 1 P.M. to 5 P.M. Closed on most city holidays. Hours of the branch locations vary. The Special Collections Department at HWLC has limited hours.

Illustrations 14.3 and 14.4: Each floor of the massive central public library is a specialty library of its own. The Municipal Reference Collection, for example, can guide you to information about city workers and students in city schools. Exterior photo by Phil Moloitis; interior photo by Nancy Beskin.

Illustration 14.4

Fees:

There are no fees to research. Photocopy fees apply; currently there is no charge for copies from microfilm, but this is subject to change.

Rules of Use:

Microfilm readers and printers are on a first-come, first-served basis. You will need to provide an ID to use materials that are in the closed reference areas. Open-stack reference books do not circulate. Circulating books require a Chicago Public Library card. If you live outside Chicago, you can get a library card if your library belongs to the Illinois Intersystem Reciprocal Borrowing Covenant. A list of member libraries is posted at www.chipublib.org/003cpl/reciprocal.html.

Holdings Summary:

• **Third Floor**—Newspapers and General Periodicals, Microform Room: U.S. census records from 1840 to 1930; census indexes from 1880 to 1930; Chicago city directories from 1839, 1843 to 1917, 1923, and 1928–29 (complete run—all available years); Chicago telephone directories from 1878; various suburban telephone books beginning in 1928; and other various Illinois city telephone books. Also available are Illinois county histories from the late nineteenth and early twentieth centuries. Some indexes to passenger lists are also held in the Microform Room. Complete runs of most Chicago newspapers and some suburban papers are here as well.

• **Fourth Floor**—Business, Science, and Technology: Fire insurance maps.

• **Fifth Floor**—Municipal Reference Collection: City of Chicago documents including the *Chicago City Council Proceedings* beginning in 1858, Civil Service Commission annual reports from 1896 to 1925, and some Chicago Board of Education reports including names of high school graduates from 1867 to 1895.

• **Sixth Floor**—Chicago History Collection: Books and other reference materials on Chicago history, politics, and culture. Limited biographical resources are also available.

• **Ninth Floor**—Special Collections: Archives on neighborhood histories, especially South and West Side neighborhoods, and general Chicago history. Sulzer and Woodson regional libraries also have special collections with a focus on the North Side neighborhoods and African-American history in Illinois, respectively.

Services:
Librarians are available for reference assistance and will provide guidance on what resources are available and where they are located. Beginning genealogists should start on the sixth floor in the Social Sciences and History Division. There is a copy center on the fourth floor that can also make copies, including color copies, for a fee. The library offers a circulating book collection, interlibrary loan, and computers with free Internet access.

Contact:
The Chicago Public Library Web site is www.chipublib. org. Click the link "Selected Internet Resources" and then "Genealogy" for a description of genealogy-related material. Telephone numbers at HWLC are: Social Sciences and History: 312/747-4600; Government Publications: 312/747-4500; Special Collections: 312/747-4875; Newspapers and General Periodicals: 312/747-4340. The telephone number at Sulzer Regional Library is 312/744-7616. The telephone number at Woodson Regional Library is 312/747-6900.

Clerk of the Circuit Court
of Cook County Archives

Location:
Clerk of the Circuit Court of Cook County Archives
Richard J. Daley Center
50 W. Washington Street, Room 1113
Chicago, IL 60602

Illustration 14.5: The third-floor Microform Room at HWLC holds complete runs of many Chicago newspapers. It is also the place to view city directories and census schedules. Photo by Nancy Beskin.

The building is easily accessible by public transportation; public parking garages are available nearby.

Hours:
Open Monday through Friday from 8:30 A.M. to 4:30 P.M. Closed on court holidays.

Fees:
There is no charge to use the archives in person. For research conducted by mail, separate fees apply for each year searched in indexes and certified copies of documents (payable in advance). Photocopy charges for informational uncertified copies of documents requested by mail are set by Illinois statute (payable after copies are made). Self-service copies made on-site cost much less. Fees are subject to change without notice.

Illustration 14.6: The Circuit Court Archives is located at the nexus of city, county, and state government in downtown Chicago, next to the famous Picasso statue. Because the Daley Center acts as a county courthouse, you must pass through metal detectors in the lobby (seen at left) before taking elevators to the 11th floor. Photo by Nancy Beskin.

Rules of Use:

There is a security check in the main building lobby before you access the building elevators. Once in the archives reading room, you will need to register in a logbook. All archives case files must be requested through the completion of an Archives Reference Request Form. Once your file is available, you will need to sign an Agreement for Use of the Clerk of the Circuit Court of Cook County Archives form. All documents must remain in the archives reading room. Indexes to archive information are available on a self-serve basis. Smoking, food, and beverages are not allowed in the reading room.

Holdings Summary:

The Circuit Court Archives contains the *National Archives Soundex Index to Naturalization Petitions for the U.S. District and Circuit Courts, Northern District of Illinois and INS District*

Illustration 14.7: I've found the Circuit Court Archives to be one of the most helpful government offices. The staff there deal with an amazing amount of traffic—and requests that run the gamut—every day, and they are unfailingly respectful of patrons. Photo by Nancy Beskin.

#9—*1840–1950*. It covers northern Illinois and parts of Iowa, Wisconsin, and Indiana. The Circuit Court Archives also holds naturalization records of the Superior, Circuit, County, and Criminal Courts of Cook County from 1871 to 1929 (these may include declaration of intent, petition, and/or court order).

Indexes for probate cases include probate deceased indexes from 1871 to 1975 and a wills index from 1850 to 1993. Records span 1871 to 1975, with some wills dating from 1850. There is also an index to incompetents from 1911 to 1975 and an index to minors under guardianship from 1871 to 1976. Divorce cases are available from 1871 to 1986. Criminal felony cases are available from 1871 to 1900 and 1927 to 1983 (cases between these dates may be re-created from court docket books and indictment records); indexes for these cases are available from 1873 to 1983. Juvenile cases, adoption cases, and mental health cases are closed.

Services:

If you do not have a specific case number, you can request case searches in person or by mail. If you cannot visit the archives in person, it's best to call, as the staff can give you the specific procedures for obtaining the information you want. Search request forms are available on the archives Web site, and requests can be mailed with a check for the search fee. It generally takes two to ten days to receive the case file, and it is advisable that you call before going to the archives to ensure that your case file has arrived. Case files are only held for 30 days from date of receipt.

Contact:

General information can be found online at www.cook countyclerkofcourt.org; click on the "Archives" link. You can also call 312/603-6601 for reference assistance.

Cook County Bureau of Vital Statistics

Location:

Cook County Bureau of Vital Statistics
County Building
118 N. Clark Street
Chicago, IL 60602

Use the Randolph Street entrance and take the escalator down to the lower (concourse) level. There are also connecting tunnels from the Daley Center and the State of Illinois building (Thompson Center). The building is easily accessible by public transportation; public parking garages are available nearby. There are also five suburban locations. (Additionally, some Chicago-area currency exchanges offer vital records services for an additional fee.)

Hours:

Open Monday through Friday from 8:30 A.M. to 5 P.M. Closed on county holidays.

Illustration 14.8: If you're downtown researching at the Circuit Court Archives, the Cook County Bureau of Vital Statistics is right across the street in the City Hall–County Building at Clark and Randolph. This photo shows the Clark Street facade. Go to the Randolph Street entrance and take the escalator down to the lower (concourse) level. There are also connecting tunnels from the Daley Center and the State of Illinois building (Thompson Center). Photo by Nancy Beskin.

Illustration 14.9: Bring cash and a photo ID to place orders for vital records at the Cook County Bureau of Vital Statistics. Staff will tell you whether your order will have to be retrieved from the warehouse and mailed to you. More recent records may be available on a "will call" basis or possibly pulled while you wait, if you provide all the necessary information for searching. Photo by Nancy Beskin.

Fees:

A lower fee applies if you can provide the state file number (certificate number) with your request. See Chapter 12 ("Nuts and Bolts of Birth and Death Records") for ways to obtain these numbers. There is a small charge for additional copies of a birth or marriage certificate; a slightly higher charge applies for additional copies of a death certificate. A convenience fee applies to documents ordered over the phone or the Internet through VitalChek.

Rules of Use:

All searches are conducted by staff and are dependent

on the information you provide. Give as much as you can, including alternate spellings of names. Most genealogical requests will have to be retrieved from the warehouse and mailed to you. You must complete a Genealogical Request Form to receive copies of certificates. If you go in person, be prepared to show a photo ID and bring cash payment (no bills larger than $20)—no checks or credit cards are accepted.

Holdings Summary:

For genealogical purposes, the Bureau of Vital Statistics has birth certificates older than 75 years and dating back to October 1871; marriage certificates older than 50 years and dating back to October 1871; and death certificates older than 20 years and dating back to October 1871. Some still-born birth records are available post-1936 when there was a burial. For more recent birth and death documents, you must prove that you are a close relation to the person about whom you are requesting the document.

Services:

Requests can be made in person or through the mail (request forms are available on the Web site). Fees must be paid at the time of the request. The certificates will be mailed within three to four weeks, according to officials; in practice, it is often six to eight weeks or more. Telephone and Internet orders can be placed using VitalChek.

Contact:

General information and request forms are available online at www.cookctyclerk.com/sub/vital_records.asp; click on the "Genealogy Requests" link. You can also call 312/603-7790. Or send a request by mail to:

Cook County Clerk
Bureau of Vital Statistics
Attn.: Genealogy
P.O. Box 642570
Chicago, IL 60664-2570

If you wish to order documents through VitalChek, you can call 312/603-7799 or log on to www.vitalchek.com.

Family History Center (FHC)—
Wilmette, Illinois

Family History Centers are affiliated with the Church of Jesus Christ of Latter-day Saints. The main Family History Library is in Salt Lake City, Utah, and the FHCs around the country obtain much of their material from that library. There are ten centers in the Chicagoland area; Wilmette's is the oldest and largest. All of the centers have access to the same material but may not have as many holdings on permanent loan from the main library.

Location:
Family History Center
2727 Lake Avenue
Wilmette, IL 60091

The Wilmette Family History Center is located in the southwest corner of the church building on the corner of Lake and Locust. You go in through a doorway adjacent to the parking lot. Ring the doorbell for entry. The center is also accessible by public transportation by linking CTA train service with the PACE suburban bus system.

Hours:
Open Tuesday through Thursday from 10 A.M. to 3 P.M. and 6:30 P.M. to 9:30 P.M.; Saturday from 9 A.M. to 1 P.M. Closed on Monday, Friday, and Sunday. Call ahead during inclement weather, as the center may be closed.

Fees:
There is no charge to use the reading room. Different charges apply for microfilm copies, photocopies, and computer printouts. If you are ordering microfilm or microfiche from Salt Lake City, small fees apply for the initial order and each

Illustration 14.10: The Wilmette Family History Center has many Cook County vital records on microfilm. You can save time and money by going here instead of the Cook County Bureau of Vital Statistics for certificates from the nineteenth and early twentieth centuries. Photo by Nancy Beskin.

Illustration 14.11: Family History Centers like the one in Wilmette (shown here) are open to anyone doing genealogy research, not just members of the Church of Jesus Christ of Latter-day Saints. Other centers in the Chicago area are located in Buffalo Grove, Chicago Heights, Crystal Lake, Hyde Park, Joliet, Naperville, Orland Park, Schaumburg, and Westchester. Photo by Nancy Beskin.

renewal. Orders must be placed in person and paid in advance. You will be notified by postcard when your order arrives.

Rules of Use:

Coats must be stored in the coatroom outside of the Family History Center. Sign your name in the log book upon arrival. No smoking, food, or drink is allowed in the center. Small children are discouraged.

Holdings Summary:

The Family History Library catalog is available on microfiche and CD-ROM (current to 1998) and is accessible through the Internet (updated daily) using the computers available in the center. This catalog lists all the holdings of the library, many of which can be ordered through the local Family History Centers. The FHC in Wilmette has, on permanent loan from the library, substantial microfiche and microfilm resources related to Chicago and Cook County. These include indexes to birth, death, and marriage records, as well as many of the birth and death certificates and marriage licenses themselves. Some marriage information from as far back as 1833 is available. Besides death indexes and certificates, the FHC has such things as cemetery records, coroner's death certificates from 1879 to 1904, and records of funerals for the Norwegian community for 1899 to 1972. Birth information is generally available up to 1922 with some limited information for later years. The FHC has some Cook County Circuit Court documents from 1871 to 1929 (including naturalization records and probate court records). The center holds microfilm from the Roman Catholic Archdiocese of Chicago up to 1915, including information from all the Polish parishes. Besides the Chicago and Cook County information, the FHC has noncirculating guides to genealogy, reference books, and numerous indexes to international records.

Services:
Public-access computers have links to the Family History Library catalog, the Internet, and a full subscription to Ancestry.com (including indexes to passenger records). Access to microfilm and microfiche is self-service. Helpful volunteers staff the center and have limited ability to provide services by telephone; however, they will tell you if a specific microfilm is available at their location or if it will need to be ordered. The center cannot respond to mail inquiries because of limited staff.

Contact:
The Family History Library catalog and useful research information are available at www.familysearch.org. The phone number for the Wilmette Family History Center is 847/251-9818.

Illinois Regional Archives Depository (IRAD)

The Illinois Regional Archives Depository at Northeastern Illinois University is one of seven regional depositories of the Illinois State Archives.

Location:
Illinois Regional Archives Depository
Northeastern Illinois University
5500 N. St. Louis Avenue
Chicago, IL 60625

IRAD is located on the lower level of the Ronald Williams Library. Street parking is available on Bryn Mawr and St. Louis Avenues. University lots may be used with the purchase of a daily parking permit (available at the kiosk located near the south end of the main parking lot).

Hours:
Open Monday through Friday from 9 A.M. to 4 P.M. Closed on state holidays and during the university's winter break.

Illustration 14.12: Because IRAD is housed in a university library, it's a good idea to call ahead and make sure you won't be tripped up by a school or holiday closing. Photo by Nancy Beskin.

Illustration 14.13: You can always find plenty of room to work at IRAD. More people should know about the unique Chicago and Cook County materials here. Photo by Nancy Beskin.

Fees:
There is no charge to use the reading room. There is a small minimum charge for photocopies from microfilm, microfiche, and printed materials.

Rules of Use:
Sign in at the desk upon your arrival. IRAD Patron Use Forms must be completed in order to obtain material in the archives.

Holdings Summary:
A complete listing of IRAD's holdings is available at the reference desk and is also online at the Illinois State Archives Web site (www.cyberdriveillinois.com/departments/archives/irad/iradholdings.html).

IRAD has a limited collection of vital records holdings for Cook County and Chicago. A birth record index for Cook County covers the years 1871 to 1916, and birth registers are available from 1871 to 1915. The *Cook County Death Index*, available at IRAD and partially online at the Illinois State Archives Web site, covers the years 1871 to 1916. This should be completely online by early 2005. The *Illinois Death Index* is available at IRAD and online for the years 1916 to 1950. The marriage record index for Cook County is available for the years 1871 to 1904, and marriage licenses are available for the years 1871 to 1900.

Other records at IRAD include naturalization records (1871–1906), coroner's inquest records (1872–1911), and Cook County Hospital patient registers (1872–1948).

IRAD holds many original documents relating to Chicago and Cook County local governments. The *Chicago City Council Proceedings* from 1833 to 1944 include such things as licenses, petitions, and appointments; names may be searched through an index available at IRAD and on the state archives Web site. Proceedings and minutes for annexed towns and villages (for example, Hyde Park and Rogers Park) are also available at IRAD.

The *Chicago Board of Elections Registered Voters Index* (also known as *Record and Index of Persons Registered and*

Poll Lists of Voters) for the years 1888, 1888 to 1890, and 1892 are housed at IRAD both in hard copy and on microfilm. This provides valuable demographic information for 1890, the year for which the national census is unavailable.

IRAD also has copies of Sanborn fire insurance atlases for Chicago, created 1906 to 1950 with updates through 1972.

General genealogy and Chicago history books are available for use in the reading room.

Services:

Microfilm and microfiche readers are available. Staff (graduate student interns) will assist with inquiries in person, by mail, and over the telephone at no charge. Requests should be limited to three names at a time; response time is approximately one to two weeks.

Contact:

Additional information about IRAD can be found at www.cyberdriveillinois.com/departments/archives/archives.html. The telephone number for IRAD is 773/442-4506.

National Archives and Records Administration (NARA)— Great Lakes Region

The Great Lakes branch is one of NARA's 18 regional facilities.

Location:

National Archives and Records Administration
Great Lakes Region
7358 S. Pulaski Road
Chicago, IL 60629

From Pulaski, turn west onto 75th Street; NARA is located one block west on the right. The entrance to the research areas has a burgundy awning. Public transportation is available; a parking lot is adjacent to the building.

Illustration 14.14: It's nice to have convenient access in the Chicago area to federal records of historical value. Entrance to the NARA reading rooms is off the parking lot to the right of the building. Photo by Nancy Beskin.

Hours:

The Microfilm Reading Room is open Monday through Friday from 8 A.M. to 4:15 P.M. On the first Tuesday of each month, the room is open until 8:30 P.M. The Textual Research Room is open Monday through Friday from 8 A.M. to 4:15 P.M.; requests for original records must be received by 3:15 P.M. for same-day service. Closed on federal holidays.

Fees:

There is no charge to use the research facilities. Different fees apply for self-service copies of nonrecord material from paper and from microfilm. Higher fees apply for records that staff is required to copy; more for oversized documents. Certified copies incur a photocopying charge per page and a certification fee. There is a minimum mail order fee. Microfilm rolls can be purchased from NARA in Washington, D.C. Photographs, sound recordings, and other nontextual archival materials are copied using outside vendors with prices determined by the vendor; NARA charges an additional handling fee per item to coordinate the reproduction.

Rules of Use:
All visitors must sign in and sign out in the main lobby and in the Microfilm Reading Room. Reservations are encouraged if using the Microfilm Reading Room, but they are not mandatory. Those using the Textual Research Room must fill out an application and show a photo ID to obtain a researcher card, which is good for one year. If researching in the Textual Research Room, it is advised to call ahead and talk to a staff member, who may be able to discuss what is available on-site and possibly have it ready for use. Smoking, food, beverages, gum, and pen use are not allowed in the Textual Research Room. Complete regulations are published in *Code of Federal Regulations*, 36 CFR, Chapter XII.

Holdings Summary:
Microfilm: The Great Lakes Region has the 1790–1930 censuses for all states as well as 1885–1940 Indian censuses for Michigan, Minnesota, and Wisconsin. Some pre-1900 military service records (including some pension records) are available as are some World War I draft cards for Illinois, Indiana, Michigan, Minnesota, Ohio, and Wisconsin and World War II draft cards for older men for those states except Minnesota. Selected passenger arrival records and indexes for vessels arriving at various U.S. ports are available, as are selected naturalization indexes. There is a small collection of nonfederal research aids, including some Chicago city directories and Chicago voter registration records for 1888 to 1890 and 1892.

Original Records: NARA holds bankruptcy, civil, and criminal case files, as well as naturalization records from the U.S. District Courts in the Great Lakes Region. Noncourt holdings include records for federal agency offices in Illinois, Indiana, Michigan, Minnesota, Ohio, and Wisconsin.

Illustration 14.15: The newly renovated Microfilm Reading Room is where you'll research the census, passenger lists, and other records preserved on film. It also has Internet access. You sign in first at the main desk (left foreground) and then at the Reading Room desk. Photo by Nancy Beskin.

Illustration 14.16: The Textual Research Room (renovated in spring 2004) is the designated place to look at original records (such as naturalizations) on paper. You'll need to obtain a researcher card on your first visit. No food, drinks, or pens are allowed in the room, to safeguard the records. Photo by Nancy Beskin.

Services:
The Microfilm Reading Room has two computers with public Internet access and a full subscription to Ancestry.com (including indexes to passenger records). The room is staffed by both NARA personnel and volunteers. Limited reference assistance will be provided over the telephone. A listing of researchers for hire is available on the NARA Web site.

Contact:
The NARA Web site, www.archives.gov, contains a great amount of helpful general information, as well as access to the online catalog. The Great Lakes Region-specific Web site, www.archives.gov/facilities/il/chicago.html, provides information on the local facility and its holdings. The general telephone number is 773/948-9000. The Microfilm Reading Room can be reached at 773/948-9020 and the Textual Research Room at 773/948-9019. The fax number is 773/948-9050.

Newberry Library

Location:
Newberry Library
60 W. Walton Street
Chicago, IL 60610

The Newberry is located between Clark and Dearborn, a few blocks west of the 900 N. Michigan shopping mall. CTA bus numbers 22 and 70 stop in front of the door. For the cheapest parking in the area, go to the 100 W. Chestnut garage (the entrance is on Clark Street just north of the traffic light at Chestnut); have your ticket validated at the Newberry lobby kiosk. Metered parking on Walton has many restrictions and is heavily patrolled.

Hours:
Open Tuesday through Thursday from 10 A.M. to 6 P.M.; Friday and Saturday from 9 A.M. to 5 P.M. Closed Sunday and Monday.

Illustration 14.17: Not many people realize that the imposing building fronting Washington Square Park is open to ordinary people research-ing their families. More than a century's worth of black soot was cleaned off in the 1990s. Photo by Grace DuMelle.

Illustration 14.18: The second-floor reading room, shown here, is where you'll be doing the bulk of your research. Some material is available for browsing, but most items must be brought to your assigned seat. Courtesy the Newberry Library, Chicago.

Fees:

No charge to use the reading rooms. Pay for computer printouts, photocopies, microfilm or microfiche copies, photo or slide reproductions, "Quick Search" services, and loans of Church of Jesus Christ of Latter-day Saints microfilm.

Rules of Use:

Bring a photo ID your first visit to obtain a reader's card, good for one year. Coats, briefcases, backpacks, umbrellas, and similar items must be stowed in free lockers. You may take your laptop. All items are inspected at the guard desk when leaving. Pencils rather than pens must be used. No food or drinks allowed, including bottled water. Materials do not circulate and are not interlibrary loaned. To obtain most books, maps, and manuscripts, you'll fill out call slips to have them brought to your assigned seat. Most microfilm and microfiche is open-shelf (self-service); you'll need to obtain a carrel assignment to look at them.

Holdings Summary:

The Local and Family History section is on the second floor. There is a reference desk that is always staffed when the library is open. The Newberry is good for census, city directory, and biographical research. It holds all available U.S. censuses for Illinois and extensive indexes. In city directories, it has a complete run of Chicago city directories as well as many for Cook County towns. The *Cook County Biography and Industry File* indexes many biographical dictionaries published in the late nineteenth and early twentieth centuries. It has a growing body of Chicago Lutheran church records and some cemetery records. You'll find indexes to vital records but not the records themselves. Some Chicago newspapers are available on microfilm or hard copy up until 1964. The fully searchable version of the *Chicago Tribune* 1890–1946 from *ProQuest Historical Newspapers* has recently been added. There is also a good collection of maps and local histories.

Services:

Public-access computers with links to genealogy Web sites (both free and subscription). "Quick Search" services for a fee (obituaries, census, Chicago church records, Cook County birth and death indexes, city directories, and phone books). Genealogy reference questions are answered by librarians at genealogy@newberry.org or by mail. A list of professional researchers is available. Guides to Chicago and ethnic genealogy are on the Web site and at the library. The Newberry has a loan program with the Church of Jesus Christ of Latter-day Saints for microfilmed materials.

Contact:

For general information, go to www.newberry.org and click on "Genealogy," or call the Local and Family History reference desk at 312/255-3512.

University of Illinois at Chicago (UIC) Richard J. Daley Library

Location:

Richard J. Daley Library
University of Illinois at Chicago
801 S. Morgan Street
Chicago, IL 60607

The library is located between Taylor Street and Harrison Street, just south of Greektown and the Eisenhower Expressway. Public transportation is available via CTA bus and train; visitor parking lots are located on Halsted and on Harrison.

Hours:

Open seven days a week when school is in session. Times vary according to school schedules. Call to check hours on the recorded message before going: 312/996-0304.

Illustration 14.19: The main library at the University of Illinois at Chicago is centrally located and open to the public. You don't have to look hard to find a wealth of family history resources behind its concrete walls. Photo by Grace DuMelle.

Illustration 14.20: The Microforms section has easy access to Chicago newspapers and city directories. It's usually open in the evenings and weekends, when other research facilities are closed. Photo by Grace DuMelle.

Fees:

No charge to use the library. Pay for photocopies, computer printouts, microfilm or microfiche copies, and photo or slide reproductions.

Rules of Use:

Because UIC operates with public funds, it is open to the public, not just students and faculty. Most materials are open-shelf and can be browsed. Staff reshelves material; leave items on tables when you are done.

Holdings Summary:

The Richard J. Daley Library is good for newspaper and city directory research, as well as research into your ancestor's house. In the Microforms section on the second floor you'll find complete runs of many Chicago newspapers, all the Chicago city directories, and the U.S. census for Cook County 1840 to 1920 (with the exception of 1890; also, no Soundexes). You can look at fire insurance maps for Chicago and suburbs and Chicago building permits 1872 to 1954.

The Maps section on the third floor has one of the largest collections in the area, including ward maps of Chicago and topographic maps showing cultural and other features over time. In the Documents section (also on the third floor), browse proceedings of Chicago and Cook County governmental units that may have references to your ancestor's employment.

"Genealogical Resources at the UIC Library" is a nice summary guide developed by the Newberry Library and available at the Newberry's Local and Family History section.

Services:

Public computers on every floor feature library resources and Internet access. From the library home page, you can use FirstSearch, an online subscription gateway to many academic databases. One of the databases, WorldCat (short for "World Catalog"), helps you locate materials in libraries across the United States. You can also use the electronic resources that the library subscribes to. FirstSearch and other subscriptions are not available outside the Daley Library if you are not a UIC student, alumnus, or employee. Printed guides to different types of research (biographical, architectural, Chicago history) are available near the second-floor reference desk.

Contact:

Digital reference services are available from the library's home page, www.uic.edu/depts/lib, or call 312/996-2726. For the Documents/Maps Department, call 312/996-2738.

What to Expect at Chicago-Area Research Facilities

Points to Remember

Some items are not specifically mentioned in this chapter but are discussed in other chapters.

❏ *Chicago Historical Society*
top resources:

- complete run of Chicago city directories
- complete run of Chicago telephone directories
- extensive Chicago newspaper holdings
- fire insurance maps
- *Chicago Tribune Historical Archive*

❏ *Chicago Public Library*
top resources:

- complete run of Chicago city directories
- Chicago and suburban telephone directories
- U.S. census records and indexes for Illinois
- complete runs of most Chicago newspapers
- City of Chicago documents

What to Expect at Chicago-Area Research Facilities

❑ *Clerk of the Circuit Court of Cook County Archives top resources:*

- naturalization index and records
- probate and wills indexes and records
- divorce indexes and records
- criminal felony indexes and records
- minors under guardianship index and records

❑ *Cook County Bureau of Vital Statistics top resources:*

- birth certificates
- marriage certificates
- death certificates
- stillborn birth records (some)

❑ *Family History Center— Wilmette, Illinois top resources:*

- Cook County vital records and indexes
- Cook County cemetery records
- Polish Roman Catholic parish records
- Hamburg emigration lists index
- full subscription to Ancestry.com

(Continued next page)

What to Expect at Chicago-Area Research Facilities

❑ *Illinois Regional Archives at Northeastern Illinois University top resources:*

• Limited collection of Cook County vital records and indexes

• naturalization index and records

• Cook County Coroner's inquest records and index

• Cook County Hospital patient registers

• Chicago City Cemetery records (in *Chicago City Council Proceedings*)

❑ *National Archives and Records Administration—Great Lakes top resources:*

• all available U.S. censuses for all states

• selected passenger lists and records

• naturalization records for the region

• World War I and World War II draft cards for the region

• full subscription to Ancestry.com

What to Expect at Chicago-Area Research Facilities

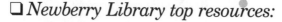

❑ *Newberry Library top resources:*

• complete run of Chicago city directories

• all available U.S. censuses for Illinois and extensive indexes

• many Chicago Lutheran church records

• extensive map holdings

• public-access computers with links to paid and free Web sites, such as ProQuest's *Chicago Tribune* 1890–1946

❑ *University of Illinois at Chicago Richard J. Daley Library top resources:*

• complete runs of many Chicago newspapers

• complete run of Chicago city directories

• fire insurance maps

• Chicago building permits

• extensive map holdings

• Internet access throughout the library; FirstSearch's WorldCat and other subscription databases

15   Top Web Sites for Chicago-Area Research

by Jack Simpson
Curator of Local and Family History,
the Newberry Library

Genealogy is one of the most popular uses for the Internet. This ranking is partially a result of the growing popularity of genealogy, but it also reflects a close compatibility between Internet technology and the needs of genealogical researchers. In other words, the Internet is particularly well suited to solve some of the problems genealogists face. Genealogical research requires searching massive amounts of raw data: long lists of names, thousands of pages of newsprint, or multiple book indexes. The search technology of the Internet eliminates much of this tedious, eye-straining work. Researching family history means searching for information held by distant cousins or other researchers, and the Internet helps researchers make these connections. Finally, genealogy research requires searching libraries and other repositories scattered around the globe; for those of us without a private jet, the Internet is one of the easiest ways of spanning physical distance.

In an earlier chapter, I warned that the Internet is not a good place to start your research. However, once you have a grounding in the basics of genealogical research, the Internet will become your best friend, albeit a sometimes difficult one. This chapter will cover some of the best genealogy Web sites and other Internet resources for Cook County research.

Local Institutional Web Sites

Some of the most useful Web sites for Cook County are hosted by research institutions that hold genealogical records.

Illinois State Archives
www.sos.state.il.us/departments/archives/archives.html
The Illinois State Archives is one of the most aggressive state repositories in the nation at making governmental records available online. The State Archives in Springfield has built a number of databases that cover statewide records. The local branches of the State Archives are known as the Illinois Regional Archives Depositories (IRAD), and they have also created databases of local governmental records. (These are described separately after the Illinois State Archives discussion.) Following are some of the most useful databases for Cook County researchers.

Illinois Marriage Index
www.sos.state.il.us/departments/archives/marriage.html
This database indexes marriage records statewide covering the period 1763 to 1900. For Cook County, the database covers 1833 to May 1895, but the bulk of records are from 1871 to 1895. Because all civil marriage certificates in Cook County were destroyed in the Chicago Fire of 1871, the earlier index references are taken from *Sam Fink's Index*, which was compiled from marriage notices in pre-Fire Chicago newspapers. As with any database, it is worth learning about the specific search functionality of the marriage database. Note that you can search by both the surname of the groom or the bride's maiden name. If you don't get results with the groom's name, try the bride's name. Also, note that you can type in a partial surname, and all of the surnames that start with those letters will return.

Illinois Death Index 1916–1950
www.sos.state.il.us/departments/archives/idphdeathindex.html
The Illinois Department of Public Health began recording deaths statewide in 1916, and this database indexes those records. As with any database, you will find misspellings and omissions in this record set, but overall it is a relatively exhaustive list of deaths in Illinois during this period.

Pre-1916 Illinois Death Index
www.sos.state.il.us/departments/archives/death.html
The State Archives is coordinating a large volunteer project to enter the pre-1916 death indexes of Illinois counties into one database. Currently, volunteers are making rapid progress entering in the *Cook County Death Index 1871–1916*, and this portion of the database may be complete by the time this book is printed.

Other Statewide Databases at the State Archives
The Illinois State Archives has created a number of other databases that are useful to Cook County researchers:

www.sos.state.il.us/departments/archives/data_lan.html
The *Illinois Public Domain Land Tract Sales* database records the initial purchasers of land sold by the federal or state government. If you have ancestors who settled in Cook County from 1830 to 1870, this database might show you where they held property.

www.sos.state.il.us/departments/archives/databases.html
The State Archives also created a number of databases that give information on Illinois veterans of military conflicts, including the War of 1812, the Civil War, the Spanish-American War, and World War I.

Illinois Regional Archives Depository at Northeastern Illinois University
www.sos.state.il.us/departments/archives/irad/neiumap.html
Currently, there are three databases indexing Cook County records created by the Northeastern Illinois

University branch of IRAD: *Chicago City Council Proceedings Files, 1833–1871*; the *Cook County Coroner's Inquest Record Index, 1872–1911*; and the *Chicago Police Department Homicide Record Index, 1870–1930*.

www.sos.state.il.us/departments/archives/chicago_proceedings/ proceedings_intro.html

The *City Council Proceedings* database describes topics covered at council meetings up to 1871. The database is a great source for early Chicago historical research but has limited usefulness for genealogists. It includes some personal names and can help lead particularly intrepid genealogy researchers to some early Chicago records, but for most Chicago researchers it is not a commonly used resource. An exception is records of the Chicago City Cemetery contained in the *Proceedings*. See Chapter 8, "When Did My Ancestor Die and Where Is My Ancestor Buried?".

www.sos.state.il.us/departments/archives/cookinqt.html

The *Coroner's Inquest* database indexes individuals whose deaths were investigated by the Cook County Coroner. The coroner's office investigates mysterious deaths, including accidents and suspected homicides or suicides. The database is useful to researchers whose ancestors may have died violently or accidentally. The database is also useful as an alternate source for death information, as it indexes a different set of records than the Cook County and Illinois death indexes. We have found examples where individuals who are not listed in the death certificate indexes show up in the *Coroner's Inquest Record Index*.

www.sos.state.il.us/departments/archives/homicide.html

The *Chicago Police Department Homicide Record Index* lists the names of homicide victims from 1870 to 1930. Given Chicago's less than pacific history, this database gets a fair amount of use. An expanded transcription of the police department homicide files went online June 2004 at http://homicide.northwestern.edu.

IRAD Local Governmental Records Holdings Database
www.sos.state.il.us/departments/archives/irad/iradholdings.html
The Illinois Regional Archives Depository System has a descriptive inventory of its records online here. By selecting "Cook" in the "County" field of this database, researchers can generate a list of Cook County records held by IRAD in Chicago. Here are some examples of entries in the database:

• License Record, Horse-Drawn Vehicle (Chicago), 1897–98

• Local Improvements Registers (Lakeview), 1872–90

• Village Trustees' Proceedings Files (Rogers Park), 1874–95

Unlike most of the other databases already described, the inventory does not list personal names—you won't be able to determine who received horse-drawn vehicle licenses in Chicago using the database. However, for researchers who are willing to travel to IRAD and dig through primary records, this is a valuable tool. By seeing what type of records are available and their date spans, you can investigate ones that hold promise for your ancestors.

Newberry Library Web Site

www.newberry.org
The Newberry Library holds the largest genealogy collection in the Chicago area, and the genealogy section of its Web site has a great deal of useful information. The site contains a number of guides for researchers on a variety of genealogical topics. Census holdings, city directory holdings, Chicago church and synagogue records, Chicago maps, and Chicago neighborhoods are all covered. While the guides focus on the Newberry's collection, they also provide links to other institutions and Internet databases. Additionally, there is a partial catalog of the library's holdings; items acquired since 1980 are described online. The library is adding the older card catalog records to the Web site, and the online catalog should be complete by about 2008. The Web site also gives researchers tips on preparing for a visit to the library. For

researchers who cannot visit, the Web site describes fee-based "Quick Searches," including obituary and city directory searches for Chicago.

Chicago Historical Society (CHS) Web Site

www.chicagohs.org/collections/index.html

The Research Center at the Chicago Historical Society holds a great deal of valuable Chicago history sources: manuscript collections, books, photographs, maps, and other artifacts. A portion of the collection is now described in the society's online catalog, "Archie."

The society has also added a number of other useful databases and images to its Web site. Recently, CHS placed digital versions of some commonly used Chicago reference sources online: the "Address Conversion Guides" of 1909 (www.chsmedia.org/househistory/1909snc/start.pdf) and 1911 (www.chsmedia.org/househistory/1911snc/start.pdf) and the "Street Name Changes" list (www.chsmedia.org/househistory/nameChanges/start.pdf). These resources are essential for figuring out where old addresses were located in Chicago. (Note: the files are quite large and take much time to load and work with.) CHS also placed the 1928 to 1929 Chicago criss-cross directory online (www.chsmedia.org/househistory/polk/Menus/Polks.pdf) and a database of building permits listed in *American Contractor* from 1898 to 1912 (www.chsmedia.org/househistory/1898-1912permits/search.asp).

Perhaps the most fascinating database from CHS is the *Chicago Daily News* photograph collection. In collaboration with the Library of Congress, CHS digitized more than 55,000 images taken by *Chicago Daily News* photographers from 1902 to 1933. These images are now available online in a searchable database (http://memory.loc.gov/ammem/ndlpcoop/ichihtml/cdnhome.html). Your chances of finding a photo of your ancestor in the database are fairly slim, but the image database is a useful tool for those researching Chicago history, neighborhoods, or institutions.

Illinois Newspaper Project
www.library.uiuc.edu/inp
The Illinois Newspaper Project is part of a nationwide effort on the part of the Library of Congress and collaborating institutions to inventory newspaper holdings at libraries. The Illinois Newspaper Project database, which resides on the University of Illinois at Urbana–Champaign Web site, describes newspaper holdings at libraries across the state of Illinois. For example, by entering "Cicero" in the "Area of Coverage" field of the database, I found 12 different Cicero newspapers held at six different libraries across the state.

Other Local Institutional Web Sites
www.chipublib.org/cpl.html
The Chicago Public Library's site has a good description of its neighborhood history collections and an online catalog.

www.cookctyclerk.com/sub/vital_records.asp
www.cookcountyclerkofcourt.org/Archives_/archives_.htm
The Web sites of both the Cook County Bureau of Vital Statistics and the Cook County Circuit Court Archives describe their holdings and offer printable search request forms.

Church of Jesus Christ of Latter-day Saints

There's a good reason why this church has been frequently mentioned in *Finding Your Chicago Ancestors*. A key belief of Latter-day Saints is that families can be united eternally after death, including deceased generations. Hence the importance members place on identifying ancestors, and the church's development as a major force in genealogy.

Microfilming crews sponsored by the church work around the globe, preserving all sorts of genealogical records. Family

History Centers operate in 64 countries, open to the public as well as church members. Church volunteers worked for 17 years on the every-name CD index to the 1880 U.S. census. Eleven years of labor went into putting the Freedman's Bank records on CD, a breakthrough for African-American research. These and other tools are sold at cost and often made available online for free.

FamilySearch Web Site

www.familysearch.org

In May 1999 the Church of Jesus Christ of Latter-day Saints launched its Internet genealogy service, called FamilySearch. 110,000 people visit each day. The Web site includes a number of genealogical databases, under the heading "Search for Ancestors." These include some databases where information is submitted by researchers, such as *Ancestral File* and *Pedigree Resource File*. Other databases index original records, such as the *International Genealogical Index*, which is compiled from church and vital records.

The Family History Library catalog is also available on the Web site. By entering "Chicago" or "Cook" as a place search, you will be able to see the wealth of Cook County records held by the library, the most important repository for genealogical records in the world. There is also a database of Family History Centers around the country where researchers can borrow the library's microfilmed records for a small fee.

Free Internet Sources

One common misperception among novice genealogy researchers is that everything on the Internet costs money. Commercial genealogy services advertise a great deal on the Internet, so if you are surfing the Web without much direction, you are likely to end up on a pay site. However, if you know where you are going, you will find a great deal of free information on the Internet.

USGenWeb

www.usgenweb.org/states
USGenWeb is a network of sites created and run by genealogy volunteers around the country. Sites are arranged into a hierarchy—there is a page for each U.S. state and then a page for each county. The "Cook County IL GenWeb" page offers links to Cook County research institutions, lists lookup volunteers, and gives researchers a place to post genealogical data. For researchers getting started, USGenWeb is a good place to browse, although the mix of links and posted data can be somewhat confusing.

Cyndi's List of Genealogy Sites on the Internet

www.cyndislist.com
Genealogist Cyndi Howells maintains more than 235,000 categorized links on this site. If you are searching for a set of relevant Web sites on a particular genealogical subject, Cyndi's List is the place to go. To find a set of links for Cook County research, look in the Main Category Index under United States, then Illinois localities, and then Cook County.

A Look at Cook

www.alookatcook.com
A Look at Cook is a site run by a former Chicagoan who created maps of the Chicago wards and *enumeration districts* (areas assigned to the enumerator, or census taker) for the censuses of 1870 to 1930. Enumeration district maps are a vital tool for urban census research, and Chicago researchers are lucky to have this free resource—currently, no comparable site exists for other large cities.

Cook County Mailing List on RootsWeb.com

http://lists.rootsweb.com/index/usa/IL/cook.html

E-mail lists, or mailing lists, are a great way for a community of researchers to share information. The Cook County mailing list hosted by RootsWeb.com is an example of a useful list. Follow the instructions on the Web site above to subscribe to the list. Once you are a member of the list, you can send questions to the list, and all of the people on the list will receive it. Similarly, you will receive any messages sent to the list by other subscribers. To cut down on the amount of e-mail you receive, you might opt to receive the messages in a daily digest. By joining the list, you will be able to connect to a large group of Cook County researchers, including some who have much experience dealing with local genealogical records. The archived messages of the list (available via a link on this same site) are a great source of answers to difficult Cook County research questions.

Subscription Databases

While many of the most useful Web sites are available for free, there are other important sites that are only available to home subscribers or in subscribing libraries.

Ancestry.com

www.ancestry.com

Ancestry.com is a commercial Web site that provides a wide variety of databases for home subscribers and libraries. The company has scanned in digital images of every U.S. census and has created nationwide indexes for many of the census years, including 1870, 1880, 1920, and 1930 (at the time this book was published). Ancestry.com also offers a number of databases of particular interest to Cook County researchers, including those described in the following sections.

Chicago's Irish Families Database

This database indexes a variety of records relating to Chicago's Irish community in the late nineteenth and early twentieth centuries: obituaries, gravestone transcriptions, church records, and published biographical sketches.

Chicago Voters Registration for 1888 to 1890 and 1892

These records gathered information on registered voters in Chicago and the then-suburban localities of Lake View, Hyde Park, and the Town of Lake. Details include names, addresses, nativity, and naturalization status. The database consists of an index linked to digital images of the original rolls.

Chicago Obituaries

Ancestry.com has indexes to obituaries in the *Chicago Sun-Times* for 1988 to 1995 and the *Chicago Tribune* for 1988 to 1997.

Notable Digitized Books

Ancestry.com has digitized many published books. For Cook County research, some of the significant titles are *Cook County, Illinois History*, which was originally published in 1884 by A.T. Andreas; *Chicago and Cook County: A Guide to Research* (1996) by Loretto Szucs; and *Prairie Farmer's Reliable Directory: Will and Southern Cook County, Illinois*, originally published in 1918.

HeritageQuest Online

www.heritagequestonline.com

HeritageQuest Online is a subscription Web site available through libraries; some libraries allow their members access from home. Like Ancestry.com, HeritageQuest has digitized the entire census and has created indexes to a number of them: 1860, 1870, 1900, and 1910. The Web site also contains a large collection of digitized books.

OCLC FirstSearch

www.oclc.org/firstsearch

FirstSearch is an online subscription service to academic databases in science, humanities, business, and other subjects. It was created by OCLC (Online Computer Library Center), a non-profit library consortium. One of the databases in FirstSearch is called WorldCat. It is a *union catalog* (a listing of everything known to be held on a particular topic) of library holdings around the country. Most large public libraries and academic libraries belong to WorldCat and offer it on their public access computers. While WorldCat is not specifically created for genealogists, it is a very useful tool for family history research. By searching WorldCat for a particular title, you can see which libraries nationwide hold the book. By searching the database for a particular subject, you can see what works are available on that topic. To learn more about it, click on the link "See sample screens from FirstSearch" on the page referenced above.

Top Web Sites for Chicago-Area Research

Points to Remember

❑ *16 Home Pages to Bookmark*

• Illinois State Archives
www.sos.state.il.us/departments/archives/archives.html

• Illinois Regional Archives Depository
    at Northeastern Illinois University
www.sos.state.il.us/departments/archives/irad/iradhome.html

• Newberry Library
www.newberry.org (go to genealogy section)

• Chicago Historical Society
www.chicagohs.org/collections/index.html

• Illinois Newspaper Project
www.library.uiuc.edu/inp

• Chicago Public Library
www.chipublib.org/cpl.html

• Cook County Bureau of Vital Statistics
www.cookctyclerk.com/sub/vital_records.asp

• Cook County Circuit Court Archives
www.cookcountyclerkofcourt.org/Archives_/archives_.htm

Top Web Sites for Chicago-Area Research

- Genealogy site of the Church of Jesus Christ of Latter-day Saints
www.familysearch.org

- USGenWeb
www.usgenweb.org/states

- Cyndi's List of Genealogy Sites on the Internet
www.cyndislist.com

- A Look at Cook
www.alookatcook.com

- Cook County Mailing List on RootsWeb.com
http://lists.rootsweb.com/index/usa/IL/cook.html

- Ancestry.com
www.ancestry.com

- HeritageQuest Online
www.heritagequestonline.com

- OCLC FirstSearch
www.oclc.org/firstsearch

16   Ethnic Resources

by Jack Simpson
Curator of Local and Family History,
the Newberry Library

Imagine that you are a recent immigrant to Chicago from Poland. You came to Chicago because you believed there would be work available here and because you have friends and family who live here. Upon arriving in Chicago, you get an apartment near your family in a neighborhood where many of your fellow Polish immigrants reside. Not only is your neighborhood close to your friends and family, but it also is very convenient for you. The local market sells the kind of food you are used to eating, its owner speaks Polish, and he sells Polish-language newspapers. When you watch TV, you watch a local Polish-language television network, which provides local news as well as Polish news and entertainment. You might belong to a club or social organization of your fellow immigrants, and you attend a church where the minister speaks your language.

By simply changing a few details, the same story applies to Mexican or Korean immigrants today, or to Germans in the 1850s or Italians in the 1890s. Immigrants build their own communities within Chicago, with their own social organizations, newspapers, and churches. To a great extent, the same pattern holds for African-Americans, whose segregation led them to build their own institutions. The records of these ethnic institutions are a vital source for researching immigrant ancestors. This chapter will describe methods for researching ethnic ancestors and will identify some specific sources for heavily researched ethnic groups.

General Resources

It helps to get an overview of your ancestor's group, both in Chicago and in the country of origin. For example, knowing the events that precipitated immigration, such as the Mexican Revolution or the potato famine in Ireland, can help you target when your ancestor came to the United States. Learning language patterns, for instance name endings that indicate marital status, can unlock clues in records. The research facilities listed below can point you to histories, genealogy guides, maps, gazetteers, and much more. Studying these kinds of materials about the "old country" will help you understand your ancestor's world at a certain time in history.

• The Newberry Library is a good starting point for ethnic research. The library has short *bibliographies* (printed listings of materials on a particular subject) for the following ethnic groups: African-American, Bohemian, Canadian, Cherokee, English, Germanic, Hispanic, Irish, Italian, Jewish, Polish, and Swedish. The bibliographies tend to cover major printed works and local resources for the groups. They are available in the second-floor reading room of the library and on its Web site, www.newberry.org. It is also worth searching the library's catalogs for ethnic subject headings, such as "Italians—Illinois—Chicago."

• The Chicago Historical Society has a strong collection of material about Chicago's ethnic communities. Although its collection is not focused on genealogical research, the historical material the society collects is useful for researching ethnic ancestors. For instance, a search on the keyword "Italians" in the society's online catalog showed that the library holds seven boxes of oral history transcripts for a project to document Italian-Americans in Chicago. The people interviewed in the papers are unlikely to include the ancestors of any particular Italian-American researcher, but they are still worth reading, as they will shed light on the world Chicago's

Italian immigrants lived in. The Chicago Historical Society also has a strong collection of Chicago ethnic newspapers. Ethnic newspapers are an important resource for genealogy researchers. They tend to be a better source for the obituaries of immigrants than English-language papers such as the *Tribune*. By browsing ethnic newspapers, even if you don't know the language, you'll get a feel for the concerns of the ethnic group, just by the kinds of ads and articles that are featured.

• The Cook County Circuit Court Archives, the National Archives—Great Lakes, and the Illinois Regional Archives Depository hold naturalization records. These records, particularly those after 1904–06, are extremely informative. For an in-depth discussion and examples, see Chapter 9 ("When Did My Ancestor Come to America?").

• The Chicago Public Library collects both published and archival material on Chicago's ethnic groups. The library's online catalog, at www.chipublib.org, is worth searching for specific ethnic groups. The Vivian Harsh Collection at the Woodson branch is an important resource for researching African-Americans in Chicago.

• The Family History Library in Salt Lake City has a large collection of church and civil records from other countries that can be loaned to local Family History Centers or the Newberry Library. Once you find information about the town or region your ancestors immigrated from, you might check the Family History Library catalog online (www.familysearch.org) and see whether the library has records of that place.

• *Ethnic Chicago*, 4th edition, edited by Melvin G. Holli and Peter d'A. Jones, 1995, is a good overview of Chicago's ethnic groups. It contains histories on many of Chicago's ethnic communities and essays on ethnic institutions. It also contains some useful tools for genealogists, such as a list of Chicago cemeteries by ethnicity.

Resources by Ethnic Group

Chicago is a very diverse city. It is not possible to cover every ethnic group here, so the following sections will focus on the groups most researched by genealogists. It's worth joining a society or museum devoted to a particular group and exploring its resources and publications for a year.

African-American

• The Afro-American Historical and Genealogical Society is a national organization based in Washington, D.C., and dedicated to scholarly research. Its Chicago branch, the Patricia Liddell Researchers, meets regularly, holds an annual conference, and publishes books on Chicago's African-American history. Contact:

Patricia Liddell Researchers
P.O. Box 43862
Chicago, IL 60643
773/821-6473
http://family.freesitenow.com/plr/page1.html

• As noted earlier, the Vivian Harsh Collection at the Woodson branch of the Chicago Public Library holds a large collection of material related to African-American genealogy. Chicago resources in the collection include newspapers, directories, yearbooks, and church records.

• The *Chicago Defender*, established in 1909, is a major African-American newspaper. The Chicago Historical Society, the Chicago Public Library, and the University of Illinois at Chicago hold microfilm copies of the *Defender* dating back to the early twentieth century. There is a published obituary index to the *Defender* covering the years 1910 to 1935 by Lori Husband, in two volumes. The index is available at the Newberry Library, the Chicago Public Library, and the Chicago Historical Society. The Patricia Liddell Researchers published an additional obituary extraction for the years 1936 to 1939.

African-American cont.

• The Newberry Library collects material on African-American genealogy. The publication *A Bibliography of African American History at the Newberry Library*, available at the Newberry and on the Newberry Web site, contains sections on Chicago and Illinois.

Chinese

• The National Archives—Great Lakes holds a number of Chinese Exclusion Act case files documenting Chinese immigrants to the Chicago area from 1898 to 1940. There is an online index to these records at www.archives.gov/research_room/finding_aids/chicago/chinese_files_chicago.html.

Czech and Slovak

• The Czech and Slovak American Genealogy Society of Illinois is a great resource for researching Czech and Slovak ancestors. The society maintains a library for genealogical research. It publishes *Koreny*, a journal on the history of Czechs and Slovaks in Illinois, and has also indexed the obituaries in the *Denni Hlasatel*, a Czech newspaper from Chicago. The society's Web site includes an index to *Koreny*, a list of Chicago's Czech and Slovak churches, and helpful links. Contact:

Czech and Slovak American
Genealogy Society of Illinois
P.O. Box 313
Sugar Grove, IL 60554
630/906-8175
www.csagsi.org

German

• There are substantial collections of Chicago German Lutheran congregation records at both the Archives of the Evangelical Lutheran Church in America and the Newberry Library. The Newberry Library also holds microfilms of

Waldheim, Forest Home, and Wunders cemeteries, where many German-Americans are buried, and also holds a number of nineteenth-century German-American newspapers from Chicago. Contact:

Archives of the Evangelical Lutheran Church
in America
321 Bonnie Lane
Elk Grove Village, IL 60007
847/690-9410
www.elca.org/archives/index.html

• The Goethe–Institut Chicago promotes German culture and language. While it focuses on present-day connections between Chicago and Germany, its Web site and library have some information about the history of Germans in Chicago. Contact:

Goethe–Institut Chicago
150 N. Michigan Avenue, Suite 200
Chicago, IL 60601
312/263-0472
www.goethe.de/uk/chi/enindex.htm

Irish

• The Irish-American Heritage Center in Chicago holds genealogy events and is building a library. Contact:

Irish-American Heritage Center
4626 N. Knox Avenue
Chicago, IL 60630
773/282-7035
www.irishamhc.com

• *Chicago's Irish Families* is a database of Irish-American death notices, gravestone transcriptions, and other sources, available to subscribers of Ancestry.com. The Ancestry.com Web site is accessible for free at many libraries, such as the Arlington Heights Memorial Library, the Elmhurst Public Library, and the Newberry Library.

Italian

• Chicago's Italian Genealogy Station (www.angelfire. com/il/ChicagoItalians) is a volunteer-run Web site with information about the history of Italian-Americans in Chicago and its suburbs. The site contains some genealogical material, such as a list of Italians in *Who's Who in Chicago*, published in 1926.

• POINTers in Person is an Italian-American genealogy organization. (POINT = Pursuing Our Italian Names Together.) Its Chicago branch has regular meetings and an informative Web site (www.rootsweb.com/~itappcnc), with lists of city and suburban Catholic churches, for instance. Contact:

pipnorth@attbi.com.

Jewish

• The Chicago Jewish Archives, at the Asher Library of Spertus Institute of Jewish Studies in Chicago, collects organizational records and personal papers documenting Jewish Chicago. The Chicago Jewish Historical Society (http://chicagojewishhistory.org), which is also located in the Spertus Institute, collects historical material, sponsors lectures, leads tours and publishes a newsletter on the history of Chicago's Jewish community. Contact:

The Chicago Jewish Archives
Spertus Institute of Jewish Studies
618 S. Michigan Avenue
Chicago, IL 60605
312/322-1741
www.spertus.edu/asher/cja.html

Chicago Jewish Historical Society
618 S. Michigan Avenue
Chicago, IL 60605
312/663-5634

• The Jewish Genealogical Society of Illinois holds conferences, publishes a newsletter, and has a small noncirculating reference library. Contact:

Jewish Genealogical Society of Illinois
P.O. Box 515
Northbrook, IL 60065-0515
312/666-0100
www.jewishgen.org/jgsi

Lithuanian

• The Balzekas Museum of Lithuanian Culture in Chicago has a research library with historical and genealogical resources relating to Chicago's Lithuanian community. These include institutional records, yearbooks, death notices, and a collection of information on Lithuanian immigrants to the United States before World War I. Contact:

Balzekas Museum of Lithuanian Culture
6500 S. Pulaski Road
Chicago, IL 60629
773/582-6500
www.lithaz.org/museums/balzekas

Polish

• The Polish Genealogical Society of America is located in Chicago and is a very active group. It works closely with the Polish Museum of America and its library and archives. The museum allows PGSA to use its address as a mailing address. PGSA maintains a useful Web site with a number of extremely informative databases:

—*Dziennik Chicagoski Death Indexes, 1890–1971:* This database is an indispensable tool for researching Polish Chicagoans. For Polish immigrants, it was common to run an obituary in the Polish paper rather than the *Tribune* or other English-language newspapers.

—*Marriage Index for Polish Parishes in Chicago Through 1915:* This database indexes marriage records from Roman Catholic parishes. Marriage records from Polish churches often contain detailed genealogical information, so this index can lead to valuable records.

Polish cont.

Researchers who are planning extensive research on Polish ancestors should also consider joining the society or attending its annual conference. Contact:

Polish Genealogical Society of America
984 N. Milwaukee Avenue
Chicago, IL 60622
PGSA has no phone number; use e-mail:
PGSAmerica@aol.com
www.pgsa.org

• The Polish Museum of America maintains archives dealing with the history of Poles and Polish-Americans. Many Illinois and Chicago organizations and publications are represented. The museum library has a microfilm collection of the Polish press published in the United States, including the *Dzennik Chicagoski* from 1890 to 1971. A *List of the Genealogical Holdings of the Polish Museum of America Library* was published in 2001. Contact:

Polish Museum of America
984 N. Milwaukee Avenue
Chicago, IL 60622
773/384-3352 (both library and museum)
http://pma.prcua.org

Swedish

• The Swedish American Museum Center features exhibits on Swedish-American history, including a great Children's Museum of Immigration. It also has a genealogical collection, including a subscription to an online service that allows access to church records from Sweden. Call ahead for a research appointment. Contact:

Swedish American Museum Center
5211 N. Clark Street
Chicago, IL 60640
773/728-8111
www.samac.org

• The F. M. Johnson Archives and Special Collections of North Park University holds the Swedish-American Archives of Greater Chicago. This collection of organizational records and personal papers documents the history of Swedish immigrants in Chicago. The Web site of the Special Collections Department provides an overview of the archives and finding aids for some of the papers. Contact:

F. M. Johnson Archives and Special Collections
North Park University
Brandel Library
3225 W. Foster Avenue
Chicago, IL 60625-4895
773/244-6223 or 773/244-6224
www.northpark.edu/library/archives/index.htm

• The Swenson Swedish Immigration Research Center at Augustana College in Rock Island, Illinois, is a major national library for researching Swedish genealogy. The center holds a number of important records for Cook County research, including many records of Chicago's Swedish churches. Contact:

Swenson Swedish Immigration Research Center
Augustana College
639 38th Street
Rock Island, IL 61201-2296
309/794-7204
www.augustana.edu/administration/SWENSON

Cultural Organizations

There are many ethnic societies in the Chicago area with a mission of connecting immigrants, expatriates, and interested Americans with the culture or language of a particular country. The Goethe–Institut Chicago and the Irish-American Heritage Center (both listed earlier) perform this function for Germany and Ireland, respectively. Similar societies exist for many other ethnic groups, such as the Illinois St. Andrew's Society (Scottish), the Alliance Française de Chicago (French), the Netherlands Club of Chicago (Dutch), and many others. These societies tend to focus on promoting ethnic culture rather than researching genealogy; nevertheless, they are worth contacting for information about local researchers, translators, and genealogy interest groups. You can also learn more about the land of your ancestor's birth and what it's like today. Contact:

Alliance Française de Chicago
810 N. Dearborn Street
Chicago, IL 60610
312/337-1070
www.afchicago.com

Illinois St. Andrew Society
The Scottish Home
28th and Des Plaines Avenue
North Riverside, IL 60546
www.chicago-scots.org

Netherlands Club of Chicago
The Regal Knickerbocker Hotel
163 E. Walton Street
Chicago, IL 60611
www.dutchclubchicago.com

Ethnic Resources

Points to Remember

❏ *Strategies for researching an ethnic group:*

• Look for an overview, such as in *Ethnic Chicago*. When did the group start coming to the area? Why? Where did they first settle? What institutions did they create? What was their world like at a certain point in time?

• Look for a society or museum devoted to the group. Join for a year and explore their resources and publications.

• See what is available at general research facilities, such as the Chicago Public Library, the Chicago Historical Society, and the Newberry Library.

• Browse ethnic newspapers, even if you don't know the language, to get a feel for the issues and concerns of the group during your ancestor's time.

• Try connecting with a cultural organization to learn more about the area your ancestor came from and what it's like today.

• Study maps and histories of the "old country" for a broader view of your ancestor's role in that time and place.

Beginner's Bookshelf

These are the reference books mentioned in the text, with publication information provided so you can locate them in libraries and bookstores. I used many of these titles when I was learning, and I still turn to them today.

American Map Corporation. *Chicagoland Atlas 2003.* Addison, Illinois: Creative Sales Corporation, 2003.
  Spiral-bound, covers all collar counties, shows locations of cemeteries and schools.

Bochar, Jack. *Locations of Chicago Roman Catholic Churches, 1850–1990,* 2nd edition, revised to 1997. Edited by George and Louise Rokos. Sugar Grove, Illinois: Czech and Slovak American Genealogy Society of Illinois, 1998.

Burroughs, Tony. *Black Roots: A Beginner's Guide to Tracing the African American Family Tree.* New York: Fireside Book, 2001.

Colletta, John P. *They Came in Ships: A Guide to Finding Your Immigrant Ancestor's Arrival Record,* 3rd edition. Orem, Utah: Ancestry, 2002.

Hayner, Don, and Tom McNamee. *Streetwise Chicago: A History of Chicago Street Names.* Chicago: Loyola University Press, 1988.

Hinckley, Kathleen W. *Locating Lost Family Members and Friends: Modern Genealogical Research Techniques for Locating the People of Your Past and Present.* Cincinnati: Betterway Books, 1999.

Holli, Melvin G., and Peter d'A. Jones, editors. *Ethnic Chicago: A Multicultural Portrait,* 4th edition. Grand Rapids, Michigan: William B. Eerdmans Publishing Company, 1995.

Newman, John J. *American Naturalization Processes and Procedures, 1790–1985.* Indianapolis: Family History Section, Indiana Historical Society, 1985.

Schaefer, Christina K. *Guide to Naturalization Records of the United States*. Baltimore: Genealogical Publishing Company, 1997.

Sommer, Barbara W., and Mary Kay Quinlan. *The Oral History Manual*. Walnut Creek, California: AltaMira Press, 2002. Detailed instructions, many illustrations, reproducible forms.

Szucs, Loretto Dennis. *Chicago and Cook County: A Guide to Research*. Salt Lake City, Utah: Ancestry, 1996.

Thackery, David T. *A Bibliography of African American History at the Newberry Library*. Chicago: Newberry Library, 1993. Updated with materials added since 1993 at the genealogy section of the library Web site, www.newberry.org.

Index

To find illustrations, look under the appropriate category and the term "example" or "photographs of." For instance, "baptismal register, example" or "Chicago Public Library, photographs of."

neighborhood, 206–207
obituary indexes, 209
overview, 202–203
Polish, 206
Scandinavian, 206
where to find, 203–207
newspapers, Evanston, 210
newspapers, Oak Park, 210
newspapers, Skokie, 210
newspapers, suburban, 210
newspapers, Winnetka, 210
Northeastern Illinois University.
   See Illinois Regional Archives
   Depository (IRAD)
Northwestern Memorial Hospital, 219

O

oath of allegiance, example, 157
obituaries
   Chicago Sun-Times, 296
   Chicago Tribune, 296
   example, 59
   search services, 210–211
   searching tips, 131–132
   sibling information, 55–56, 58
Oral History Manual, The, 4, 313

P

passenger lists
   Chicago and Midwest
      holdings, 170–171
   ethnic indexes, 166–167
   example, 162–163
   obtaining copies of, 169–170
   overview, 161–166
   port indexes and holdings,
      167–169
   where to find, 170–171
Patricia Liddell Researchers, 303
Petition for Naturalization, 152
   example, 155
POINTers in Person, 306

Polish Genealogical Society of
   America, 211, 307–308
Polish Museum of America, 308
Polish resources, 307–308
port indexes and holdings, 167–169
Pre-1916 Illinois Death Index, 288
pre-annexation records, 85
primary sources, 244
probate case files, Cook County, 60
probate records, sibling information,
   58
professional directories, 121
proof of heirship, 58
   example, 61–62
property photograph sources, 93–94
Pullman Car Works, 117–118
Pullman Company, 118
Pullman porter record, example, 119

Q

Quinlan, Mary Kay, 4, 313

R

Railroad Retirement Board, 116
railroad workers, 116–119
   pensioner's record,
      example, 117–118
*Record and Index of Persons
   Registered and Poll Lists of
   Voters*, 144, 148, 270–271
religion, determining from ethnicity,
   36
religious records, 20, 50–51, 77, 84,
   148–149
*Report of the Fire Marshal
   (Chicago)*, 116
research facilities, tips, 250
reverse directory. *See* Chicago
   criss-cross directory
Roman Catholic Church of Chicago.
   See Archdiocese of Chicago,
   Roman Catholic
RootsWeb.com, Web site, 295

About the Author

Grace DuMelle studied writing and history at Dominican University in River Forest, Illinois. As part of her program, she conducted extensive primary research in England on Charles Dickens. Not surprisingly, after a successful period as an advertising copywriter, Grace returned to her first love, historical research. She launched Heartland Historical Research Service in 1995, conducting original research for house histories. As Grace's knowledge of genealogy grew, she also began accepting family history projects, including oral histories helping families document stories from loved ones. Heartland's projects have taken Grace to libraries and government offices across the Chicagoland area on behalf of her clients. Heartland has been featured in the *Chicago Tribune* and the *Daily Southtown* and on WGN radio. Its clients have included the United States Department of Justice, the Museum of Broadcast Communications in Chicago, the Niagara Falls Museum in Ontario, Canada, and Graystone Communications in North Hollywood, California (parent company of The History Channel). Currently, Grace is on staff at the Newberry Library, one of the country's foremost genealogical libraries.

Photo by Bob Nick and Liz Sloan.

Notes

Notes

Notes

Notes

Notes

Notes

Notes

Also From Lake Claremont Press

**The Streets & San Man's
Guide to Chicago Eats**
Dennis Foley

A Cook's Guide to Chicago
Marilyn Pocius

**Great Chicago Fires:
Historic Blazes That Shaped a City**
David Cowan

**The Firefighter's Best Friend:
Lives and Legends of Chicago
Firehouse Dogs**
Trevor and Drew Orsinger

**Chicago's Midway Airport:
The First Seventy-Five Years**
Christopher Lynch

**The Chicago River:
A Natural and Unnatural History**
Libby Hill

**Literary Chicago: A Book
Lover's Tour of the Windy City**
Greg Holden

**The Hoofs and Guns of the Storm:
Chicago's Civil War Connections**
and
**Hollywood on Lake Michigan: 100
Years of Chicago and the Movies**
Arnie Bernstein

**The Golden Age of Chicago
Children's Television**
Ted Okuda and Jack Mulqueen

**Chicago Haunts:
Ghostlore of the Windy City**
and
**More Chicago Haunts:
Scenes from Myth and Memory**
and
Creepy Chicago (for kids!)
Ursula Bielski

**Graveyards of Chicago:
The People, History, Art, and Lore
of Cook County Cemeteries**
Matt Hucke and Ursala Bielski

**Muldoon:
A True Chicago Ghost Story:
Tales of a Forgotten Rectory**
Rocco and Daniel Facchini

**Near West Side Stories: Struggles
for Community
in Chicago's Maxwell Street
Neighborhood**
Carolyn Eastwood

**A Native's Guide to Chicago,
4th Edition**
Lake Claremont Press

**A Native's Guide to
Northwest Indiana**
Mark Skertic

COMING SOON

**The Politics of Place: A History
of Zoning in Chicago**
Dana Caspall and
Joe Schwieterman

**Wrigley Field's Last World
Series: The Wartime Chicago
Cubs and The Pennant of 1945**
Charles N. Billington

**Chicagoland's Best Services &
Professionals: Discriminating
Advice from the Gold Coast**
Christopher Luis

Other Lake Claremont Press Books

Regional History ─────────────────────────

Chicago's Midway Airport: The First Seventy-Five Years
by Christopher Lynch
Training ground of heroes and daredevils. Transportation hub to the nation. Heart of a neighborhood. Outpost of glamour. Crossroads of the world. Birthplace of the major airlines. Contemporary success story. Learn why Midway Airport may be Chicago's most overlooked treasure and the country's most historic airport with this collection of oral histories, historic narrative, and fascinating photos. As recommended in the *Chicago Sun-Times* and several aviation magazines.
1-893121-18-6, Jan. 2003, oblong, larger format softcover, 201 pp., 205 historic and contemporary photos and artifacts, $19.95

The Hoofs and Guns of the Storm: Chicago's Civil War Connections
by Arnie Bernstein, with foreword by Senator Paul Simon
Put Chicago's Civil War history into your hands with this comprehensive popular history/guidebook that shows you familiar memorials, old gravesites, and everyday streets in fresh perspective. While America's Civil War was fought on Confederate battlefields, Chicago played a crucial role in the Union's struggle toward victory. *The Hoofs and Guns of the Storm* takes you through a whirlwind of nineteenth-century people, places, and events that created the foundation for modern-day Chicago. Recommended by top Civil War historians, authors, and Civil War round tables!
1-893121-06-2, Sept. 2003, softcover, 284 pp., 82 photos, $15.95

Great Chicago Fires: Historic Blazes That Shaped a City
by David Cowan
As Chicago changed from agrarian outpost to industrial giant, it would be visited time and again by some of the worst infernos in American history—fires that sparked not only banner headlines but, more importantly, critical upgrades in fire safety laws across the globe. Acclaimed author (*To Sleep With the Angels*) and veteran firefighter David Cowan tells the story of the other "great" Chicago fires, noting the causes, consequences, and historical context of each. In transporting readers beyond the fireline and into the ruins, Cowan brings readers up close to the heroism, awe, and devastation generated by the fires that shaped Chicago.
1-893121-07-0, Aug. 2001, oblong, larger format softcover, 167 pp., 80 historic photos, $19.95

The Chicago River: A Natural and Unnatural History
by Libby Hill
Hill presents an intimate biography of a humble, even sluggish, stream in the right place at the right time—the story of the making and perpetual re-making of a river by everything from geological forces to the

interventions of an emerging and mighty city. Winner of the 2001 American Regional History Publishing Award (1st Place, Midwest) and the 2000 Midwest Independent Publishers Association Award (2nd Place, History), and nominated for best public works book of the year. 1-893121-02-X, Aug. 2000, softcover, 302 pp., 78 maps and photos, $16.95

The Golden Age of Chicago Children's Television
by Ted Okuda and Jack Mulqueen
Behind-the-Scenes Stories of the Golden Age of Chicago Children's Television as Told by the People Who Lived It! At one time every station in Chicago—a maximum of five, until 1964—produced or aired some programming for children. From the late 1940s through the early 1970s, local television stations created a golden age of children's television unique in American broadcasting. Though the shows often operated under strict budgetary constraints, these programs were rich in imagination, inventiveness, and devoted fans. The mere mention of their names brings smiles to the faces of Midwestern Baby Boomers everywhere: *Kukla, Fran, & Ollie, Super Circus, Garfield Goose, Bozo's Circus, Mulqueens' Kiddie-A-Go-Go, BJ & Dirty Dragon, Ray Rayner and Friends*, and a host of others. Discover the back stories and details of this special era from the people who created, lived, and enjoyed it—producers, on-air personalities, and fans. As seen in *Chicago Magazine*. 1-893121-17-8, June 2004, softcover, 251 pp., 78 photos, $17.95

Regional Travel & Guidebooks By Locals _____

The Streets & San Man's Guide to Chicago Eats
by Dennis Foley
Tongue-in-Cheek Style and Food-in-Mouth Expertise Certified by the City of Chicago's *Department of Lunch*. Quickly becoming a cult classic among city workers! Streets & San electrician Dennis Foley shares his and his co-workers' favorite lunch joints in all reaches of the city. Enjoy Chicago's best mom-and-pop eateries at fast-food prices and never eat in chain restaurants again! Warning: requires a sense of humor, a sense of adventure, and a large appetite. As seen in the *Chicago Tribune, Chicago Sun-Times*, and many more. 1-893121-27-5, June 2004, softcover, 117 pp., 83 reviews, 23 detours, 25 coupons, $12.95

A Cook's Guide to Chicago: Where to Find Everything You Need and Lots of Things You Didn't Know You Did
by Marilyn Pocius
Chef Marilyn Pocius takes food lovers and serious home cooks into all corners of Chicagoland in her explorations of local foodways. In addition to providing extensive information on specialty food and equipment shops (including gourmet stores, health food shops, butchers, fishmongers, produce stands, spice shops, ethnic grocers, and restaurant supplies dealers),

Pocius directs readers to farmers markets, knife sharpeners, foodie clubs, cooking classes, and culinary publications. Her special emphasis on what to do with the unfamiliar items found in ethnic supermarkets includes "Top 10" lists, simple recipes, and tips on using exotic ingredients. A complete index makes it easy to find what you need: frozen tropical fruit pulp, smoked goat feet, fresh durian, sanding sugar, empanada dough, live crabs, egusi seeds, mugwort flour, kishke, and over two thousand other items you didn't know you couldn't live without! Recommended in the *Chicago Sun-Times, Chicago Tribune,* and many others. Second edition available, April 2005.
1-893121-16-X, June 2002, softcover, 275 pp., $15

A Native's Guide to Chicago, 4th Edition
by Lake Claremont Press, edited by Sharon Woodhouse
Venture into the nooks and crannies of everyday Chicago with this one-of-a-kind, comprehensive budget guide. Over 400 pages of free, inexpensive, and unusual things to do in the Windy City make this the perfect resource for tourists, business travelers, visiting suburbanites, and resident Chicagoans. Called the "best guidebook for locals" in New City's "Best of Chicago" issue!
1-893121-23-2, Nov. 2004, softcover, 468 pp., 22 photos, 10 maps, $15.95

A Native's Guide to Northwest Indiana
by Mark Skertic
At the southern tip of Lake Michigan, in the crook between Chicagoland and southwestern Michigan, lies Northwest Indiana, a region of natural diversity, colorful history, abundant recreational opportunities, small town activities, and urban diversions. Whether you're a life-long resident, new in the area, or just passing through, let native Mark Skertic be your personal tour guide of the best The Region has to offer. With regional maps, chapters on 31 communities, and special sections on antiques, boating, gaming, golf courses, the lakeshore and dunes, shopping, theater, and more. As seen in *Lake Magazine.*
1-893121-08-9, Aug. 2003, softcover, 319 pp., 62 photos, 5 maps, $15

Ghostlore and Haunted History _____

Chicago Haunts: Ghostlore of the Windy City
by Ursula Bielski
Bielski captures over 160 years of Chicago's haunted history with her distinctive blend of lively storytelling, in-depth historical research, exclusive interviews, and insights from parapsychology. Called "a masterpiece of the genre," "a must-read," and "an absolutely first-rate-book" by reviewers, *Chicago Haunts* continues to earn the praise of critics and readers alike.
0-9642426-7-2, Oct. 1998, softcover, 277 pp., 29 photos, $15

More Chicago Haunts: Scenes from Myth and Memory
by Ursula Bielski
Chicago. A town with a past. A people haunted by its history in more ways than one. A "windy city" with tales to tell . . . Bielski is back with more history, more legends, and more hauntings, including the personal scary stories of *Chicago Haunts* readers.
1-893121-04-6, Oct. 2000, softcover, 312 pp., 50 photos, $15

Creepy Chicago: A Ghosthunter's Tales of the City's Scariest Sites
by Ursula Bielski, illustrated by Amy Noble
Chicago's famous phantoms, haunted history, and unsolved mysteries for readers ages 8–12. *Chicago Haunts* for kids!
1-893121-15-1, Aug. 2003, softcover, 19 illustrated stories, glossary, tips for young ghosthunters, 136 pp., $8

Haunted Michigan: Recent Encounters with Active Spirits
by Rev. Gerald S. Hunter
Hunter shares his investigations into modern ghost stories—active hauntings that continue to this day—and uncovers a chilling array of local spirits in his tour of the two peninsulas.
1-893121-10-0, Oct. 2000, softcover, 207 pp., 20 photos, $12.95

More Haunted Michigan:
New Encounters with Ghosts of the Great Lakes State
by Rev. Gerald S. Hunter
Rev. Hunter invited readers of *Haunted Michigan* to open their minds to the presence of the paranormal all around them. They opened their minds . . . and unlocked a grand repository of their own personal supernatural experiences. Hunter investigated these modern, active hauntings and recounts the most chilling and most unusual here for you, in further confirmation that the Great Lakes State may be one of the most haunted places in the country.
1-893121-29-1, Feb. 2003, softcover, 231 pp., 22 photos, $15

Muldoon: A True Chicago Ghost Story: Tales of a Forgotten Rectory
by Rocco A. Facchini and Daniel J. Facchini
Poverty, crime, politics, scandal, revenge, and a ghost: Fresh out of the seminary in 1957, Father Rocco Facchini was appointed to his first assignment at the parish of St. Charles Borromeo on Chicago's Near West Side. Adjusting to rectory life with an unorthodox, dispirited pastor and adapting to the needs of the rough, impoverished neighborhood were challenges in themselves. Little did he know that the rectory and church were also being haunted by a bishop's ghost! These are the untold stories of the last days of St. Charles parish by the last person able to tell them. Called "The hot new read among Chicago priests" in the *Chicago Sun-Times*. Recommended by Catholic and secular publications alike.
1-893121-24-0, Sept. 2003, softcover, 268 pp., 44 photos, $15

Order Form

Finding Your Chicago Ancestors	_____ @ $16.95 =	_____
The Golden Age of Chicago Children's Television	_____ @ $17.95 =	_____
A Native's Guide to Chicago	_____ @ $15.95 =	_____
Literary Chicago	_____ @ $15.95 =	_____
The Chicago River	_____ @ $16.95 =	_____
Great Chicago Fires	_____ @ $19.95 =	_____
Chicago's Midway Airport	_____ @ $19.95 =	_____
The Hoofs & Guns of the Storm	_____ @ $15.95 =	_____
Graveyards of Chicago	_____ @ $15.00 =	_____
A Cook's Guide to Chicago	_____ @ $15.00 =	_____
_____	_____ @ $____ =	_____
_____	_____ @ $____ =	_____

Subtotal: _____
Less Discount: _____
New Subtotal: _____
8.75% Sales Tax for Illinois Residents: _____
Shipping: _____
TOTAL: _____

Name _____

Address _____

City_____ **State**_____ **Zip** _____

E-mail _____

❏ *Add me to the LCP monthly customer e-mail newsletter list.*

Please enclose check, money order, or credit card information.

Visa/MC/AmEx/Discover#_____ **Exp.** _____

Signature_____

Discounts when you order multiple copies!
2 books—10% off total, 3–4 books—20% off,
5–9 books—25% off, 10+ books—40% off

—Low shipping fees—
$2.50 for the first book and $.50 for each additional book,
with a maximum charge of $8.

Order by mail, phone, fax, or e-mail.
All of our books have a no-hassle, 100% money back guarantee.

4650 N. Rockwell St.
Chicago, IL 60625
773/583-7800
773/583-7877 (fax)
lcp@lakeclaremont.com
www.lakeclaremont.com